FOUR VOICES

Managing love, loyalty, family wealth and
succession through the generations

JOHN VAMOS

This book is dedicated to the many families that have embraced, tested and applied the approach described in these pages; families that have evidenced that the formula described in *Four Voices* works.

They have shown, without qualification, that the *Four Voices* approach can successfully bring rigour, accountability, harmony and sustainability to families that share love, loyalty … and wealth.

– John Vamos

First published in 2022 by John Vamos

A catalogue entry for this book is available from the National Library of Australia.

ISBN: 978-1-922764-07-2

Project management and text design by Publish Central
Cover design by Pipeline Design

Contents

Acknowledgements

I would like to thank the many families that have put their collective future and harmony in my hands.

Our shared learnings have shaped the thoughts and pointed me in the direction of the science that this book promotes.

Their application of the solutions outlined prove the efficacy of the model and will hopefully help many other families that face similar challenges.

This book has come to life over a number of years thanks in large part to my friend, colleague and co-author Karen McCreadie. Her patience, powers of interpretation and sharp filter for what matters and what doesn't has brought both my thoughts, and the Jackson Family, to life. The book would never have seen the light of day without her.

Thanks also to Lesley Vamos for her wonderful illustrations. They truly capture the moment and make the Jackson Family very, very real!

About the Author

John Vamos has worked alongside businesses for over 35 years, including many of Australia's most successful, wealthy and enduring family dynasties. Regarded by many as the father of business coaching in Australia, John was certainly the first to apply 'business coaching' as a professional designation. Over three decades he has also been the lead strategic facilitator for many of Australia's top 200 public and private companies.

A law graduate with 15 years of financial advisory experience overlapping 35 years as a business coach, John has witnessed first-hand the unique and especially complex issues that face family enterprise. He has met countless struggling business leaders inside family enterprise who are confused by the reality they find themselves in – everything from succession issues to business dysfunction to sibling rivalry to family disunity and fracture.

The creator of the highly successful Thinking System suite of tools, John uses these tried-and-tested techniques to address these and other thorny family business issues. The Thinking System can liberate any type of business from any type of challenge, but the rewards of resolution can be especially miraculous in family business.

John is the author of three books. The first, *You Don't Think as Smart as You Are*, explored how our being human challenges productivity. The second, *Elephants and the Business Laws of Nature*, looked more closely at these issues in the context of business management. And this book, *Four Voices* – his magnum opus – is dedicated to unravelling how those same human issues play out in family enterprise. And more importantly, this book explores and explains exactly what to do to defend love, loyalty, family wealth and succession through the generations.

> *Over a number of years, together with colleagues at the Centre for Management and Organisation Studies at the University of Technology, Sydney, I have been researching the field of business coaching. While there are many offers in the marketplace, our findings are that none is as distinctive, nor more useful in terms of business improvement, as the methodology of organisational coaching that John Vamos has pioneered. Having watched his coaching in action, we can see that the questions that have been devised [in the Thinking System] act as prompts to unlock potentials that were already there but otherwise lying dormant.*
> – Professor Stewart Clegg

About You

Let me tell you a really quick story. If you relate to it or resonate with it in any way, read the book. If you don't, use it as a door stop and move on ...

While attending a family business conference held at a stunning resort I got chatting to an older bloke who had a very successful manufacturing business employing around 2,000 people. After telling me a little about his business, he asked what I did. So, I explained that I work with businesses just like his to help them navigate the additional challenges of family enterprise. He was intrigued and went on to outline some of the challenges he was facing in his own family business. His wife had been instrumental in the business – in fact, she had started it, but he had turned it into something that was scalable. He employed his sister, who worked in operations, as well as his daughter and his son. His son had made a significant contribution, having created a proprietary process that was now the business's main point of difference in the marketplace; and his daughter was also making a positive impact, leading the traditional front end of the business. He also had two other children who were not involved in the business. Although his son and daughter's roles were fairly clear and didn't really cross over, there was unspoken angst around what was going to happen in the future. What he described was the typical Gordian Knot of complexity that weaves through every family business.

It was clear these issues were causing him deep concern. After a few minutes he turned to me and said, 'So, what do I do?'

By the time we arrived at the new venue for the next session, a walk of about 15 to 20 minutes, I had outlined what he should do and in what order. Essentially, I explained what's in this book – giving him a snapshot of the importance of eliciting the four voices from the business and family, and why.

He looked shocked. Grabbing my arm, he spun me around so we were no longer walking side by side but facing each other. Clearly, he had thought his question was rhetorical.

'So, hang on – are you telling me there is a way do to this? For years I've been told by accountants, consultants and lawyers that this is just the way it is in family business. Some sort of pecking order would sort itself out eventually. Are you telling me that's not true? Are you telling me there is a proven way, a system or formulae, that will sort it out?'

'Yes. That's exactly what I'm saying. There is always a best way to do anything – including a best way to manage love, loyalty, family wealth and succession. All you need to do is apply "thinking systems" to the Gordian Knot and the challenges unravel.'

This book is that best way.

If you want to know how to unravel that Gordian Knot right now, once you've read the introduction and chapters 1 and 2 you could skip forward to part III and read from there. You will get the answers you are looking for. But you won't fully grasp the problems. This is a little like the parable about giving a man a fish versus teaching him to fish. If you skip to part III, and I fully appreciate your desire to do so, the book will give you the fish. But because you don't fully understand why the Gordian Knot was created in the first place, you may find yourself repeating patterns and behaviours that made the knot in the first place. As such you may not reap the full benefits of the book.

I get it. You're busy. Businesses don't run themselves and family businesses, as this book will attest, bring exponential issues to deal with. But I strongly recommend you learn how to fish. Read part I and part II because they set the scene and allow you to fully appreciate why the answers laid out in part III onwards actually work.

What you will read in these pages, wherever you decide to start, is the story of families in business – including the management of their wealth and effective succession. It is also worth noting that the value in these pages magnifies as the wealth, sustainability and complexity of a family business increases.

Like beauty, most of us recognise that wealth is relative and it can mean different things to different people. Wealth may mean a level of freedom to spend quality time with those you love. For others wealth could simply be measured in dollars and cents. No one version is any better or worse than any other. Just because a family has money does not make them superior to a family with limited resources. This is especially important to remember, should you find yourself marrying into a family with different financial resources than those you grew up with.

This is not opinion and nor is it any type of social commentary. There is no inference or suggestion that wealthy people are better, smarter, more important or happier than those who are not wealthy. In fact, the irony is that the only category of people in the world who know for sure that money doesn't buy happiness is the wealthy!

But for the purposes of this book, let's define wealth in a way that further helps you decide if you will benefit from reading it:

- **Establishment wealth (level 1):** This is the wealth created by the founder of the business. The challenges we explore in these pages are unlikely to derail establishment wealth. But if you're at level 1 and want to make sure you reach level 2 and level 3 then you *should* read this book.
- **Foundational wealth (level 2):** This is the wealth that extends beyond the founder. Typically, this means more than enough has

been made for the founder to live comfortably and have sufficient resources to help their children, parents or siblings. If the foundational wealth is wrapped up in a business you want to pass on to the next generation, then you will almost certainly be subject to some of the challenges in this book. You *must* read it.

- **Generational wealth (level 3):** This is the wealth that extends beyond the family. If you have more money than you or your children could *ever* reasonably use or spend in your lifetimes, you have accumulated generational wealth. If you find yourself in this position, then you face the challenges that inspired me to write this book! And you will be subject to ALL the problems and opportunities we are about to explore. You are also most at risk of the family business curse (more on that shortly). *You can't afford not to read this book.*

Bottom line: financial wealth can be a blessing or a curse. Whether it ends up being a blessing or a curse for you and the people you love is inextricably linked to your understanding of and appreciation for the four voices.

IF YOU HAVE MORE MONEY THAN YOU OR YOUR CHILDREN COULD EVER REASONABLY USE OR SPEND IN YOUR LIFETIMES, YOU ARE AT GREATEST RISK OF THE FAMILY BUSINESS CURSE AND YOU CAN'T AFFORD TO IGNORE THE CONTENTS OF THESE PAGES.

Introduction

There is an ancient Arabian parable that explains what typically happens to the wealth generated by family business:

> The first generation retains the desert qualities, desert toughness, and desert savagery ... they are brave and rapacious ... the strength of group feeling continues to be preserved among them. They are sharp and greatly feared. People submit to them.

> Under the influence of royal authority and a life of ease, the second generation changes from the desert attitude to a sedentary culture, from privation to luxury and plenty, from a state in which everybody shared in the glory to one in which one man claims all the glory ... others are [in] ... humble subservience ... the vigour of the group feeling is broken ... But many of the old virtues remain ... because they [the second generation] had direct personal contact with the first generation ...

> The third generation, then, has completely forgotten the period of desert life and toughness ... Luxury reaches its peak among them ... Group feeling disappears completely ... People forget to protect and defend themselves ... In the course of these three generations, the dynasty grows senile and is worn out.[1]

In the United Kingdom there are various versions of this idea but my favourite is the Lancashire proverb, 'There's nobbut three generations atween a clog and clog.' In Italian it is *'Dalle stalle alle stelle alle stalle'* ('From the stables to the stars to the stables'). In Mexico it's *'Padre noble, hijo rico, nieto pobre'* ('Noble father, rich son, poor grandson'). In China, '富 不过三代' (*'Fu bu guo san dai'*) is straight to the point – 'Wealth does not pass three generations.'

In essence, when it comes to family wealth there is a curse active throughout the world. Namely, that the first generation makes it, the second generation enjoys it and the third generation destroys it! Rags to riches and back again in three generations.

One of the most well-known and often cited examples of this phenomenon is the Vanderbilt empire.

Back in the late 19th century, Cornelius Vanderbilt – known as 'Commodore' – was the Jeff Bezos of his day. He was worth US$105 million – equivalent in today's money to about $205 billion.[2] Starting with a borrowed stake of $100 from his mother he piloted a passenger boat on Staten Island in 1810. He expanded into the steamboat business and went on to build a railroad empire. When he died in 1877, he was the richest man on earth. Despite Cornelius believing his sons were not up to snuff, William Vanderbilt expanded the railroad business and doubled the family fortune. But it didn't last.

Within just 30 years of the old man's death, no member of the Vanderbilt family was among the richest in the United States. It has been observed that by 1972, when 120 of his descendants gathered for a reunion at the Vanderbilt University, not one of them was a modern 'millionaire'. One of his grandchildren is said to have died penniless.

In less than three generations a business empire and its fortune were gone.

William K Vanderbilt, one of Cornelius's grandsons, even went so far as to say, 'Inherited wealth is a real handicap to happiness. It is as certain a death to ambition as cocaine is to morality.' It is easy to scoff at William's statement believing it was him and his fellow third generation (G3) that destroyed an empire. And yet, my experience has proven, without qualification, that this is rarely G3's fault. It's the behaviour, attitude and actions of the founder – or generation one (G1), in this case Cornelius Vanderbilt – that determines whether their legacy will be preserved or not.

IT'S THE BEHAVIOUR, ATTITUDE AND ACTIONS OF THE FOUNDER – OR GENERATION ONE (G1) – THAT DETERMINES WHETHER THEIR LEGACY WILL BE PRESERVED OR NOT.

This book explains the practical science and psychology of why this happens and most importantly how to use governance to avoid it. Governance is the systematic process that seeks to fully answer the question, 'How do we make decisions?'

Of course, the curse is not inevitable – G2 and G3 may be as successful as, or even more successful than, the founder. When we investigate those who *are*, we discover that their success is always aided and abetted by G1's positive actions. These actions are only possible – or, at least, are far easier to accomplish successfully – in the hands of the founding generation (G1).

Too often, the generation that seeds the wealth (G1) thinks the critical rules and lessons learnt in the making of the money are the same as the knowledge needed for the defence of the money. And yet, the management of an enduring multigenerational family business and the governance of wealth is a completely different science to the science of entrepreneurship and making money. While each generation must learn the ropes of their respective industry or business – be that property development, hospitality or constructing railways – there are very few lessons to be learnt about the starting of that business that are necessary or applicable to family governance, succession or continued growth. The inventor or founder of a business is never going to successfully transition that business to the next generation and beyond by teaching those individuals how they invented a product or started that business. The information and knowledge needed to develop a business, take it forward and maintain and develop wealth for each successive generation are very different from the entrepreneurial mindset so often present in the founder.

If G1 is serious about succession and wants to create an enduring legacy, their job is to master stewardship and put things in place that will allow G2 (and beyond) to be ready for succession.

Like so many G1s, Cornelius Vanderbilt believed his children unworthy. He was irritated by what he perceived as a lack of appreciation for the hard work he'd put in to create his business. In his eyes he'd cut the ground and made all the sacrifices and they couldn't even be trusted to do the easy bit – maintain and build upon what he had created. He didn't appreciate that maintenance and building is every bit as challenging as creation – just different. Vanderbilt was also still locked in money-making mode and, as a result, he didn't pay attention to the governance of his wealth or ensure the readiness of his heirs which could have, in turn, ensured the survival of the empire. This is often G1's error.

The error G2 and beyond make is that they believe that they can inherit their father or mother's job. Just because someone had the same surname as the founder does not entitle them to take over the reins of that business when G1 steps down or passes away. G2 can inherit shares, rights and influence but they can't inherit a job – they can only earn it. This fact is obvious in all areas of life – except family business. If one of your parents is an eye surgeon and they die suddenly, you don't expect a phone call from their hospital to say you are now their go-to eye surgeon and you are expected in theatre in two hours. The idea is ludicrous and yet it is expected and almost inevitable in family business.

(As an aside, apologies to the G2 reading this who may be offended by the notion that G1 was the 'lone' wealth creator. I feel you. You were there too!)

It's impossible to dismiss the universal aphorisms that speak of family business failure as old wives' tales or stories such as the Vanderbilts' as anomalies, because the curse is also borne out in statistics. In Australia, for example, although the estimated wealth in the family business sector is $4.3 trillion, the first-generation wealth is $3 trillion, second-generation wealth is $987 billion and third to fifth generation wealth $346 billion.[3] The wealth of the family deteriorates significantly from one generation to the next. In Australia, the average age of a family business is just 32 years.[4] Effective succession is clearly still an issue in family business; and yet the sector and each individual business offers huge advantages to the family, the economy and the wider community. Finding a genuine solution that can reverse the decreasing wealth trend from generation to generation is paramount – hence the motivation for this book.

While we may think of family business in terms of the millions of small and medium-sized operations that underpin many global economies, almost 35 percent of Fortune 500 companies are family owned or controlled. Family businesses account for 50 percent of United States gross domestic product (GDP), and they generate 60 percent of the country's employment and 78 percent of all new job creation.[5] In Australia, family businesses account for around 72 percent of all businesses.[6] And yet, when you look at the generational shift of those businesses, 60 percent are first-generation family businesses, 24 percent are second generation and just 14 percent are family businesses that have survived into the third generation or later.

If the curse is true, and the statistics certainly indicate that it is, then the shirt sleeves to shirt sleeves boomerang represents a colossal waste. Not just the staggering loss of the accumulated wealth but the human cost too – the people who are no longer employed by these businesses, the communities they no longer serve and the breakdown of family connection, love and loyalty that the curse renders inevitable.

But it doesn't have to be this way.

Managing love, loyalty and family wealth successfully generation after generation comes down to your willingness and determination to allow four distinct voices to be heard:

1. The business (or balance sheet) must have a voice.
2. The individuals (founder and family members) must have an individual voice.
3. The family must have a collective voice.
4. The family community (spouses and generations that follow) must have a voice.

Governance and stewardship are what facilitate the emergence of these crucial voices and we will explore these in much more detail later in the book. But first, we must push past the symptoms of the curse to reveal the real cause of failure and family disintegration.

How Our Minds Work Against Us

Before everything – our role in the family, our role in the business, our level of wealth – we are all Homo sapiens. As such we are equipped with a brain, and yet we are not taught how that brain works, how best to use it or how to navigate its quirks. Most of us have next to no scientific or psychological insight or understanding of how our brain operates, so we don't understand its significant neurological and evolutionary limitations. And we certainly don't appreciate that many of the problems we face in all aspects of our life, from relationships to business challenges or financial worries, can be traced back to these limitations! We constantly look outside for solutions or reasons for the various challenges we face and yet most of them emerge from the six inches between our ears.

WE CONSTANTLY LOOK OUTSIDE FOR SOLUTIONS
OR REASONS FOR THE VARIOUS CHALLENGES WE FACE
AND YET MOST OF THEM EMERGE FROM THE SIX INCHES
BETWEEN OUR EARS.

You may have bought this book expecting answers about family business, and it *will* deliver those answers – but you will need to be patient. Most of the problems you face inside and outside the family business are because you and everyone you interact with is a human being. Once you understand a little more about how your brain works (chapter 2) and the five limitations this creates (part I), you will be able to recognise their influence and, perhaps for the first time, appreciate their impact. Without this insight it's impossible to help the founder and members of the family to find their own individual voices. Understanding the human dimension helps to elicit these crucial voices.

This insight also allows you to appreciate that when you are dealing with a family that is bound together by blood and history, where everyone is in possession of an unruly and undisciplined brain, any illusion you harboured about how the process 'should be easy' can finally be laid to rest.

To make these limitations more real for you, I've introduced a fictional family, the Jacksons (you will meet and get to know them in chapter 1). I've chosen to create the Jacksons to better illustrate the unique and complex challenges faced by many of the well-known family businesses I work with, while also seeking to protect those families' lives, experiences and identities. It is the universal experiences, or what is shared by family enterprise, that are important, rather than who the families are. We will come back to the Jacksons time and time again throughout the book to demonstrate the various issues, their implications and more importantly what every family business can do to navigate the inevitable landmines hidden in every family enterprise.

If you belong to a family that has worked with me, and you happen to be reading this book, you can relax now … you aren't in it!

By anchoring to the limitations of the human mind and explaining how they play out in the world of the Jacksons, I'll show you how, left unchecked, our humanness can and will negatively impact a family business and succession while magnifying the problems of wealth management and defence.

You will, for example, meet the Jacksons again in part II, when we unpack happiness. Why? Because, in my experience, it's a fundamental lack of happiness that often triggers my first meeting with a prospective family. The founder or husband-and-wife team are invariably wealthy. They have worked hard, battled the odds, raised a family and founded a successful business – often creating the type of wealth many people only dream of. And yet they are not happy, and neither are their descendants.

They know they should be happy. Often, they will even say so – 'It shouldn't be like this. We should all be happy' – notwithstanding everything they've accomplished and all of the joys and benefits they experience in their lives. I have sat with countless families, seeing the pain and the burden etched on parents' faces as they tell me of the dysfunction among their children. I have also seen the distress etched on G2's faces as they explain the dysfunction and rage either among their siblings or directed towards a parent.

We need to understand happiness far better than we currently do. More specifically we need to appreciate the twin enemies of happiness that are amplified by wealth, not solved by it. Namely, uncertainty and complexity.

WE NEED TO APPRECIATE THE TWIN ENEMIES OF HAPPINESS THAT ARE AMPLIFIED BY WEALTH, NOT SOLVED BY IT. NAMELY, UNCERTAINTY AND COMPLEXITY.

Uncertainty and complexity are increasing for all of us in modern life. We have to make more decisions by breakfast than our ancestors made in a month! These forces are amplified still further in family business and jacked up on steroids where wealth is added to the mix. Part II is therefore about recognising that in a family business you've got all of these diverse forces, each ramping up the complexity and uncertainty. As a result, the business also needs a voice to dial down the noise that can come from the competing individual voices of the founder(s) and family members.

Most of us say we want to be happy or happier. It is a universal goal, and yet we don't appreciate how these forces impact that goal. Too often we assume that money is the answer. As a result, those that don't have enough money set their targets on the wrong goal and those who have achieved wealth get to feel especially guilty because they have what everyone else wants and they are still miserable! That is often what leads them to me. Part II shines a much-needed light on the forces of uncertainty and complexity. It will begin to familiarise you with the first mathematical model that explains the family business issues that are ubiquitous and inescapable. Part I and part II therefore outline the problems and consequences.

Part III explores the solutions: namely governance and stewardship. I show you what the entire governance process might look like, using the Jacksons while also covering the most common variations and the key distinctions that make governance work. In business, especially family business, founders (G1), next gen (G2) and beyond are constantly hoodwinked into believing that their situation is unique. And yet, although the particular family's dynamics or the nature of the industry may be different, the themes, challenges and dysfunction rarely are. Governance and stewardship are always the solutions. The institution of a Family Charter can ensure that the third voice, the voice of the family, is heard. Think of this voice as the collective voice of the whole family. The charter brings individual voices together and is the expression of the vision, values and rules of engagement amongst the family, and between the family and the wealth.

Part IV spells out the processes and techniques used to ensure that the four crucial voices are heard in the business and the family. Again, we will be using the Jacksons to demonstrate the process used to ensure:

- the business has a voice (achieved by the strategic plan)
- the founder and individual family members have a voice (achieved by the personal plans for all Jackson family members and their partners)
- the family has a collective voice (achieved by the Family Charter)
- the family community has a voice (achieved by the Family Retreat).

This success toolkit provides a path to engineered objectivity and decision-making protocols that can ensure your family business and/or balance sheet becomes a tale of success and not another statistic of the curse. Examples of the relevant documents for the Jacksons around the four voices are included in the appendices.

It never ceases to amaze me that when it comes to family business, 'we're family' is uttered as an endlessly hopeful statement about that family's ability to weather the frequent family and business storms they encounter. Implied in that statement, often uttered with a mix of desperation and confusion, is that employed family members or those benefiting from the balance sheet will do what's right; that the family *and* the business will therefore endure, and the wealth will grow for future generations. Essentially, it will work, because 'we're family'.

This hypothesis is wrong. It is a classic example of one of my favourite quotes from American scholar HL Mencken: 'For every complex problem there is an answer that is clear, simple, and wrong.'

Family with multigenerational wealth is a *very* complex problem. Assuming that somehow 'it' (whatever 'it' is today) will work itself out because 'we're family' and 'blood is thicker than water' is clear, simple and wrong. The assumption that a wealth creator is by definition motivated to see their heirs replicate or exceed their accomplishments is also clear, simple and wrong. From Sigmund Freud to Eric Berne's transactional analysis this falsehood is well articulated.[7] Family business is astonishingly complex because of psychology more than commerce.

Bottom line: if you don't understand certain things about who you are as a human being regardless of your role or position in the family or the business, you are doomed. If you don't understand the forces at work that can impact your quality of life and happiness, you are doomed.

If you don't understand certain things about the principles of governance, which provide a robust, proven solution to any problem not caused by the human condition, or you refuse to apply governance, you are doomed. The curse will become a reality – the family will fracture; the balance sheet will deteriorate; and the wealth will disintegrate.

CHAPTER 1

Introducing the Jacksons

John Jackson arrived in Australia from England with his parents and two brothers when he was five years old. He doesn't remember England and his family rarely went back because of the distance and the expense.

His relationship with his brothers was fairly typical – friendly one minute, knocking seven bells out of each other the next. His parents were strict and uncompromising – they had to be. Arriving in a new country with three children, their only advantage was that they spoke the language. John's father worked long hours in a warehouse – he didn't see him much. His mum stayed at home but worked a part-time job in the evenings once her husband came home. John saw how hard they worked and was keen to do better and enjoy life a little more.

John's first job out of school was in construction and he bought his first property in the inner west of Sydney when he was 22. It was definitely a fixer-upper. That was a steep and expensive learning curve but he enjoyed the process and wondered if there was scope for more. At 24 he married Ayesha, who was four years his junior. They met in the suburb John grew up in. Ayesha was born in Australia; her parents were from Sri Lanka, arriving in Australia in the mid-1960s. Like John's parents, Ayesha's carved out a life in Australia through sheer hard work. Their children called Australia 'home'.

John and Ayesha were happy. They bought another property together as the family home and set about renovating it. Coming from different backgrounds was a source of amusement for both of them as they would bump up against different ideas, customs and value systems. The difference was cute – almost adorable.

Then they had children.

What's fascinating about families is that different value systems are often a source of endearment and attraction when two people meet; but as soon as children come along, those same endearing differences can easily become a source of tension, as both parents seek to raise the children from within their own value system. The way we see the world is coloured by our own upbringing or a deliberate deviation from it. In other words, we adjust how we raise our children based on what we think worked in the way we were raised by our parents, *and* what we think didn't work. We believe our upbringing was the 'right way' – even if we recognise that it was flawed. Alternatively, we rail against it. Either way, it is rare that two parents from two different backgrounds with different value systems will agree on how best to raise their children.

The Jacksons' first 'child' was Jackson Developments & Construction, which they created together in 1983. Their first project was a house on a large block of land in Maroubra, New South Wales, which they demolished and built a duplex in its place. It was a nerve-wracking time but also exhilarating when it all came together.

Christopher was born in 1985. Having a child was nerve-wracking for different reasons! Becoming a parent for the first time was certainly daunting. Priya followed a year later, then Nathan and Anika. Ayesha continued to work after Christopher was born but stopped once Priya arrived. By the time Christopher arrived, John had progressed his foray into building property. Initially he focused on subdividing large garden blocks and building another house, or flattening the existing house and creating a duplex or small block of apartments. Sydney was booming so business was thriving. Once the children were all at school Ayesha went back to work in the family business doing the books, scheduling tradesmen and organising deliveries to the various sites. Raising four children alongside her work in the business helped her develop expert negotiation and organisational skills. She would drop the children at school and go on to the office. If any of the children were sick, the school nurse put them in a taxi, they would arrive at the office and be tucked up in the break room with a blanket, a mug of steaming Heinz tomato soup, some toast and the remote control for the TV. If it was more than a sniffle Ayesha would take them home along with a pile of folders.

As they got older the boys were expected to work on the various building sites, although Ayesha would frequently argue that Priya also wanted to help. Priya was strong and sporty and was obviously interested in the family business. She would constantly ask if she could go with her dad. Sometimes she was allowed, but John secretly wished that it was Christopher or Nathan that showed as much interest. He was sure his inner thoughts were his own – but Priya knew. As far as she was concerned his indifference oozed from every pore. She knew he loved her but he frequently dismissed her because she was a girl or it simply didn't even cross his mind to invite her. If Priya challenged him on his attitude or a dismissive comment, John would say he was 'just joking' and that she shouldn't get so defensive – 'it's just banter'. It didn't feel like banter to Priya.

In fairness to John, he grew up with two brothers; he didn't really understand girls. His relationship with his mother had been good but he'd only really experienced her at home. By the time she went out to work in the evenings, he was in bed. As a result, John's 'right way' was that women belonged at home raising the family. He only agreed to Ayesha helping in the business because he needed the help and didn't want to pay an extra salary – although he wouldn't admit that to his wife. She had surprised him and become invaluable in the growth and development of the business, but his cultural upbringing still limited his opinions of how his own daughters might be involved – especially since it was a construction business. Besides, they would just end up leaving to get married and have children – right?

As for Chris, he just confused John. For a start, he hated being called Chris and insisted on Christopher, which John thought odd. Christopher and John were not alike. As a child, Christopher wasn't sporty and would avoid being outside if he could help it. He preferred drawing or coming up with short animated films. Nathan was more like his father, and he would follow him around as a child. John would put him in the pick-up truck on a Saturday morning and the two of them would go and visit various work sites or drive around a suburb looking for potential property to develop. Anika couldn't care less about the family business – she wanted to be a chef. By the time John and Nathan arrived home she would have prepared a family lunch for everyone. Priya would arrive home from hockey and Christopher would emerge from his room – enticed out by the smell of something tasty from the kitchen.

Academically Priya was the smartest of the four children; she was certainly smarter than Nathan, who appeared to be the one most likely to take on the family firm. Christopher was bright but his talents went towards creative pursuits. He was much more interested in how something looked than how it was built. It was pretty clear that John didn't even consider the girls as potential successors to what was now a very successful property development empire making tens of millions of dollars a year in net profit. John and Ayesha would often argue about it, with Ayesha constantly trying to get John to see each of the children for their unique gifts. Yes, Nathan was more like John and that could be useful; but Christopher could easily be part of the business using his design and creative skills, perhaps through architecture. And there was certainly no reason in the modern world where machines did the hard work that either of the girls couldn't run a property development business.

Most of it fell on deaf ears. As a result, all the weight of expectation regarding the business was heaped on the shoulders of Christopher and Nathan.

Cultural expectations of firstborn children created an underlying narrative that Christopher would take over the business – even though Christopher himself clearly showed little interest, and there was a huge amount of resentment from Nathan and Priya who *were* interested in taking the business forward. Christopher and Nathan never really got on. They were reasonably friendly when they were young – although Nathan, who was physically bigger – often bullied Christopher. Once the testosterone arrived it got worse and the 'alpha male' competition started as they jostled for position. They were constantly fighting during their teen years. It was a source of stress for Ayesha but it didn't bother John. He felt it was just normal male behaviour. He fought with his brothers all the time at that age. Besides, it demonstrated aggression and fighting spirit – both of which John believed necessary for success in business. John was secretly proud. Until, of course, their aggression turned towards him as they entered adulthood and were not so happy to be pushed around by dad anymore.

Christopher would accommodate his dad's aspirations for him to join the family business because he loved him and wanted his approval, but he still didn't really see himself in construction. That said, the pressure to conform was intense and relentless. If asked, John would wax lyrical about how he encouraged his children to pursue their dreams and made it clear they could do whatever they wanted – but the truth was very different. There were no ultimatums or screaming matches, but the boys were under no illusion they were expected to take over once John decided he'd had enough. The girls could do something in the business if they *really* wanted to, but their role was never going to be CEO. Maybe HR, business development or something like that.

Today John is 63 and Ayesha is 59. They are very wealthy. The children are doing their thing including building families of their own. All are married with at least one child, except Priya who is engaged to her partner Delvyn. But they are all confused about what's going to happen with the wealth and the business. Anika still has no interest in the business and, with a little help from her parents, opened her own restaurant a few years back. Christopher is doing his best to appease his dad but is conscious he's not really considered up to snuff. Nathan is irritated that he can't just be fast-tracked to John's 2IC. And Priya is pretty angry that despite doing a master's in engineering she is still seen as the tea lady.

John and Ayesha talk about wanting to step back from the business and enjoy life a bit more; at least Ayesha does. She is keen for John to take it a bit easier – he had a heart scare when he was 58. Surely, it's time to pass the business to G2. In theory, John agrees and quite likes the idea of more golf and travel, but he doesn't know how to do it. He doesn't know who he should appoint in his place and besides, he doesn't want to step away completely. It's his business; his blood, sweat and tears went into it. He's not even convinced that any of his children have what it takes to run the business, never mind develop it further.

The Jacksons are stuck. John is stuck because he doesn't know what to do and doesn't really trust his children to be as good at the business as he is. Ayesha's stuck because she can see what the situation is doing to John *and* their children. Christopher's stuck living a half life, trying to keep his father happy but do what he wants as well. Priya is stuck because she can't get her dad to take her seriously, but if she leaves the business, she might never get back in. Nathan is stuck because he believes he's entitled to take over the business now – because he just is, and besides, he sees himself as the favourite. Why should it matter who was born first? And Anika is stuck because her siblings make her feel guilty about the help she received to open the restaurant.

This scenario or some version of it is very common in the family businesses I work with. A founder, or founding husband-and-wife team, co-create not only a business but a family. The business becomes very successful and the children grow up.

And then the fun starts.

We will come back to the Jacksons throughout the book. There is also a short biography on each family member at the end of chapter 14 as a helpful reminder of who's who.

But first, we need to unpack the mind. The next chapter covers the human source of much of our misery. We will then explore the five human limitations the mind creates and how they actually play out in a family business environment. These limitations cause problems in life, regardless of whether you work in a family business or not. But, for reasons I will explain and demonstrate via this hypothetical family, the dysfunction they can create in a family business is significant. At least they are when the family is not aware of them, and hasn't yet taken active governance steps to counteract their negative influence.

Of course, the point must be made: you are not the Jacksons. But the differences are irrelevant – it is the similarities that really matter. I may or may not know you personally but I DO know this: you are human, you have relationships and you probably have a business. Or, you have a balance sheet that must be managed. It may be a very successful business or a significant balance sheet. More than likely, you have siblings and/or children managing or relying on this wealth and you are trying to make this work while growing the love, loyalty and family wealth!

It's tough. But there is a proven path through.

CHAPTER 2

Introducing Your Mind

The common denominator between family, business and wealth and the myriad challenges they generate is *people*. This is so obvious that we disregard its relevance, but to do so is a profound mistake. Most of the issues we face in life, family, business and beyond are down to our ignorance or dismissal of the human component. It's a component that is not unique to each family or to individual personalities, but common amongst our species. As Professor Nigel Nicholson once said, 'You can take the person out of the Stone Age, but you can't take the Stone Age out of the person.'[8]

As I said in the introduction, we are constantly looking outside for solutions or reasons for the various challenges we face, and yet most of them arise from the six inches between our ears. I first wrote about this reality and its impact on business management in my first book *You Don't Think as Smart as You Are* back in 2000. Ten years later my second book, *Elephants and the Business Laws of Nature*, looked more closely at how those six inches impact the performance gap, productivity and business success. And this book examines the impact these six inches have on love, loyalty and wealth in family business, while offering a blueprint on how to mitigate our brains' most disruptive tendencies.

It makes sense, then, to embark on a whistle-stop examination of those six inches. It may seem unnecessary in a book about managing wealth through generations, but I promise, once you understand your mind, *everything* else – from business management to productivity to relationships to family dynamics to wealth management and beyond – makes much more sense. The way our brain develops creates five limitations – which we will unpack in part I – which, in turn, create so much of the dysfunction that is common in family business. The way the human brain develops is actually the reason why family business so often falls prey to the curse – shirt sleeves to shirt sleeves in three generations.

THE WAY OUR BRAIN DEVELOPS IS THE REASON WHY FAMILY BUSINESS SO OFTEN FALLS PREY TO THE CURSE – SHIRT SLEEVES TO SHIRT SLEEVES IN THREE GENERATIONS.

I'm sure you will agree it is therefore well worth a not-so-small detour. I make no apologies for diving deep into the machine that came without instructions.

Thanks to the field of evolutionary psychology, we understand much more about psychological structures from a modern evolutionary perspective. The field itself, which has emerged over several decades, is a convergence of discoveries in genetics, neuropsychology and paleobiology amongst many other sciences.

According to evolutionary psychologists a great deal of human behaviour is the result of psychological adaptations that evolved to solve recurring problems in our ancestral environment.[9] While we may look a little different to our cave-dwelling ancestors – we may wear nicer clothes and eat more interesting and tasty food – our brain is much the same.

The reason for this is three-fold. First, humans started to disperse from their point of origin across the globe, which alleviated territory constraints. Second, there was also no consistent environmental crisis that demanded evolution to deal with changing circumstances through increased thinking capacity. Together, this meant that natural selection didn't always kick in. Natural selection states that in response to a particular environmental or survival challenge any species, including Homo sapiens, will adapt in some way to survive in the new environment. For example, Darwin discovered that there was a finch on Wolf Island in the Galapagos that adapted over time to survive on an island with very little fresh water. This particular finch is called the vampire finch because it has a very sharp beak that it uses to puncture other birds' skin and drink their blood. For humans, there was no recurring problem to solve in our ancestral environment; this meant there was no 'burning platform' caused by lack of food or space, or some environmental crisis, to trigger an evolutionary jump in our intellectual capacity. We didn't need to be smarter so we didn't get smarter.

And third, human beings only really started to take control of their environment through the cultivation of agriculture some 10,000 years ago, and 10,000 years isn't long enough to see any significant alterations to mental capacity. As a result, our software might be evolving through increased access to knowledge but our hardware is still upgrading at a glacial pace.

The fact that we are human beings is the source of a great deal of our problems, regardless of what those problems might be. These challenges are caused and amplified by our innate human nature and unconscious programming, not by the myriad reasons, explanations, excuses or justifications that we so readily come up with to explain our various predicaments.

Much of the humanness I am referring to emerges from the fact that human beings are driven by the biological imperative, or our drive to survive. The definition of the biological imperative is the 'needs of living organisms required to perpetuate their existence: to survive. It includes the following hierarchy of logical imperatives for a living organism: survival, territorialism, competition, reproduction, quality of life-seeking, and group forming.'[10] Interestingly, when diagnosing the challenges in family business, the issues ultimately fall under one of these subconscious and hardwired drivers.

We are intrinsically wired to find and consume food, defend territory, congregate in groups, find a partner and produce children. We are not naturally wired to do just about anything else – including business.

WE ARE INTRINSICALLY WIRED TO FIND AND CONSUME FOOD, DEFEND TERRITORY, CONGREGATE IN GROUPS, FIND A PARTNER AND PRODUCE CHILDREN. WE ARE NOT NATURALLY WIRED TO DO JUST ABOUT ANYTHING ELSE – INCLUDING BUSINESS.

Although human beings today inhabit a world that bears almost no resemblance to the one inhabited by our Stone Age ancestors, we are navigating this new world with the ingrained mentality and instinctive drives Stone Age hunter-gatherers possessed. For example, finding food used to be a daily problem fraught with all manner of potentially lethal dangers from toxic berries to sabre-toothed tigers. Today we go to the supermarket or order online and someone will deliver food to our door. And yet, in the intermitting 200,000 years or so, we've had marginal, if any, biological or neurological upgrades. Hence Professor Nicholson's statement, 'You can take the person out of the Stone Age, but you can't take the Stone Age out of the person.'[11]

This is the core of the problem.

Any problem.

Human Beings Are Not Born Ready

A baby antelope or bison is running alongside its mother within minutes of birth. A baby tortoise hatches from an egg, digs itself out of the sand and scuttles to the ocean by moonlight without any parental supervision whatsoever. But a human baby is utterly useless for the first few years of its life (for some it can be much longer!).

When a human baby is born their brain is around 350 cc in size. This is pretty much the maximum possible size because of the diameter of the female pelvis. The pelvis can't go beyond a certain size because such adaptations would create walking problems which would bring a new set of survival issues. So, 350 cc is about as good as it's going to get for any baby. That's about the same size as the brain of a baby chimpanzee. But, to be considered 'ready', a human being needs a much bigger brain than the one they are born with so growth after birth becomes paramount. For the chimpanzee, life is fairly straightforward – find food, protect the group, defend territory, find a mate, reproduce (much like us except for our highly complex 'quality of life-seeking'). As a result, the chimpanzee's brain will grow a further 100 cc by the time it reaches adulthood. The typical human brain on the other hand will grow another 1,000 cc at least. In terms of mass most of that additional growth will occur before the age of four or five.[12] In terms of capability the growth and development will occur over a couple of decades. In fact, the human brain isn't fully 'ready' until we reach our early to mid-20s.

From an evolutionary perspective our brain consists of three areas – the reptilian brain, the midbrain (also known as the mammalian brain or limbic system) and the neocortex (see figure 2.1 overleaf).

The reptilian brain includes the brainstem and the cerebellum and appeared in early humans over 500 million years ago. This part of the brain is responsible for coordination and body movement and function. In a baby this is present but underdeveloped – hence why you can put a baby down in a room and go back 10 minutes later and they haven't moved beyond waving their arms and legs around.

The midbrain appeared some 300 to 150 million years ago. This adaptation wraps around the brainstem and has developed significantly over the last three million years! The midbrain is home to our involuntary, *autonomic nervous system* and is also sometimes referred to as the emotion centre of the brain. It regulates chemical production and therefore has an impact on the body's internal state. Again, a baby is born with the midbrain intact but underdeveloped. Together the reptilian brain and midbrain make up most of what we refer to as the subconscious mind. These brain structures are doing their thing without our conscious effort or even awareness.

Figure 2.1: The Human Brain

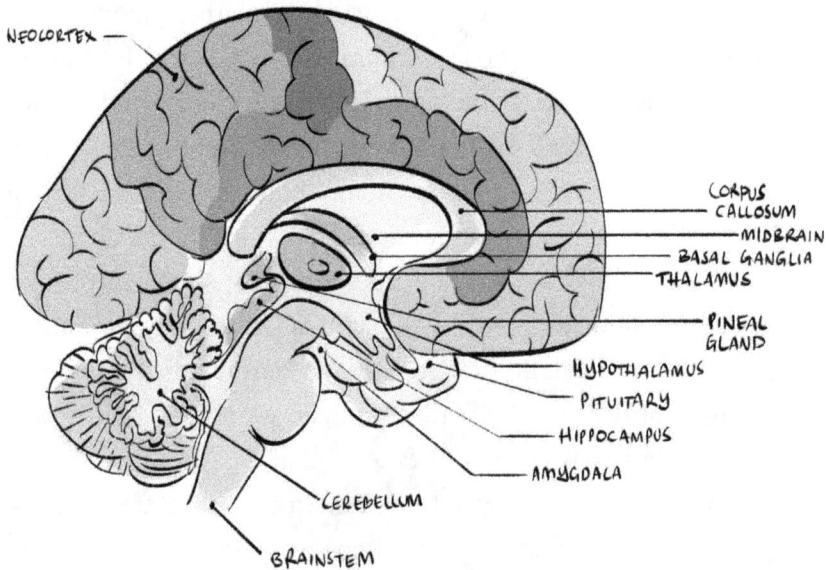

There are two types of consciousness.[13] The first, which is primarily taken care of by the reptilian brain and the midbrain, is known as *objective consciousness* or *subconscious*. This objective consciousness is not only a vast repository of information but it is also the intelligent awareness that gives us life every day and keeps our bodies working. It pumps blood and processes millions of automatic functions without us having to 'do' anything.

It is our objective consciousness that ensures that each and every blood cell makes a complete circuit through our body every 20 to 60 seconds. In doing so, those blood cells travel some 6,000 miles through our vascular channels which account for about 3 percent of our body's mass. There are 100,000 chemical reactions taking place in every one of our estimated 70 to 100 trillion cells every second. Around 10 million of those cells die every second and are swept up and eliminated. At the same time, 10 million new cells take their place. Our kidneys are filtering our blood faster and more efficiently than the most sophisticated dialysis machines on the planet and communication between our cells occurs faster than the speed of light.[14] All this, together with countless other processes, is occurring 'behind the scenes' without any intervention or effort whatsoever on our part. We don't need to remember or add these things to our 'to-do list' – objective consciousness has it covered.

Meanwhile, the second type of consciousness is known as *subjective consciousness*. It's subjective consciousness that is aware of reading these words. It maintains our individual free will and allows us to express ourselves as self-conscious identities. This type of consciousness is only possible with the addition of the last evolutionary adaptation in our brain – the neocortex.

The neocortex appeared about 3 million years ago and moulded itself around the other two layers of the brain. This is the seat of our conscious awareness. Most of the 1,000 cc plus of brain growth occurs in the neocortex, especially the frontal lobe. It is the frontal lobe of the neocortex that gives us unique capabilities over our chimpanzee cousins. It is also the frontal lobe that is the 'I' we recognise as self. It is what facilitates self-awareness – where we are aware of our actions, thinking, behaviour, feelings and our environment.[15]

Whereas the neocortex of other mammals accounts for between 10 and 40 percent of the brain, it starts at 50 percent in primates and rises to about 80 percent in Homo sapiens. Most of our adult brain is made up of neocortex. Research conducted by British anthropologist and evolutionary psychologist Robin Dunbar has demonstrated that neocortex volume correlates with social complexity especially in relation to the frontal lobe.[16] Essentially, it is our advanced frontal lobe that separates us from primates and embodies all that we associate with 'being human'. It is the neocortex that gives us gifts that only human beings enjoy, such as feelings of uncertainty and doubt, the combination arising out of our uniquely conscious sense of the future.[17] What makes human beings different from every other species? We know there is a tomorrow.[18]

Although the other lobes of the neocortex – the parietal lobe, occipital lobe and temporal lobe – are involved in creating the pictures, ideas and abstract concepts we have, and they are involved in the filtering of data through the senses to give us what we view as reality, it is the frontal lobe that decides what to do with that information. The other lobes may alert us if we are too hot or too cold, but it's the frontal lobe that comes up with the solution to turn up the heating or put a sweater on. As the seat of our conscious awareness, the frontal lobe is responsible for the meaning we attach to those pictures and ideas and the ability to hold them wilfully in mind. It is in charge of all the so-called higher functions such as reasoning, planning, intellectualising, learning and remembering, creating, analysing and verbally communicating, to name a few.

Both subjective and objective consciousness are amazing and incredibly useful at keeping us alive and functioning in the world, but they also create some challenging side effects which I'll explain in part I.

These challenges are made worse because the neocortex doesn't come fully installed. The journey towards 'ready' from helpless infant to mature adult requires an astonishing amount of growth and learning which complicates things still further.

The Creation of Default Settings

If we are not born ready, how do we get ready?

Basically, we learn really quickly and create what are effectively default settings that determine how we live our lives. Think of these brain default settings in the same way you would consider default settings on your computer. When you buy a new computer, you remove it from its box and plug it in – it's ready to go. The software on the hardware is already configured to do what most users would want to do with that type of computer, whether that's prepare documents or play graphics-heavy games. The manufacturer knows what the user wants and has set the system up for that purpose with the option of changing various settings should they wish. This makes the user experience much easier and faster and ensures customers don't screw up their new machine and clog up support lines with stupid questions. It's plug-and-play and most users want plug-and-play. If we bought a new computer and we had to load all the software and fiddle around with the settings most of us would lose the will to live. So, all that is taken care of for us. We can change the settings, but most users never do. Most of us have absolutely no idea the extent of the additional functions, bells and whistles that even a mid-range computer could deliver if we changed the default settings the machine comes with initially.

And the same is true with the brain. Its default settings are developed over time as a result of the learning process. The cerebellum plays a crucial role in the development of default settings as it coordinates movements and facilitates automatic hardwired memories and behaviour. The hippocampus is also involved as it formulates experiences with associated emotional memories, for processing vital information during learning and for encoding long-term memories.[19]

Human beings learn through associative conditioning. This is often called Hebb's Law – what fires together wires together.[20] In 1949, Donald Hebb, a Canadian neuropsychologist, presented a theory of learning suggesting we learn new information when our brain forms new synaptic connections – increasing our capacity to remember by forming associations between the known and the unknown. (This is why metaphor and analogy work so well as a communication tool – they compare something that is known to something that is unknown, narrowing the comprehension gap.)

What we believe about the world – what is 'right', 'wrong', 'acceptable', 'unacceptable', 'possible', 'impossible', 'good' or 'bad' – is learned through this conditioning process. If we look at John Jackson, for example: he never considers his daughters as legitimate potential heirs to his business, because he never saw women in leadership roles or witnessed women adding value anywhere outside the home. John's world view is myopic – women's potential is evident throughout society and across every culture – but his personal defaults, also known as prejudices, have blinded him to that fact. These conditioned stereotypes are reinforced by the nature of his business, which he believes to be dirty male-dominated work. It never crosses his mind that the brawn that was required to be successful in his profession when he started has been replaced by machinery that anyone can operate, or that brains, male or female, are now the most important ingredient for his business's success.

Conditioning is an automatic learning mechanism born out of the biological imperative – the drive to survive. It kicks in almost as soon as we are born and long before we can speak. John was never consciously taught his conditioned beliefs about women; he simply picked them up from the environment he grew up in.

The purpose of conditioning is to assess incoming signals, determine whether those signals pose a threat and classify that information for later use. This process is facilitated by the amygdala – the body's emotional early warning system.

The amygdala is one of the few parts of the brain that is fully developed and fully functional at birth. The amygdala *is* born ready. It's doing its thing – alerting us to danger – before the part of the brain we use to recognise ourselves is even active!

From an evolutionary psychology perspective this associative learning model is referred to as *classification before calculus*.[21] In an effort to make sense of changing and uncertain events and circumstances, the human brain classifies all experiences instantaneously so that in the future it doesn't have to calculate whether the information is important or not. Because of the sheer volume of information in our modern environment this skill has become extremely well honed, and we have developed prodigious capabilities for sorting and classifying information.

This ability to classify everything in a nanosecond was once useful not only in terms of whether to eat the red berries or the blue ones, but also who in the tribe to align with. Instantaneous assessment of people still occurs today as we make immediate judgements about everyone we meet.

This ability to classify without real thinking is the biological basis of the default settings we create. Essentially, these act as predetermined conclusions that are derived and stored from thoughts of the past. They free us from having to consciously process the vast majority of the data we receive in the present.

In theory, this is an amazing superpower of human evolution. In reality, it's a recipe for disaster. We think we are making decisions based on logic and reason when actually we are simply reacting to long-forgotten events or situations that were sufficiently challenging that they created a default setting to help us avoid the same or a similar event in the future.

There are two types of conditioning – single trial and multiple trial. As the name suggests, single trial conditioning occurs very quickly as a result of a single exposure to a stimulus. The most obvious examples are when a child burns their fingers on a stove or from messing about with matches. Going back to the Jacksons, let's say that child is Nathan and he's burned himself on the stove. The physical pain and corresponding emotional pain of being yelled at by Ayesha is enough to burn that learning into Nathan's brain. This means he will not have to repeat the event and therefore re-experience the pain – thus ensuring his safety and survival into the future.

Science has proven a correlation between the number of 'markers' that occur in an event or situation and the creation of learning. The more markers – such as fear, pain or environmental or situational data points – that are involved, the greater the fusion of neural patterns and the faster the learning.[22]

Essentially, in that learning moment at the stove, Nathan's brain scanned the environment and collected all the information that set the moment apart, recorded it and classified it. Nathan doesn't remember this and wasn't even aware of it at the time, but his brain logged everything from what Ayesha was wearing when she shouted at him, to what was on the radio in the background, to what he was wearing, to the temperature in the room, to who else was present, to any smells and sounds that could be identified. What his brain was doing was cataloguing the event to map its characteristics and parameters so that it could alert him to danger should a cluster of those same or similar parameters show up again in a future situation. What fires together wires together – so these disparate characteristics of the episode are forever connected or wired together, thus ensuring ongoing safety, survival and pain avoidance.

The second type of conditioning is multiple trial conditioning. It is often less dramatic or memorable but its impact is every bit as powerful. Again, as the name would suggest, it relates to all the things that are learned through repetition. Essentially, when we are told something enough times, or we experience something enough times, whether our frontal lobe believes it or not, it has a formative impact on us.

Like any family, the Jacksons have plenty of default settings created through multiple trial conditioning to contend with. Christopher received the message from his dad that he was a bit 'soft'. He was the whinger. Nathan would constantly point out how nothing was ever quite right for 'St Christopher'. Priya's consistent messaging was that she wasn't quite as good as the boys. She played sport so she could get closer to her dad but he never really saw past her gender. John didn't know it but by constantly diminishing Priya's genuine interest for the business he limited both of their options. He limited his own options for effective succession and he limited his daughter's appreciation of what she was capable of. Anika was always just 'the baby' and remained so even into her late 20s. On the rare occasions John would ask her to come to the yard and help out, how was she ever supposed to be taken seriously? Her parents and siblings sometimes even called her 'the baby' in meetings.

These stereotypes translated into playful or even loving monikers may be cute at home but they are not when they spill into the family workplace. They are essentially default settings created by multiple trial conditioning where family members are markers of the default. And, of course, those family members are the same people everyone is now trying to run a business with! Every family member takes on a role in that family – the joker, the black sheep, the difficult one, the aggressive one. For family members who are not in business together these defaults become the fodder for the clinical psychologist they may visit later in life. But when these defaults are 'trapped' inside a shared business it's like putting them in a kiln – they become baked in!

Imagine a business meeting with various key players attending. John is chairing the meeting and Christopher, Nathan and Priya are involved. Christopher is making an important point and Nathan says, 'Okay, St Christopher, no need to get your knickers in a knot.' How does that change the meeting? How does Christopher feel? Is that likely to get the best thinking out of the group? Would Nathan say that to an unrelated colleague? If Nathan is uncouth or uncultured by nature, he might. But a civil Nathan would never dream of directing such a statement towards an *employee* – and yet he feels totally comfortable directing it towards his *brother*. Is Christopher going to bring his A-game or is he going to simmer with resentment? He may look like the 35-year-old that entered the meeting half an hour early but physiologically, emotionally and intellectually he's not.

He's been transported back to the countless fights he had as a young child fighting with his younger but physically bigger brother in their shared bedroom; fights that would involve Nathan criticising Christopher's creativity and basically bullying his older brother. Nathan's 'funny' comment about the knickers triggers a default setting that's been running since they were children and neither of them even realise it.

I remember as a child my parents used to say I was prone to histrionics. I honestly don't remember it but apparently I was a bit of a drama queen and would make a fuss if I didn't get my own way. My Dad called me 'Hystika', a Hungarian quirk of adding 'ka' to the end of words as a term of affection. I wouldn't quite go so far as tantrum but my behaviour was certainly in that ballpark. Fast forward 30 years and my dad came to work with me. According to all who met him, Pete was one of the smartest, most balanced, honourable and kind human beings one could meet. But, imagine the damage he could have caused if, after I had pulled a staff member aside and had a word with them about their performance, or if I had given a passionate and rousing speech to my team demanding more effort, Dad had told everyone, 'Oh, don't take it too seriously – he's always been a bit prone to histrionics! Settle down Hystika.' From that point forward my staff might simply dismiss any forceful intervention on my part, regardless of how valid it was.

Learnings from the Field: King of Catastrophe

Imagine the damage that is done when a very successful G1 refers to his son as the 'King of Catastrophe'. Standing with his leadership team as his son approaches, G1 announces to the group, 'Oh look, here comes the King of Catastrophe'. His leadership team members laugh – why not? It is quite funny. But his son who is just out of earshot has no idea why the group is laughing. He can take a pretty accurate guess based on past experience that it has something to do with him. This is a fair assessment considering his dad has no qualms about sharing the 'King of Catastrophe' moniker with others, and he eventually learns of it through the grapevine. There is no malice from G1 – he just thought it was funny. But stop for a moment and imagine how it must feel for his son to find out his dad holds that opinion, and worse, openly shares it with G2's colleagues and subordinates? Would it improve his confidence and standing in the firm, or diminish it? Would it bolster G2's self-esteem, or damage it? It would hurt and negatively impact how G2 feels and how others view him. I assure you, this type of retro role-playing happens all the time in families.

As we grow up, we grow into a role or stereotype based on myriad factors and influences. It doesn't matter how old we are: as soon as the family is together again, each parent and child will take on their role – forever pigeonholed as 'the baby' or 'St Christopher' or 'aggressive' or 'the King of Catastrophe'. That's hard enough in a family setting; it can be infuriating, condescending and humiliating in a family business setting.

Of course, having a commercial business that includes family members can make the business more personal, inspiring and meaningful. It can also make it more fun. But if we don't first appreciate the human dynamics at play, trouble is inevitable. The mere presence of a family member can trigger all sorts of long-forgotten memories, feelings, reactions and default settings, polluting our ability to access our best thinking and smartest decisions. This can and does result in arguments, resentments or the emergence of familiar behaviour patterns and family stereotypes that are more often than not counterproductive to business success and happiness.

Collectively these conditioning processes create myriad default settings – automatic responses that are triggered by the presence of particular markers from the past that alert the amygdala of impending danger. Think of your amygdala as an auto-activated chemical plant that relies on suspicion, not fact, as the trigger.

Our default settings are made visible in the world via reflex actions.

Reflex Actions

When something is repeated over and over again (multiple trial conditioning) it becomes a conditioned response or reflex response. Ivan Pavlov is the man who alerted us to the power of these neurological constructs. Initially studying digestion and using dogs as subjects, Pavlov noticed that if his Alsatians were fed at the same time as a bell was rung or a whistle was blown and that was repeated over time, the dogs would make a connection between the two separate events (being fed and the sound of a bell). After a relatively short period of time the dogs would salivate at the sound regardless of whether they were fed or not.[23]

THINK OF YOUR AMYGDALA AS AN AUTO-ACTIVATED CHEMICAL PLANT THAT RELIES ON SUSPICION, NOT FACT, AS THE TRIGGER.

There is no logical, rational or useful connection between whistles or bells and salivation and yet repetition created one. It may be fascinating and remarkably clever but it also highlights the shortcomings of the conditioning process and the default settings it creates. Conditioning is blunt, often wildly inaccurate and profoundly unsophisticated. By its very nature conditioning matches stimuli, information or data and connects them when they are not necessarily connected. In the case of Nathan's 'stove incident', his unfinished and unready brain connected the fact that Ayesha was wearing jeans and a red t-shirt, it was a cold day so he was wearing a blue fleece top, and *I don't like Mondays* by the Boomtown Rats was playing on the radio. Obviously, Nathan wasn't consciously aware of any of this and certainly didn't know who the Boomtown Rats were, but his mother was enjoying it – until he burned his fingers. Those 'markers' plus myriad other data points were stored in Nathan's brain and permanently connected. Remember: what fires together wires together.

Fast forward nearly 30 years and Nathan is working in the family business. He has managed to secure a meeting with a prospect but it can only happen on Sunday. Nathan agrees and they arrange to meet in a local café. Nathan decides that he will have the meeting and then go to the gym so he grabs a blue fleece top as it's a cold day. The prospect arrives wearing jeans and a red t-shirt and they order coffee and sit down. The radio in the café is playing in the background and the DJ is inviting listeners to 'guess the year'; then *I don't like Mondays* starts playing. For some reason Nathan feels off. He was really excited about this meeting but now he's filled with foreboding that he can't explain. He presses on and makes his pitch but he doesn't seem to be getting through to the prospect. Nathan's brain goes into overdrive – 'What was I thinking? I should have dressed smarter than this – I look like an amateur.' Nathan rationalises the outcome and assumes it didn't go well because he wasn't prepared and, with hindsight, he was dressed inappropriately – but actually, it didn't go well because several of the markers that wired together when he was four years old were activated in the café and that default setting put him on edge and made him feel the way he did when his mother shouted at him for playing with the stove! His amygdala sounded the alarm which simultaneously shut down access to his frontal lobe and readied him for a survival response. A tad over the top considering he was having a chat with a possible client in a café! Without access to the thinking part of the brain, the presentation was awkward – Nathan effectively froze, and later blamed the aberration on the fact that he was dressed too casually.

We mistake the work of the midbrain as being 'I', when it is in fact 'I robot' or perhaps more accurately 'AI robot'. One of the most extraordinary characteristics of artificial intelligence (AI) is its speed at data assessment and the application of algorithms. And yet our amygdala is just as fast and equally capable of instantly matching the vast repository of internal nonsense we accumulate during the conditioning process to any manner of external nonsense, arriving at a conclusion before the thinking brain is even in gear.

The faulty explanations we then use to explain that nonsense away is an example of ethnomethodology – the study of the methods we use to understand life and make sense of our experiences. Developed by sociologist Harold Garfinkel, ethnomethodology upends the idea that 'everything happens for a reason' and states instead that stuff happens and then we rationalise it and explain it to ourselves so that it makes sense.[24]

> *Life is understood backwards, but must be lived forwards.*
> – Søren Kierkegaard

Everything Happens for a Reason

The idea that everything happens for a reason is just lazy thinking. Let me prove it. If everything happens for a reason, why does reason always follow the event?

By definition, the 'reason' is how we explain, justify or create context for what 'just happened'. Our amygdala, in its eternal pursuit to learn from or categorise an experience, provokes us to find the invented 'method in the madness' of reality.

Understanding how the manifestations of our brain work allows us to lift our thinking beyond everything from the platitudes such as 'everything happens for a reason' to the dribble dished out in books like *The Secret*.

Here's the real secret: all you attract is a function of all you do. What you do impacts others' reflex responses. Behaviours that drive 'attraction' are functional and factual manifestations of our reflex responses.

If you don't believe me, read anything by Derren Brown to fully understand the science of our perceptions.

As for Christopher, his default was triggered in the meeting by the fact that the point he was making was related to a creative idea, and his brother had mocked his creative tendencies since they were children. The presence of even a couple of similar markers were enough to trip Christopher's default setting, with the corresponding reflex response of silence and withdrawal. As an adult he should be able to recognise that his brother is deliberately trying to undermine him, but the default is too powerful – especially when he doesn't know about it. Instead, he does what he has always done – he withdraws. Others in the meeting may be able to sense a shift in the energy, but even if John or Priya admonish Nathan for being unprofessional, the default has tripped and there is nothing anyone can do about it.

And in case you are reading this thinking, 'I would never do that' or 'This doesn't apply to me because I had a good upbringing and get on with my family' – no one can avoid conditioning. We can't reach adulthood without these default settings – it's biologically and neurologically impossible. And it doesn't matter how good or otherwise our upbringing was or how we get on with our family. Defaults exist in all of us and they trigger actions and reactions that we have very limited control over.

The default settings that are created by conditioning and manifest in reflex actions are often extremely unhelpful. There is no causation between blue fleece tops or red t-shirts and fear or foreboding – or between creativity and being bullied by your brother – but the brain creates a connection that becomes an automatic response when those markers appear in adult life. We don't question them; we don't understand them and often we don't realise what has just happened. All we know is we feel worse than we did a few minutes ago. Christopher might know he feels terrible but he doesn't really know why, other than Nathan being Nathan.

It's like when you go to the doctor and she whips out her trusty rubber hammer and taps your knee. Your knee kicks out automatically. You have no control over it and can't claim it as your own action. It just happens. It has nothing to do with your 'I'. You don't say, 'See what I just did – bet that's the fastest you've seen – right?' It's just the automatic output of a rubber hammer input.

We have thousands of these automatic outputs (reflex responses) triggered by thousands of rubber hammer inputs that coincidentally match enough data points in the default setting to trigger their response. It's all because of the conditioning process.

We all have these reflex responses and they will all be triggered by events at some point or another. But, in family – especially family business, where family members are working alongside each other as adults – they can be triggered almost daily. Each sibling or parent is effectively a little rubber hammer whose mere presence can and does trigger all manner of reflex responses. 'Dad, why are you always late?' is a common phrase uttered in the Jackson business. John Jackson tends to be late for meetings, and Priya always complains about it. She isn't aware of why it upsets her so much, but it's because he was supposed to collect her after school camp when she was six years old, and Priya was the last one to be collected. Her teacher had to call John to find out where he was which made Priya feel uncared for and forgotten. 'Nathan is unreliable' is another common refrain. Actually, Nathan isn't unreliable – it's just that Anika has never quite forgiven him for going to his friend's 10th birthday party instead of helping her fix her bike. Family is a minefield of reflex responses borne out of conditioning that no one in the family even remembers! Most of this conditioning occurs before we are six years old – a time when we spend the vast majority of our time with parents or siblings – which means that a huge number of these automatic default settings will involve a family member. This is why even the mere presence of family automatically increases the likelihood of a reflex response being triggered.

Unfortunately, it Gets Worse

Remember, we are not born ready. In those early years as the brain is growing and absorbing huge amounts of information it is doing so in a catch-22 situation. We need to learn more stuff to become ready, but we don't actually have the neurological equipment to ensure that what we are learning is accurate, valid or useful.

EEG readings of the human brain show that neural electrical activity correlates with different states of awareness and development. There are at least five different frequency levels each associated with a different brain state:

1. **Delta:** 0.5–4 Hz – Sleeping/unconscious
2. **Theta:** 4–8 Hz – Imagination/reverie
3. **Alpha:** 8–12 Hz – Calm consciousness
4. **Beta:** 12–35 Hz – Focused consciousness
5. **Gamma:** > 35 Hz – Peak performance.

Adults can shift from state to state over the whole range of normal brain functioning because they have a finished, fully functioning brain. Children don't. As a result, their brain displays very different behaviour in accordance with their level of development. During the first two years of life a human infant operates largely from delta. Between two and six years old the brain activity ramps up and the infant experiences theta. We see this as small children play make-believe and mix reality with imagination. This is the stage of fairy princesses and imaginary battles. Alpha capabilities come online after six years old and beta at about 12 years old.

What's really interesting is that delta and theta brain frequencies are known collectively as 'hypnagogic trance'.[25] If the phrase sounds familiar it's probably because it's the same neural state that a stage hypnotist accesses to make a volunteer from the audience cluck like a chicken whenever they clap their hands and shout 'cauliflower' – much to the amusement of the rest of the audience.

This means that during the first six years of our lives we were effectively being hypnotised by the people around us – mainly parents and siblings (hence their propensity to trigger default settings and emotional reflex responses in later life). This also explains why sibling relationships can be so formative: we spent more time with them. But other care providers, friends, pre-school teachers and the culture we lived in also played a part. We learned what was right, wrong, good, bad, acceptable, not acceptable, normal and abnormal by what we heard, saw, felt and experienced in those early years of life. And we've been clucking like a chicken whenever anyone says 'cauliflower' ever since.

Most of the information and signals we receive via our five senses that are instrumental in the conditioning process and therefore the creation of default settings and reflex responses don't even register with us consciously – even as adults. For example, we already know that the central nervous system is only capable of processing a tiny fraction of what it *could* be aware of via our senses. The retina transmits data at 10 million bits per second, our other senses process one million bits per second, and yet only 40 bits per second reach consciousness.[26] Forty! That's pathetic! Our subconscious mind – the mind that's taking care of all sorts of stuff like pumping blood, regulating temperature and extracting nutrients from food – is capable of processing 20 million environmental stimuli per second, against the dismal 40 environmental stimuli that our conscious mind is processing.[27]

This is a double whammy. We are being programmed by a colossal amount of information and data at a time when we don't yet have the brain capability to consciously scrutinise that information and data for accuracy. Infants don't yet have a functioning frontal lobe. This means that any one of those millions of data points and spurious correlations could have created a conditioned response or default setting that will then trigger a decision, emotional response or behaviour without us knowing why. As an adult, we might be able to come up with a rational explanation for the decision or action using our now-developed frontal lobe, but the reality is we have acted or made a decision based on a conditioned response or programming that was formed before we could even speak! And certainly before we had the cognitive capability to assess its accuracy and validity. To make matters worse, the automatic response of a default setting is always significantly faster than the rational response. Which means our rational self is constantly trying to talk our irrational self off the ledge – preferably before the irrational self has done or said something stupid.

As a 63-year-old man, John has a fully developed frontal lobe so he is able to rationalise that he didn't offer the IT job to Trevor because his résumé was just not up to snuff – but the real reason is that Trevor reminded him of his Uncle Marvin, who used to tweak his nose when he was three years old and it really hurt. This may sound ridiculous and frankly it is but it's a neurological reality, because the amygdala has a comparative function. This means that it is constantly comparing current events, situations or experiences to all previous events, situations and experiences from the minute we were born. Every new experience (like meeting Trevor) is instantaneously, albeit unconsciously, compared to all the data in our subconscious repository at that time to ascertain if there is any danger. Poor Trevor didn't stand a chance because the minute he shook John's hand John's amygdala instantaneously made a connection between Trevor and the pain caused by Uncle Marvin! It's like a neurological game of snap – even though the snap is triggered between a Queen of Hearts and a Jack of Diamonds (the brain will often think that two high-scoring red cards is good enough). Trevor was toast and the poor guy hadn't even finished his opening pitch. John felt anxious or uneasy with Trevor and rationalised this response as 'intuition' or 'business smarts', and Trevor was shown the door as soon as possible.

John made a wholly unfair and unfounded 'decision' on Trevor based on conditioning, default settings, reflex responses and the amygdala's early warning system that had absolutely nothing to do with Trevor himself or his ability to do the job.

This is why first impressions are so unreliable. At best, first impressions should tell us what to consider but they certainly shouldn't dictate what we conclude. Chances are that the first impression – that thing we hold such great intellectual or instinctive store in – is just a default setting that's been triggered either positively or more likely negatively, influencing our 'decision'. For example, there is a guy in John's construction company who is a liability. Countless people in the business have had a quiet word in John's ear about Simon's incompetence. But John is blind to it because they go 'way back'. The first time they met Simon took him under his wing and the two of them ended up getting drunk together. When John started out on his own, Simon joined him; but Simon was always the joker, and John's soft and blind spot soon began costing the business money. John has tried moving him into new roles but it never works out – but he just can't shake his first impression and do what's best for the business.

Of course, these first impressions or gut responses can occasionally turn out to be right. But the system is still flawed. When we are proven right, we congratulate ourselves for our razor-sharp business instinct born from years of experience. We quietly (or not so quietly) celebrate our own genius as our brain is bathed in a dopamine cocktail. However, when we are wrong – which, if default settings are firing, is much more common – our amygdala ignores the new information. It doesn't relinquish or modify the default setting, it just forgets about it.

Leading into the global financial crisis, John decided to take control of a large block of land – but its value then dropped substantially. This caused severe problems for the business which needed to refinance to survive. Even though it was an intense and painful experience, John's default is that his experience and insight is second to none. This error was therefore simply an anomaly which he quickly forgot about. However, when Christopher decided to buy an extra parcel of land and it turned out to be a mistake, this was held up as evidence that Christopher doesn't have his father's business nous – even though Christopher's mistake cost the company a fraction of the amount John's mistake cost.

This rewriting of history means we are rewarded when we are 'right' but experience no negative consequences when we are wrong, which further strengthens the self-fulfilling prophecy that the default setting creates. And, worse, we carry on acting like puppets on a string. We think we are pulling the strings based on rational, verifiable data – but we're not. We are making subliminal amygdala-based knee-jerk reactions to long-forgotten events designed to protect us from things we have learnt to be scared of or upset by.

Don't get me wrong. This is not all bad. Far from it: the brain's capacity to absorb information and learn stuff is truly phenomenal, and we do learn an astonishing amount as we develop towards ready. Our brain's capacity to heal itself is also mind-blowing. It is a marvel of flexibility and adaptability, and this 'neuroplasticity' means that we really can change our minds! Not just our minds but, according to psychiatrist and author Norman Doidge, we can and do change our brains, too.[28]

But each of us arrives in adulthood with a fully functioning brain that has, in the process of development, created countless faulty causal connections. These connections can create havoc in business – especially family business, because family members are so intrinsically intertwined with the creation of those default settings.

By now I hope the picture is already building in your mind: how on earth do you reconcile these inherited forces of nature while running a business, managing wealth and dealing with the web of intrigue, real and imagined, that is often the driving force within family relationships?

Often, we can't even articulate how we feel because all that amazing learning that ends up directing our lives was done pre-speech. The language of conditioning is emotion. We feel the learning as opposed to verbalising the learning. In practice, this means that the verbal explanations of these reflex responses are correspondingly blunt and are often expressed as absolutes. You can pretty much guarantee that someone has just had a default setting triggered when they start a sentence with, 'You always ...' or 'Why is it that you never ...'

Why do you think festivals and cultural milestones that bring family together (like Christmas lunch) are a tinderbox for millions of families around the world? One hundred and twenty defaults have been simultaneously fired in the minds of every family member before anyone has even finished their hors d'oeuvres!

All this is challenging enough in normal everyday life, but attempt to run a successful family business within that context and these human characteristics can derail that business remarkably quickly – as evidenced by the frequency that shirt sleeves return to shirt sleeves in just three generations. A huge number of our reflex responses and default settings involve our parents and siblings. As a result, our amygdala is sounding the alarm on an almost daily basis in a family business because we are working with the guy who stuck a pencil in our ear when we were three years old! This doesn't happen anywhere near as often in non-family business settings. Of course, everyone will still be susceptible to an 'Uncle Marvin Moment' but it's probably not an hourly or even daily event.

What derails most family businesses in just three generations is a lack of appreciation for the profound impact our humanness can have on the family and the business. And we certainly don't appreciate that those neurological quirks and default settings are being triggered far more often in a family business than they would be in a non-family business.

However, disaster and disintegration are not inevitable. We now understand how the mind works and what we are up against. Part I drills down into the five limitations that cause most problems so we can come to appreciate their significance and learn how to successfully navigate them.

WHAT DERAILS MOST FAMILY BUSINESSES IN JUST THREE GENERATIONS IS A LACK OF APPRECIATION FOR THE PROFOUND IMPACT OUR HUMANNESS CAN HAVE ON THE FAMILY AND THE BUSINESS. AND WE CERTAINLY DON'T APPRECIATE THAT THOSE NEUROLOGICAL QUIRKS AND DEFAULT SETTINGS ARE BEING TRIGGERED FAR MORE OFTEN IN A FAMILY BUSINESS THAN THEY WOULD BE IN A NON-FAMILY BUSINESS.

PART I

Part I explores the five human limitations we must all contend with based on our human physiology, psychology and evolution. Only when we appreciate this universal challenge from which no one is immune will we be able to address the nitty-gritty issues of family, business, wealth and succession.

My objective is to expose the machine, so you can make front-of-mind decisions to mitigate back-of-mind limitations.

When it comes to sheer neurological processing abilities,
the subconscious mind is millions of times more powerful
than the conscious mind.
– Bruce H Lipton

CHAPTER 3

We Are Not in Charge of Our Thoughts

John is already in the meeting room talking with Fred and Mary (non-family employees) when Christopher arrives. Everyone settles in to discuss the agenda – the Martin project redesign. Christopher kicks off the meeting and works through the agenda.

John is clearly irritated about something and eventually turns to Christopher and asks, 'What on earth is Priya doing with the Langdon project?'

Not long after, Christopher leaves the room, visibly upset. John leaves and Fred turns to Mary and asks, 'What just happened?'

WE ARE NOT IN CHARGE OF OUR THOUGHTS.

What happened is that no one in that meeting understood the first limitation: we are not in charge of our thoughts.

Until quite recently I was convinced that we are not in charge of our thinking; indeed, I wrote about this idea in both my previous books and would frequently tell clients and workshop participants exactly that. But, on greater reflection and with the application of deeper thinking, I've come to realise that it is our *thoughts,* not our *thinking*, that we have no control over. This evolution of the idea is itself a recognition of the difference between thoughts and thinking!

In my experience, sharing this limitation over the course of 35 years, most people resist it. Often there are howls of derision, laughter and mutters of 'absolute nonsense'.

I must confess I still find it highly amusing to demonstrate its accuracy. When delivering workshops to clients about these brain limitations, I would say, 'Okay, let's assume for a moment I'm wrong. Who is in charge of your thoughts?'

'I am!' would come the indignant reply.

At which point I would pretend to look distracted as though I'd just remembered something important. Depending on what time of year it was and what events were coming up that the audience might be aware of, I would casually say to the audience, 'Hey, by the way, who do you think is going to win the next Grand Final?' Or if it's election time I may ask, 'I meant to ask, what do you think of the election candidates this time? Is anyone going to be better for business than the others?' Or if there is nothing on the horizon, I might throw in a real curve ball and say, 'I was thinking about this the other night: which religion do you think makes the most sense?'

Two things would usually happen at this point. First, some of the audience would engage. They wouldn't even hesitate to question why I had detoured into this discussion; they would launch themselves wholeheartedly into their answer. The other thing that would happen was that a few of the audience members would look genuinely confused by the diversion. I could see the bewilderment on their faces – not just at the question but the animated and engaged discussion that followed. I would normally allow the discussion to go on for a few minutes, after which time I'd ask, 'Who on their way here today thought they would be discussing these topics?'

Of course, no one did.

So, I continued … 'Then *why* did you?' Someone would always say at this point, 'Well … because *you* asked us the question.'

Without fail, the bewildered in the audience would see this as their moment to protest and point out that they didn't engage in the discussion and were confused about why the group was having it.

However, it doesn't really matter. Regardless of what anyone may have thought at the moment I asked the question, that thought – whatever it was – was triggered by *me*. My question distracted them from wherever their thoughts were to either engage in the discussion or become irritated by the discussion.

At this point, the penny usually dropped …

We are *not* in charge of our thoughts.

Our thoughts are reactions to what we see, feel, experience, hear and much more. A driver who cuts us off in traffic could steal our thoughts for an hour. The fact that our credit card bill is due and it's larger than expected could steal our thoughts for a day. If our partner forgets our anniversary, that could steal our thoughts for a month as we dissect what that might mean for the health of our relationship! Our family, staff, colleagues, even complete strangers are often much more in charge of our thoughts than we are.

Remember the difference between subjective and objective consciousness that we discussed in chapter 2? We are aware of our subjective or 'reactive' consciousness via our neocortex but we are not aware of our objective or automated consciousness. This distinction helps us understand the difference between our thoughts and our thinking.

According to biologist Bruce H Lipton:

'The conscious mind [neocortex] is the creative one, the one that can conjure up "positive thoughts". In contrast, the sub-conscious mind [midbrain and reptilian brain] is a repository of stimulus-response tapes derived from instincts and learned experiences. The subconscious mind is strictly habitual; it will play the same behavioural responses to life's signals over and over again, much to our chagrin ...'[29]

And remember, Lipton also reminds us that the subconscious mind is millions of times more powerful than the conscious mind.

This is, at best, challenging because the subconscious mind is the source of thoughts and the conscious mind is the source of thinking. In a meeting where Nathan is being loud and annoying, Christopher's thought will always be, 'F**king Nathan'; this thought always arrives faster than his thinking, which reminds him to 'Let it go and focus on the agenda.' Left to its own devices, the subconscious mind will continually hijack our thinking and send us off on some intellectual wild goose chase. It will distort reality and distract us endlessly. Without proper understanding and conscious intervention our subconscious mind will undermine even our best conscious efforts to change our lives.[30] When John walks into a meeting with his children, his mere presence as father and founder is enough to trigger every family member's most powerful 'thoughts' – good and bad.

As I mentioned in chapter 2, scientists have demonstrated that the brain processes about 11 million bits of information per second and we are aware of about 40 bits.[31]

(Please, take a moment. Now is a good time to make a cup of tea and let that simple fact sink in, if it hasn't already. If this reality doesn't astound you and give you cause to pause, then you are mighty hard to impress.)

Logic alone should tell us that if we can take more active control over our conscious mind to direct its attention towards useful discussions and thinking rather than allowing ourselves to be hijacked by randomness, we will be more effective and are much more likely to solve our problems. (This is what the practice of meditation is all about – learning how to observe thoughts and let them pass rather than becoming consumed or distracted by them.)

Consider the first thought that came into your mind this morning. Where did that come from? Did you choose it? Even if you think you did, it couldn't have been the first thing that came to mind, right? The first thing would have to have been, 'What should my first thought be this morning?' And you most certainly did not think that! Nobody in history has thought that until right now. So – ergo, whatever it was, it 'popped' into your head without your involvement or choice.

If we've been sitting on a deserted beach for several hours, or it's late at night when everyone else in the house is asleep and we haven't spoken to anyone or watched TV for at least two hours – then perhaps we may be in charge of our thoughts. But most of the time we are not. We are almost permanently distracted – a walking, talking mass of *reaction* based on the environment around us!

Imagine that John Jackson decides to hold a family meeting to discuss the business and get a sense of what his children feel about the current situation. The meeting is called for Sunday afternoon at John and Ayesha's house. Spouses and children are also invited – everyone can share a Sunday lunch and then the partners and children can enjoy a swim in the pool and G2 can have a relaxed discussion.

This is doomed from the start, because what exactly is the relaxed discussion going to be about? There is no agenda – John decides not to create one, because that seems a little too formal. There are already a bunch of distractions caused by the social nature of the lunch and the fact that partners and children are involved. G2 might come to the meeting with thoughts on what they want to say but it's unlikely they will say what they imagined. What happens instead is that the various sibling rivalries flare up. Nathan and Christopher just snipe at each other. Anika mentions her restaurant and everyone rolls their eyes. Priya tries to talk to her dad about a new project she's working on in her own time but he keeps getting interrupted by Nathan or one of his grandchildren.

No one is in charge of their thoughts and, in that moment, it could be argued they are no longer in control of anything going on in their minds. Each family member has instead had their thoughts hijacked by old grievances, slights, their spouses, their children and a thousand other things. Tempers are fraught, old wounds are reopened, emotions are reignited. The 'meeting' finally fizzles out when Anika's son, Ben, has a scare in the pool and everyone starts to drift away. Nothing is resolved. If anything, it's just made matters worse.

As Homo sapiens we are astonishingly easy to distract. It is this distraction that is, I believe, the root cause of the difference between what we want and what we achieve; between what we say is important and what we actually accomplish. This gap is often referred to as the knowing/doing gap or the performance gap. We have all experienced situations where we know what we need to do, we are committed to doing it but our execution is not as good as we hoped. This gap reflects the knowledge we all experience from time to time that 'better' was within our grasp but not delivered or applied. It is in the under-lying frustration of the statement 'I wish I had said that or asked that earlier' – it is buried in the know-how that lives beneath our skull, but is rarely applied to its full potential. We aren't robbed of this potential by our laziness. It is the engine; its design makes it hard to apply the whole of our mind to the task at hand.

And it's because we get distracted – very, very easily. Primarily because we are not in charge of our thoughts.

Learnings from the Field: My Son's an Idiot

Imagine a scenario where G2, let's call him Matthew, decides to get some external advice to help him navigate the challenges of a very successful dealership business.

Matthew had 'taken over the business' a few years earlier but had never actually been given the reigns. It was a notional changing of the guard, but everyone in the business knew who was really in charge – Matthew's father, Fergus. The business was experiencing some challenging times and Matthew, on Fergus's prompting but against his better judgement, recruited the company's external accountant to be 'joint CEO'. That appointment had not worked well. Matthew believed the accountant had no idea how to run a dealership and had been over-empowered by Fergus. Fergus thought otherwise.

I am the advisor Matthew calls for help. In our first meeting, Fergus turns to me, very serious and very sombre, and says, 'John, we've got a massive problem. And it's all my fault. I've always known that Matthew just doesn't have the ability to make important decisions and I let him make them anyway. I've got no one to blame but myself. So, if you've got a solution for giving your children more power and authority than they've got the capability to actually manage, then I'd love to hear it.'

Matthew looks at me with an expression that says, 'See what I'm up against?' He is obviously, quite rightly, also hurt and angry and the meeting is effectively over.

In this situation, Fergus has applied no thinking whatsoever to his thoughts. Can you imagine any parent saying such a thing to their adult child? Especially in front of a total stranger? And yet I've heard more versions of this story than I care to remember.

Later on, I reach out to Fergus, meet with him one to one, and repeat his words back to him. At first, he becomes angry and denies that my recollection is accurate. I ask him to share his recollection of what he actually said. He pauses, draws breath, sighs and says, 'Oh, f**k.' Together we have begun to rehabilitate his fatherly behaviours for the greater good of the family and the business.

Thoughts are what the mind serves up to us during the course of the day. We have absolutely no control over what they are; and yet, for most of us, this intellectual roulette is obscured by the thinking those thoughts then generate. We are conscious of the thinking our thoughts trigger, and sometimes we rigorously engage in that thinking. What we are less aware of is the thought that prompted the thinking in the first place. Was it the careless driver, the credit card bill, some nonsense on our social media feed, the news, a colleague, a family member or a problem at work? The list is endless. And consequently, our thinking – the activity that occurs after the thought – is endlessly hijacked by situations, people, events, experiences, moods, conversations and arguments. We are constantly distracted by random thoughts.

WE HAVE ABSOLUTELY NO CONTROL OVER OUR THOUGHTS; AND YET THIS INTELLECTUAL ROULETTE IS OBSCURED BY THE THINKING THOSE THOUGHTS THEN GENERATE.

The slightly encouraging news is that we are not our thoughts.

We Are Not Our Thoughts

We can no more control our thoughts than we can control our eye colour. They create untold distraction and send us off down irrelevant, unhelpful and frequently negative thinking tangents.

Most of us will have had the experience of saying something or sharing a thought with another person only for them to look at us in total bewilderment as they ask, 'Where the hell did that come from?' Even if we stop and really think about the answer to that question, we are rarely able to trace the mental breadcrumbs back to the source. It just appeared from somewhere and presented itself. It could have been a fleeting memory, a sound or smell; it could have been a picture in our head, or a feeling. It may have been triggered by a conversation or a news story or a passing comment by a stranger – who knows? The source remains a mystery.

This recognition can feel uncomfortable. It implies that we have far less control over what is happening in our heads than we would like to believe. It can be disconcerting to know that we are constantly at the mercy of our own, often random, thoughts. And while this is true, we can avoid the chaos this can create by first appreciating the depth of this reality. Accepting and embracing the fact that we are not in charge of our thoughts is the first step to freedom.

Ironically, when we don't know we are not in charge of our thoughts, or we resist or deny that truth, we remain at the mercy of the chaos they create. But, once we accept that we are not in charge of our thoughts, we recognise that thoughts don't really matter that much anyway.

As Buddha and the Toltecs have already worked out, who we are is not defined by our thoughts; who we are is defined by our thinking – or what happens after the thought appears.

Consider the difference between Ted Bundy and Stephen King. Stephen King has thoughts far uglier and more terrifying than Ted Bundy, but his thinking turns those thoughts into stories. As such he has entertained millions of people with his horror fiction and made a great deal of money in the process. Ted Bundy, on the other hand, chose to turn his ugly and terrifying thoughts into reality, and sadly we know how that played out. There is much more to this dichotomy, I know, sinister and functional in its form (a mind that is just not wired correctly), but the point is the point: we all have thoughts – how we apply, deny or address them is what defines our character.

In the same way that people are measured by what they do, not what they say, we are measured by our thinking, not our thoughts. The true measure of a person in terms of their value to society is what they do with those thoughts – what they choose to think about and action. It is therefore the thinking that occurs after the thought that determines who we are and what we bring into existence.

For example, Nathan's *thoughts* often mirror his dad's. As a result, his thought is often, 'Priya can't run this business.' Nathan never recognises that this is just a thought, and instead presents it as his thinking. He will frequently voice this thinking in meetings. Take a moment to consider how Priya might feel when she hears this. Take a moment to imagine how that thought couched as rational and logical thinking will impact the relationship and harmony between Priya and Nathan. Is it even remotely helpful?

But what if, after reading this book, Nathan recognises that his bias about Priya is actually just a *thought* and decides to apply some *thinking* to that thought? He might consider her engineering degree and past projects she managed to lean into the bias and test the assumptions. He might arrive at the conclusion that, actually, Priya deserves a chance to fulfil her destiny just as much as he, Christopher and Anika do. He might decide that, like him, Priya's capability won't be known unless she is given an opportunity; that the support can and should be put in place to assist all the siblings to reach their potential. Priya could also be asked to create a business plan to test her commitment.

And here's the rub. If Priya were a friend who was in exactly the same situation but inside another business, Nathan would be much more inclined to apply thinking to her challenge and offer up genuine suggestions and solutions, so that his friend could be taken more seriously by her employer and colleagues.

But Priya is his sister; he is hardwired to slip into assumption and bias, and rely on long-forgotten default settings that are represented by his thoughts (rooted in the past) and not his thinking (which should be rooted in current reality). Consider also how these thoughts, repeatedly shared, become someone else's narrative. If left unchallenged, Nathan's assumptions about Priya, coupled with similar assumptions from other family members, cluster to form a jail that Priya locks herself in.

You may at this point be wondering how the reality of Priya's adult contribution might have contributed to her reputation in Nathan's mind. Surely, he has validated adult data to temper his learnt and reflex childhood perception? Well, no. For two reasons. First, the past is promoted and protected by the far more powerful subconscious (remember Lipton); and second, we are programmed to recognise the behaviours that reinforce our perceptions and forget those that don't (remember Garfinkel). So even a grown-up Nathan will interpret all he sees in a way that augments his internal reality.

When someone is characterised in a particular way in their family, it becomes their reality, and they do one of two things. They become angry at being perceived incorrectly, or they believe it's true and play into the stereotype – which reinforces and amplifies the behaviour they are being accused of. Neither is constructive.

On one hand, thoughts don't really matter that much because they are often random and distracting. But they can and do matter in families, because those thoughts often set off a chain reaction of thinking that is deeply unhelpful in a family business setting. Imagine that John tells Priya in a meeting, 'Hey Priya, you did a really good job on that project.' The non-family attendees in that meeting might think, 'Oh, that's nice that John has acknowledged her contribution.' But Priya may be thinking, 'Finally, I'm getting some recognition', or 'That's not the first really good job I've ever done, Dad.' There are immediately layers of additional story, inference or assumption built into the statement which is simply a function of the fact that Priya is John's daughter. All everyone else heard was a compliment.

This is why so many founders feel that their children don't measure up to their employed staff. They don't appreciate the compromising nature of their presence on their child's ability to use the part of their brain that delivers results. Even if they could, their contribution would be dismissed or diminished in some way according to their preconceived impression of that child!

Thinking is our conscious response to our thoughts. Stupidity is therefore acting on our thoughts without thinking. Wisdom is knowing the difference between the two, and applying thinking to the useful and relevant thoughts or applying systems to elicit the right thinking, at the right time, in the right context.

Now ... Let's go back to that meeting between John, Christopher, Fred and Mary. Christopher now understands that we are not in charge of our thoughts. John asks, 'What on earth is Priya doing with the Langdon project?' Christopher looks up from the agenda and says, 'Dad, something about the Martin project we're discussing has obviously reminded you of the Langdon project and the problems Priya is experiencing there. I'm sure you appreciate that when you say something like that, it can lead me to think unhelpful thoughts too and neither of us have that luxury right now. So, can we please park that question, since no one in the room can answer it and we need to resolve the issues with the Martin project so we can move forward – and you won't then have to ask Priya, "What on earth is Christopher doing with the Martin project?"'

THE 'HALFWIT'...

Think about this the next time you are in a meeting with employed colleagues and employed family. The non-family members are able to be 'full minded' and apply all their thinking. Every family member is a 'halfwit' because they are always partially distracted. They can only ever use half their thinking because the other half is taken up with the burden of formative history and a fully charged amygdala on high alert.

CHAPTER 4

Hardwired Pessimism – the Greatest Default

Nathan is involved in an important project and wants to galvanise the leadership team's support of it. He calls a meeting that John needs to be part of to reinforce the importance of the project and the message.

The meeting starts and John hasn't turned up. At first, Nathan gives him the benefit of the doubt and suggests to everyone that they wait 10 minutes. John still hasn't turned up, so Nathan carries on. Unfortunately, the meeting goes badly. His father's absence leads Nathan to being distracted and unsure of himself. So Nathan winds the meeting up, having only really covered half of the agenda points, and walks out. The remaining members of the leadership team look at each other and one asks, 'What just happened?'

IN THE ABSENCE OF INFORMATION OUR BRAINS WILL
DELIVER THOUGHTS THAT INSTINCTIVELY DEFAULT TO THE
WORST PROBABLE CONCLUSION. THIS IS AMONGST THE
MOST PROFOUND EXAMPLES OF THE SURVIVAL INSTINCT.

What just happened was that no one in the meeting understood hard-wired pessimism or our greatest default.

Now that we understand a little more about the mechanics of thought and thinking and how our brain works and our mind develops, it's easier to appreciate why we encounter so many challenges in life. And it's easier to understand why we are not in charge of our thoughts. At the heart of it all are default settings. Because of the conditioning process, we are hardwired to respond to certain situations, events or perceived threats in a certain way that bypasses thinking altogether. In fact, the mind works to *prevent* thinking. It is designed this way. There is physical distance between the default factory (amygdala) and the thinking engine (neocortex) – the latter being as far as possible from the former. Also, the brain activates chemistry that neutralises the neocortex when the amygdala senses danger or threat.

But there is one default setting that trumps all others, and that is *hardwired pessimism*.

While there are some people who are naturally more optimistic than others, for the most part, *in the absence of information* our brains will deliver thoughts that instinctively default to the worst *probable* conclusion. This is amongst the most profound examples of the survival instinct. In Nathan's case, the worst probable conclusion is that his dad doesn't respect him or think his project is as important as Nathan does – maybe with a little deliberate humiliation thrown in for good measure.

When you remember the history of your own experiences and the biological imperative that is driving the process, it becomes clear that the brain is not built for sophistication – it's built for survival and protection.

For a long time, it was thought that the signals and information received from the five senses travelled to the thalamus where they were partially translated, with most of the message travelling on to the neocortex to activate an appropriate response. If there was a perceived threat, a further signal would be diverted from the neocortex to the amygdala. This would heighten awareness and help to ensure survival. The amygdala was presumed to be important but essentially subservient to the neocortex.

Neuroscientist Joseph LeDoux from the Centre for Neural Science at New York University discovered that this is not true.[32] It isn't the big, complex and highly sophisticated neocortex that's in charge – it is the amygdala. It was LeDoux who first discovered the critical role the amygdala plays in learning and 'decision-making'. He demonstrated that there is actually a neurological emergency exit connecting the thalamus to the amygdala. When signals and information are received by the thalamus via the five senses, a portion of the original transmission goes to the amygdala *at the same* time as the rest of the message goes to the neocortex. But because that message goes directly across a single synapse, it is lightening quick. In reality this means that we react to information from the hypervigilant amygdala before the rational brain even knows what's happened.

Daniel Goleman explained the consequences of this in his book *Emotional Intelligence*.[33] While on holiday in England his friend decided to work off brunch by taking a walk beside a picturesque canal. He came across a little girl frozen with fear looking at the water and immediately jumped in, fully clothed, without even asking the girl why she looked so scared. Once the man was in the water he saw that a toddler had fallen in, who he was able to save. Before he saw the toddler, the man's neocortex hadn't stopped to wonder why the little girl looked so scared or whether he should ask what had happened: his amygdala sounded the alarm, and he jumped in.

Throughout childhood we're told to 'think before you act', but neuroscience has proven this is not always possible. The amygdala is calling the shots, working in conjunction with the conditioning process to create default settings that harness the danger signals into brain shortcuts that can be used in the future to avoid similar situations! In daily life this means that when the amygdala becomes aware of something that poses a threat, it reacts. It can't *not* react. The reaction is based on the level of threat perceived, and the chosen action or intervention will be whatever pre-loaded default setting is considered the best way to minimise the threat. All this happens automatically and often below our awareness.[34]

This also means that the amygdala is hardwired towards pessimism and always errs on the side of caution. It will always throw up potential dangers, or trigger altered behaviour to avoid potential threats. Its job is to scan the environment for danger. If things are unclear or there is an absence of information, the amygdala will always raise the alarm. It will serve up the worst probable scenario to ensure we are suitably prepared and can ready ourselves for immediate action.

This is why the vast majority of the thoughts that bubble up into our conscious awareness are negative. These negative thoughts are much 'stickier' than their rarer positive counterparts because they are designed to ensure our survival. As such they are much more likely to trigger negative thinking that, with a little nudge, can spiral into all sorts of pessimistic end-of-days scenarios.

Let me demonstrate what I mean. Imagine you are driving home and on the way, an ambulance drives past you with the sirens wailing. The thought that emerges might be, 'Wow, they are really moving.' That might lead to thinking about how many people end up in accidents because of emergency service vehicles heading towards an emergency. The thinking falls away as you focus once again on the road ahead. A couple of minutes pass and a fire engine comes out of nowhere, again with sirens sounding, heading in the same direction as the ambulance. The thought that emerges now might be, 'Oh dear, that doesn't look good.' You see traffic lights ahead turning to red so your attention is moved back to your driving. A tiny bubble of thought pops into your awareness that states, 'They are travelling in the direction of my house.' The lights change to green and you dismiss the thought and carry on. You turn into your street. As you approach the bend before your home, you can hear the sirens – they are close. What thought do you have now? 'Oh no – maybe it's a neighbour.' As you round the bend, the ambulance and the fire engine that passed you several minutes ago are parked outside *your* home.

What are your thoughts now? 'Oh my god – what's happened?!' as you drive like a maniac the last few hundred metres to reach your home. During that short final leg of the journey your mind will helpfully deliver a steady stream of unthinkable scenarios – and every last one of them will be negative.

At no point does your brain serve up, 'This is probably an emergency service training initiative.' Instead, it goes straight to, 'Shit, someone's dead!'

Lack of knowledge means worst likely case; worst likely case means many things, including fear. Fear means engagement of the survival mechanism, courtesy of the amygdala. The fight/flight reflex is in effect our deepest, oldest and most instinctive response. This survival response is initiated by the sympathetic nervous system and it prepares the body for physical action by increasing heart rate, pulling the blood flow from the organs to the extremities, releasing adrenalin and opening up the lungs ready for fighting and/or running. This active survival response numbs the frontal lobe which means we are even more likely to do or say something stupid, and we are definitely more likely to assume the worst.[35]

Think about it ... when a company announces that it is going to shed 10 percent of its staff, 100 percent of the workforce worries and any meeting called by a workgroup leader invariably makes people nervous. When your child is late home, you immediately imagine the identikit picture of their kidnapper – you don't want to and you'll try to push the thought away but it will stick until your child walks in the door. If a friend doesn't return your call, once you've confirmed that they are not on leave and have received your message you start to wonder what you said or did to offend them. You rarely assume they are simply busy and will get back to you in due course. Or if you do manage to give them the benefit of the doubt that they must be busy, just wait a day or two – if there is still no contact, your amygdala will be twitching. I promise.

Because of this survival instinct, a random negative thought is much more likely to develop into thinking that is itself negative. It's our brain's way of making sure we are paying attention to potentially life threatening or distressing situations.

This means that not only are we not in charge of our thoughts, which we discussed in the last chapter, but the brain's early warning system and hardwired pessimism mean that most thoughts served up to us are negative. Negative thoughts are stickier because they are supported by more synaptic wiring. They happen more often on both a conscious and subconscious level which leads to more negative thinking, which impacts wellbeing and outcome. Hardly a winning combination!

NOT ONLY ARE WE NOT IN CHARGE OF OUR THOUGHTS, BUT THE BRAIN'S EARLY WARNING SYSTEM AND HARDWIRED PESSIMISM MEAN THAT MOST THOUGHTS SERVED UP TO US ARE NEGATIVE.

In family and in life, this uber default setting is the key to being able to predict a person's response, and manage it. And it is as dependable as the sunrise.

Imagine the day that Anika opens her restaurant. It's just a small place – 10 tables – but it's a start and she is over the moon. The whole family is invited to the opening. The evening goes reasonably well but there is a distinct undercurrent. Christopher especially seems out of sorts. Nothing is said at the time and everyone does their best to enjoy the evening and support Anika. For weeks afterwards John notices a few snipes towards her from Christopher and Nathan. Christopher mutters under his breath how nice it must be to be supported to follow your dream. Nathan makes some comment about how there seems to be plenty of money for some people in the family but not others. After a few weeks when the atmosphere hasn't lifted John calls all four children together to ask them if there is anything that is upsetting them. John listens to their concerns, which seem to be shielding a deeper concern about where the money for Anika's restaurant came from. John has a coach so he's been told about these limitations and he remembers his coach telling him how toxic a lack of transparency can be – especially in a family business. If someone believes they are being less supported it is almost always because they don't know something or have jumped to conclusions about the support other siblings or family members are receiving.

So, John takes a leap of faith. 'Hey, look, I wanted to get you all together because I get the sense that something is bothering you and it's been brewing since Anika opened her restaurant. I didn't tell you all because I just didn't think to, but it is important. I should have raised it, and I apologise for that. I want to clear up where Anika got the money to start the restaurant. Your mum and I invested 50 percent of the start-up funding and Anika is paying that money back over the next 10 years at half a percent less than her bank's interest rates. This same offer extends to all of you should you have ideas or opportunities that require investment and support. This was promised to Anika on the condition that she prepare a business and financial plan, which she did. We would expect the same of each of you.' Immediately, the mood shifts. Priya says, 'Really? Oh, right, we just thought you'd given her the money …'

Remember, *in the absence of information* our brain will deliver thoughts that will instinctively default to the worst *probable* conclusion.

Now, let's go back to Nathan's meeting with the leadership team. Nathan now understands about hardwired pessimism. When he notices five minutes before the meeting that his dad isn't there, he checks that the appointment was properly added to his diary. It was. Did he specify the time and place? Yes, he did. Did he make it clear to his dad how important it was that he be there? Yes, he did. Instead of getting anxious and assuming that it is a power play, Nathan consciously decides to press on with the meeting. Something has obviously come up that his dad couldn't change, but he's not heard anything so his dad obviously believes he can handle it.

Nathan leads a positive and constructive meeting with the leadership team and when it's over he checks his voicemail. His mum has called and left a message: Dad isn't feeling well. He's very sorry he can't make it to the meeting but has every faith in Nathan to handle it without him.

CHAPTER 5

Emotions Are Not the Product of Reality

Nathan and his mate and colleague Rod have just finished a project for the business. They know that John had a meeting with the client who commissioned the job that morning. John has sent word that he wants to see them both in the boardroom when he gets back.

Nathan panics. What happened?

EVOLUTIONARY PSYCHOLOGY SAYS THAT EMOTION
CAN NEVER BE SUPPRESSED. IN OTHER WORDS, WE WILL
NEVER STOP OR PREVENT THE EMOTIONAL SPARK.
BUT WE CAN MANAGE THE FUEL WE ADD TO THE SPARK.

What happened is a demonstration of the third human limitation: emotions are not necessarily the product of reality. What we feel often makes no sense and bears almost no relationship to reality. We certainly don't need facts for emotion to be triggered. Nathan's emotional reaction was not triggered by the reality of the project's success, but by the fear that something was wrong and his dad was about to tell him about it.

In truth, the five limitations are inextricably linked and intertwined. Sometimes it's hard to separate them. You could for example argue that Nathan's reaction was down to a triggered default – the fear that he had disappointed his dad in some way – rather than simply an inaccurate emotional reaction. Think of these limitations like blister packs of play-dough or plasticine. At first they are neatly separated into strips of bright, pure colour: red, yellow, green, blue and maybe white and purple. However, once removed from their pristine packaging and used as intended – 'in the wild', so to speak – it's impossible to separate them. They merge together and it's often impossible to know where the red stops and the orange begins. Swirls of blue twist through the yellow and pockets of white or green – even if you could find little hotspots of pure colour you could never break it down into its original separate parts. It's often the same with our human limitations.

A useful distinction to make between defaults and emotional unreliability is to view defaults as mainly survival mechanisms. They were created when we didn't have the mental capacity to differentiate between a real or perceived threat. Emotion can be triggered by those survival jitters, *or* it may simply be a response to external stimuli in the moment. Just think about it for a moment … reading or watching the news can leave us incandescent with rage (emotional reaction), a good movie can make us cry (emotional reaction with a dash of default) or we can be afraid to sleep after a particularly disturbing documentary (default).

I can vividly remember being at a football game with my team playing the enemy. In this particular game it was drawn with only seconds left on the clock. A player from my team kicked a field goal from about 30 metres out in those dying seconds and we won the game ... and I actually teared up! Now let's just think about that for a second: a guy has kicked a piece of leather filled with air between two large posts. He happened to be wearing a white jersey with a big red 'V' on it. Last year he was wearing a blue and gold jersey and three years from now he's going to be wearing a different jersey again. But for now, he's wearing 'my' jersey.

Yet when we won that game – I cried. This is not logical. If something happened to someone close to me, I'd cry. You could conclude therefore that I feel as much emotional attachment to my football team as I do to my family. Obviously, that is not true. (I prefer football!) Yet it shows how easy it is to trigger emotions – especially when the object involves sport, religion and brands. In his book *Buyology*, Martin Lindstrom explains how we buy anything that can be wrapped and presented in some form of emotional packaging.[36] The rise of fake news and online trolls is another insidious example of how emotional response is not the product of reality, as is the storming of the US Capitol building in 2021 to stop the confirmation of Joe Biden as President of the United States. Emotional response is not the product of factual reality, but innate prejudice driven by inherited defaults.

Not only are emotions subjective but they are also automatic – often triggered by one of those pesky associative connections or default settings we just learnt about. The emotional response is just the natural consequence of our reflex response. As such, without practice and genuine frontal lobe disciplines, we have no more control over our emotions than we do our thoughts.

Again, this is a survival quirk. Evolutionary psychology offers a new paradigm on how the mind evolved and suggests that the characteristic of emotion-before-reason was an essential part of survival.[37] Obviously, when facing danger, it doesn't pay to linger in decision-making mode. We don't really need to know whether the snake is a brown snake or a green snake. The fear response will flood adrenaline into the body so we get away from the snake. That way, we don't get bitten, and the type of snake it was remains irrelevant.

As a species we have survived this long because our instinct for danger is always 'on' thanks to our amygdala. Over time a multitude of perceived dangers have become hardwired into the human condition. And that fact undoubtedly kept us alive. However, like our cognitive function, our emotional response hasn't really changed much in thousands of years either.

Evolutionary psychology says that emotion can never be suppressed. In other words, we will never stop or prevent the emotional spark. But we can manage the fuel we add to the spark.

This certainly helps to explain why we witness so many sparks in the workplace – angry meetings, tantrums in the boardroom, sulking after performance reviews or storming out of meetings. In many very real ways emotion is what makes us human and yet it is often expected that as soon as we enter the workplace, we somehow turn this particular human characteristic off. We don't. We can't. And that is true regardless of gender. Emotion comes with us wherever we go and, as a result, it influences our perception of events and can seriously interfere with our thinking.

Let's go back to the Jacksons – specifically the meeting where Nathan makes the comment about St Christopher getting his knickers in a knot. Christopher is humiliated again by his brother. The overriding emotion he feels is rage, but his reflex response to this rage is withdrawal. While everyone at the table is laughing at Nathan's comment, Christopher has shut down. If you were in the meeting too you would notice that Christopher scowls at his brother, sits down and doesn't speak again. He can no longer think straight. His physiology is on high alert and he's probably had a surge of the stress hormone. He has not yet learned to instruct his frontal lobe to ignore his brother and so can't have a discussion with himself where he convinces himself that what he is feeling is an overreaction. That threat signal has already crossed the single synapse from the thalamus to the amygdala and shut down Christopher's frontal lobe before the neocortex could even come up with a smart comeback. It's all automatic and based on years of similar situations since he was a kid. His emotional reaction colours his entire perception of the situation.

Psychologists since Sigmund Freud have spoken of perception being dependant on the individual. Carl Jung said that perception was projection as he believed that what we considered to be reality was nothing more than our own traits and characteristics reflected back to us in life. And those reflections are steeped in emotion. Someone who is angry will attract, relate and engage with other angry people – just think about talkback radio or online trolls. Someone who is kind tends to gravitate to others who are also kind.

Events, experiences and situations themselves often don't mean anything until the individual applies the meaning. And that meaning is almost always coloured by the dominant emotion at that time. If Christopher's conditioning had been different and he and his brother were closer or had a more balanced relationship he would have laughed, too, then dismissed Nathan's comment and carried on with his presentation – but that didn't happen because of the emotion stirred up by the amygdala to 'help' Christopher survive.

When we unpack perception, it's clear that emotion plays a huge part in interpreting reality. How we feel at any given moment will have a large impact on how we perceive what is happening around us. What we perceive as reality is subjective. It is an emotion-fuelled interpretation, as evidenced by Christopher.

Imagine you've just got into work and are about to check your emails. At home while you were enjoying a slice of wholemeal toast and some marmalade you opened your credit card bill. It's a joint card and you noticed while sipping your English breakfast tea that your partner had put a large purchase on your joint credit card but had failed to mention it. Initially you were irritated, but you'd managed to work the irritation into full-blown anger by the time you reached the office. Remember the last limitation – irritation can quickly turn to anger in this situation because of the lack of information about the transaction. You are now distracted away from the task at hand, defaulting to the notion of dishonesty, all of which has engaged an emotional cocktail. You have not been able to talk to your partner to understand what the purchase was, so you assume the worst probable outcome. This negative valance means that you immediately rush to some additional unhelpful and accusatory thinking that drags up similar scenarios from the past.

Stewing in your own hostility, you turn on your computer in your office and open your emails. The first message is from Ahmed in accounts who is asking when you think you will get the monthly report over to him. It is a simple question – there is no hidden agenda or irritation emanating from the email – but your emotional state shoehorns one into the communication and you fire off a missive. You assume Ahmed is angry because you are angry and you are reading the email applying the emotion of anger. This context colours your perception of the email. In truth the emotion you arrived at the office feeling (anger) polluted the exchange unnecessarily.

Now imagine you are sitting in traffic; you're late for an appointment and you're getting more and more upset. Suddenly from nowhere somebody runs into the back of your car. Now you are really mad. You jump out of your car, slam the door and storm to the back of your car armed and ready with some choice expletives. But the person in the offending vehicle is … your best friend.

All of a sudden, the knuckle sandwich turns into, 'Oh no, are you okay?'

The event is the same, but the interpretation, meaning and emotions that you attached to it have completely changed. Whatever is going to happen next will be a direct expression of the chemistry your amygdala generates based on what it guesses, not what it knows.

How often do we charge into meetings with internal knuckle sandwiches and simmering resentment that can so easily distort our judgement about the real situation and affect our decision-making? Feelings that are precipitated by the mind's own version of shadow boxing?

The part of the brain that has most to do with emotion is the limbic system – specifically, our dear friend the amygdala. You'll no doubt remember the amygdala from our exploration of default settings in the previous chapter. Unlike Al Pacino in *Scarface* who only had one little friend, we have two of these little friends, one on each hemisphere of the brain. They are perched above the brainstem and while they are the size of almonds, they pack a serious neurological punch. The amygdala will hijack the brain as soon as there is even a sniff of danger, reacting before the neocortex or thinking part of the brain has any facts.

This exchange between limbic and neocortex activity is at the heart of many of our thinking challenges and goes a long way towards explaining those passionate outbursts that we later regret. Often our emotional responses are linked to past conditioning or default settings.

The presence of even one or two markers from a previous 'dangerous' situation will be enough to set off the reaction.

Emotion is the fuel we use to achieve our dreams; emotional expression is one of our greatest strengths. However, if it is allowed to become an unchallenged contributor to the decision-making process, it becomes our greatest weakness. Especially in matters of business, if not so much in matters of the heart.

Joseph LeDoux, the man who discovered the role of the amygdala, has gone so far as to say, 'Some emotional reactions and emotional memories can be formed without any conscious, cognitive participation at all.'[38] Just stop and think about that for a moment. Discussions in a family business frequently become heated between siblings or across generations; those involved believe there is a logical reason for the discussion, that the argument represents a difference of opinion. However, in fact, the emotional reaction has simply been triggered by events and experiences of the past, shared but not remembered.

And it is this non-cognitive process that forms another of our human limitations. Research quite clearly shows that emotional responses do not require facts or details prior to engagement. This means that we instinctively race to conclusions within milliseconds of any situation or event; we will unconsciously comprehend what it is, decide whether we like it or not, present that to our awareness as 'fact' and happily form an opinion about it – all in a matter of seconds! Our emotions quite literally have a mind of their own and that mind is not necessarily in sync with the mind we recognise as 'I'.

We all know that logically it's best to get all the data before we act. We are reminded not to jump to conclusions but, at least biologically, it's very difficult not to. Without the right information, Christopher, Nathan and Priya jumped to the conclusion that Anika had been gifted a lot of money for her restaurant. That assumption created emotional tension and animosity between the siblings and their parents – all unfounded and unnecessary. The associative learning and conditioning model means that our brain is herding us towards a speedy predetermined conclusion such as 'Typical! The baby gets spoilt again.' The fact is, intelligent people with similar values, given the same information, will invariably draw the same conclusion. All four children were brought up by the same parents in the same house and most likely have similar values. If there is a disagreement, then the highest probability is that the information set is different.

Like the previous limitations, the first step towards nullifying it is to realise that the challenge exists in the first place. We all know that once emotion has arrived, it is often impossible to wait for the facts – it's too late. We are already emotional and therefore we are part of the problem. We won't even recognise the difference between emotion and reality. Thus, emotions happen as part of the journey, from a thought to our thinking, and it is a speed hump on that journey. What *should* happen, in non-life-threatening situations like business, is that our thinking is ideally applied before emotion is engaged.

WHAT *SHOULD* HAPPEN, IN NON-LIFE-THREATENING SITUATIONS LIKE BUSINESS, IS THAT OUR THINKING IS IDEALLY APPLIED BEFORE EMOTION IS ENGAGED.

Understanding can so easily be warped by emotion! While this can be a valuable additional kick-start to create action, it is also the easiest and fastest way to dysfunction and manipulation.

Now, let's go back to Nathan. Nathan and Rod are in the boardroom waiting. John walks in. And under his arm is a box that contains a bottle of Grange Hermitage – a very nice bottle of red wine.

John looks at them both and says, 'The client is really happy, loved what you guys have done and he gave me this bottle of Grange. But you pair did the heavy lifting so I want you both to go out for lunch, take his bottle, share it, enjoy it and have the rest of the day off!'

Nathan looks at Rod and Rod can tell Nathan is visibly emotional and doing his best to hold back tears.

Now imagine that Nathan understands that emotion does not equal reality. When he receives the message from his dad to meet in the boardroom, he doesn't automatically get anxious but is instead able to quickly retrace the project and assure himself that he and Rod did a good job. He doesn't assume that he and Rod are about to get a roasting for something. Instead, he simply makes the conscious decision not to attach any interpretation or emotional response to the meeting until he hears what his dad has to say to them both, without fear or expectation. And this time, the emotion he feels is simply pride.

CHAPTER 6

Language Has No Universal Unambiguous Dictionary

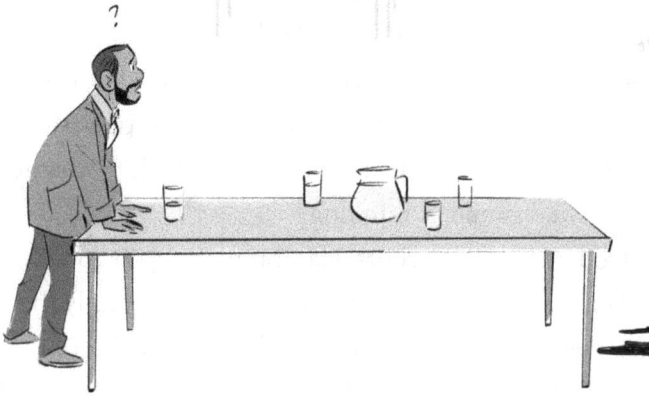

A new marketing manager, Isaac, has joined the company.

On Isaac's first day, John calls a meeting with him, Nathan and Priya to discuss the approach they should take to promote a particular development.

As they are discussing options, John says, 'I know, let's just do everything we did for Pavilion.' Nathan and Priya look at him and say, 'Yes, perfect, that will work.' The meeting ends, they all leave and Isaac is left in the room thinking, 'What just happened?'

WE ARE COMMUNICATING WITH EACH OTHER THROUGH
WORDS, BODY LANGUAGE AND NON-VERBAL SIGNALS;
BUT WITHOUT A UNIVERSAL, UNAMBIGUOUS DICTIONARY,
MISUNDERSTANDING IS INEVITABLE.

What just happened is that no one in the meeting yet understands the fourth human limitation that causes problems for us in life, business and family: language has no universal unambiguous dictionary. What is immediately obvious to John, Nathan and Priya – because they share a common dictionary – is double Dutch to Isaac. In the Jacksons' dictionary, 'Pavilion' is a particularly successful marketing initiative they ran last year. To Isaac, 'Pavilion' is a restaurant he took his partner to last week to celebrate their anniversary.

We are communicating with each other all the time, through words, body language and non-verbal signals; but without a universal dictionary, misunderstanding is inevitable. This confusion is often made worse because these forms of communication act as powerful sparks to ignite default settings and activate emotions, which then automate so much of what we assume is 'thinking'!

Most of our 'learning' occurs via conditioning before we are six years old. This means that most of our learning – certainly the learning that creates default settings – is non-verbal. Yet by the time we are a relatively small child, we are told to use our words. By the time we reach adulthood, we are expected to communicate in words. However, the reptilian brain and limbic system are not having a conversation with the frontal lobe in the way that we traditionally understand the word 'conversation'.

This conversation is all chemical, and these chemicals are the brain's vocabulary. In essence, emotions are the language of the subconscious mind signalling to the conscious mind, which is predominantly verbal.

Much of what we witness in other people who are trying to communicate with us are patterns of behaviour. They are default settings or reflex responses. A non-verbal part of their brain is seeking to get their message across to the verbal part of our brain, and we wonder why this doesn't work out so well.

Now imagine this on steroids in a family. We have lived and grown up with these people; they know our secrets and have seen us at our best and worst. We may believe that blood is thicker than water and that our familial ties make it less important that we discuss everything. We don't need to – 'we're family', right? Nothing could be further from the truth. Words have meanings; how those meanings are engineered are unique to our experience. For example, 'Pavilion' is unique to the Jacksons' work experience – it was a bonding moment for those who experienced it. In our journey to maturity, as a family, we collect a dictionary, and these words have meanings that attach to experience and become a powerful catalyst for default settings and emotions. If two people in discussion believe something different, it's likely family members – with an even greater list of assumptions and shortcuts – have arrived at even more inaccurate conclusions. Family needs more discussion, not less – as evidenced by Christopher's assumptions about how Nathan views him.

Thanks to our amazing neocortex, human beings have developed a form of communication called 'language' that is supposed to allow us to exchange views and ideas, and share information and knowledge. The concept is sound but the execution is flawed, because there is no universal unambiguous dictionary between each of us, or between the non-verbal and verbal.

To function, we need to be able to communicate with each other. In business we need to articulate our vision and our expectations to our team so that we can bring that vision into reality. We need a common language with which we can communicate those things. Yet the constraints we're discussing here make that extremely difficult – so difficult in fact that if we and our team do indeed envision the same destination it's often a miracle.

Most of us have had the experience of asking someone to do something only to have them return several hours or days later having done something that bears no resemblance to what we believed we asked for. Have you ever had to apologise to someone in a situation like this? 'Sorry, that may be what I said, but it was not what I meant'?

Imagine you, the business owner or department manager, represent the server within a local area network – and all of your staff or employees represent the workstations in your business. Separately the workstations are powerful, but together they are even more so. You need a way to connect them up into a team. The protocol that allows that to happen is language, a version of which can be thought of as software. The software we are using to write this book is English. However, there is a very important distinction between the language-as-software and real software. If I put the same information into two computers loaded with Microsoft Excel, for example, I could confidently expect the same output. But that is not the case with language software. In fact, I can put the same information into two people loaded with the same language software and I can confidently expect a different output! The difference lies within the individual using the software – where and how they grew up, cultural considerations, beliefs and value systems and the myriad default settings that direct their behaviour.

For example, if you are Australian, you probably call an apartment a unit. This is, I think, unique to Australia. If you decide to go to London for a few years, find a 'for rent' sign on a window and call the number, the owner might be very confused if you ask him how big his unit is. The language may still be English but you are now asking a very different question to the one the landlord believes you're asking!

Another example of the confusion that can occur with language is the term 'family office'. Traditionally, family office is the entity that handles investment and wealth management of the family along with other tasks. I have fought tirelessly to encourage wealthy families to appreciate the need for a family office. But universally they hate the term; so much so that they stop listening to what I am saying whenever I bring it up. In one family, the creation of a family office was seen as a way to divide the family. The firstborn CEO was deeply hostile to the fact that the second born was GM of the family office, and it was causing major headaches for the founder and fostering tension elsewhere. Everything was resolved almost overnight when a trust was formed and the second born was repositioned as the trust administrator. Nothing much had changed except the terminology, and yet it helped defuse, if not eliminate, the tension.

In another family, as soon as the term 'family office' was mentioned the founder (G1) would disengage, and everything we were seeking to do in regard to governance would slow down. Another G1 of a very successful company would just yell, 'No – not a f**king chance. We are not having an office for our family as long as I'm alive.' (He does now – but it's not called a family office!)

The reason so many G1s react poorly to the term 'family office' is that, in their internal dictionary, 'family office' means 'An expensive bureaucracy that I pay for to allow my children to avoid even more responsibility.' To a hardworking G2 it might mean, 'A way to leverage our shared resources as a family and save a lot of money.'

When two people agree on something, the only thing we know for sure is that they have two different interpretations of what has just been agreed upon. While the degree of difference varies (small to large), the fact that there *is* a difference is beyond debate. And what's the consequence for the family in business? Simple: words connect to the amygdala like a fuse to a stick of TNT.

Everybody has a slightly different interpretation of the same word. Everybody's definition of every word is based on their history, their knowledge, their education, their experience and their personality (as evidenced by the 'Pavilion' example). These definitions become shortcuts to understanding which have evolved through their own unique experience. And since no two histories are the same, no two dictionaries are the same.

Learnings from the Field: Stranger Danger

In this instance, G1 consisted of three brothers who were, to be blunt, holding the business back. They had done an outstanding job to get the business to where it was, but G2 were making huge strides in taking the business even further. G2 were often hampered by G1's outdated ideas and the notion that everything needed to be shared equally. One of the elderly G1s actually called any non-family employees 'strangers'. Yes, you read that right!

An incident arose that gave me the perfect opportunity to highlight how damaging this casual use of the word 'strangers' could be – not just to the people involved, but to the business. There was significant angst developing about a large capital investment that G1 considered essential. They had arrived at the decision – a view built more on intuition and assumption than science. The alterations they believed necessary were going to cost $3.5 million. Each G1 was to invest an equal share to pay for these alterations – a significant contribution considering their ages and impending retirement. The three brothers felt both certain and nervous about it. Meanwhile, G2, one of whom was running the business and doing an outstanding job in difficult circumstances, decided to test

G1's thinking. They wanted to find out whether the alterations their founding fathers had decided to implement were actually needed. They hired a consultant to conduct an audit and test the conclusions. G1 hated the idea. They made their feelings on the matter known. The shared (founder) sentiment was that they didn't need strangers who knew nothing about the business telling them what they should be doing.

The consultancy took a week to complete the assessment and present its findings, a service that cost $20,000. The outcome was that the business didn't need the proposed capital investment and could achieve the results with additional capacity from different alterations that would cost $500,000. G1's initial relief eventually gave way to confusion and agitation. They wanted to know how it was possible to go from the prospect of investing $1.2 million each, to half a million – an amount that could be covered by the business. How did that happen?

To which came the reply, 'It happened because G2 were comfortable to hire smart *strangers* to give us answers to questions we didn't know to ask.' The word 'stranger' has now disappeared from the family vocabulary.

To give you an idea of how much of a problem that actually is, consider this. According to Bill Bryson's book *Mother Tongue* the English language contains 615,000 words.[39] And that doesn't include technical or scientific terms, which would increase that figure to just over 1 million words. That's a lot of words that could mean different things to different people.

A family's shared history – as evidenced by John's declaration, 'Let's just do everything we did for Pavilion' – points to a family vocabulary. This is inevitable. If we live in the same space with the same people for a couple of decades we are bound to create an inner vocabulary that shortcuts thinking even further. And yet, as we learned previously, thinking is even more important with family and we must push past the convenience of that shared language and implied meaning. Such a vocabulary can not only alienate and confuse non-family members – such as Isaac, the new marketing guy – but it can easily lead to misunderstanding and upset. Do Nathan and Priya really know exactly what John means when he says, 'Let's just do everything we did for Pavilion'? Or are they just winging it? The shared vocabulary can act as a lightning rod to greater confusion, rather than greater clarity.

To add to the potential for confusion, let's apply a multiplier for each person in the equation. If I want to communicate with you, then I need your dictionary to be sure the communication is accurate, but I have no way to access your dictionary. Is it really any wonder communication is so fraught?

And yet in a family context the reverse is true, but the result is the same. Each family has a vocabulary that stimulates the emotive consequences of an amygdala hijack. The other person's dictionary and perspective is really important in business. In marketing we are constantly told to step into the shoes of our customers; so why doesn't that same principle apply across all business? Far from trying to ease understanding and mutual appreciation of the subject, in many cases 'business communication' has become an oxymoron! It is almost like we have intentionally developed this one-dimensional, flat and con-voluted way of speaking to one another – one apparent purpose of which is to devolve responsibility and increase complexity so as to deliberately diminish understanding. The legal profession is famous for hijacking language but it permeates just about every corporate memo and business letter ever written.

A Picture Paints a Thousand Words

The other challenge inherent in language is describing pictures with words. When we try to communicate using words, pictures are what we really hold in our minds. This is because of the non-verbal nature of the subconscious mind, responsible for all those default settings. However, we rarely articulate the full pictures we 'see'. Instead, we use shortcuts – words or phrases that paint more of that picture for us (such as 'Pavilion'). But those words or phrases may not paint a clear picture for the recipient. Certainly, the picture painted by John's reference to 'Pavilion' did not clarify meaning for Isaac. It might have achieved that end for Nathan and Priya – because of their shared family dictionary, John thought he could take a shortcut rather than articulating in detail exactly what he meant. But even that is fraught, because Nathan and Priya can't really be sure that their assumption of John's intended meaning is actually what he meant. As for Isaac, he's confused – and rightly so!

Because we don't get the opportunity to communicate in pictures, having to rely on words instead, our expression and explanation of what we mean is a fraction of what is required for unambiguous under-standing between the parties communicating. Figuratively speaking, if a picture paints a thousand words and we probably deploy between 70 to 100 words per picture, that means there are between 900 and 930 words that we leave the other party to make up!

Yet we often leave meetings and briefing sessions assuming the other people involved have a complete grasp of what we are saying. John certainly does. When he leaves the meeting he's absolutely sure that Nathan and Priya understand what he wants, and if Isaac's not up to speed someone will fill in the gaps. Meanwhile Nathan, Priya and Isaac are happily filling in the gaps in his communication with *their* experience, shortcuts, skills and knowledge – not with John's experience, shortcuts, skills and knowledge. This confusion and misinterpretation is common. People interact every day while missing the entire point of other people's communication.

Often a founder will hire someone based on what they perceive as careful selection and due diligence. They are confident of their choice.

Then, after one month, they will say to me, 'Not as clever as I imagined though, that new hire.' After three to five months, they will say, 'You know what? They've come good.' Now when a client tells me their new hire is 'Not as good as I thought', I suspect the right response is, 'Let's wait till they can speak our language before we judge them.'

Think of your brain as a computer and your native language as its software. The software on its own is useless until you load the data. An accounting package is useless without the numbers. A word processing package is quite useless unless you start to enter text. Your brain in this analogy relies on your life experience as data. In order to deliver an outcome of value, you actually have to provide direct, consistent and very specific language that everyone will be able to interpret in an identical fashion. And this is impossible! At least it is without the style of governance we will shortly examine.

Hidden Communication through Body Language and Tone

To make matters even trickier, body language also conveys meaning. Body language is essentially your non-verbal subconscious making itself visible. Have you noticed that from Moscow to New York, from Madrid to Chicago, everyone knows what 'angry' looks like – with or without words?

In conversation we are minimalists, so we communicate using body language and many other nuances such as tone and accent on particular words. We also interpret those same things as a way of trying to further decipher the meaning of the communication.

To demonstrate the power of vocal tonality, read the following sentences out loud, putting the emphasis on each of the highlighted words.

- *Why* did he ask me that question?
- Why *did* he ask me that question?

- Why did *he* ask me that question?
- Why did he *ask* me that question?
- Why did he ask *me* that question?
- Why did he ask me *that* question?

These identical sentences each instil radically different meanings, depending on the emphasis. And our brain tends to choose the emphasis that presents the most probable negative connotations. And that's just the variation caused by tonality and emphasis. Over 60 percent of communication is based on visual messages that are especially important in the first few moments of contact. Interestingly enough, when there is a discrepancy between what is said and what is indicated via non-verbal information, people will pay more attention to the latter.

Body language is your subconscious mind's favourite language – it will 'protect' you by ignoring the words and paying attention to everything else.

You can gauge (or guess) a person's mood, unsaid response and level of enthusiasm from body language without them uttering a single word. For example, how many times have you asked someone to stay back late at work and they have said 'Yes' but their body language is screaming 'No!'? How many times have you been in a situation where the words being spoken are not congruent with the messages being transmitted through body language? Much as we would like to, we simply can't dismiss body language as being an unimportant part of the message. In the meeting where Nathan remarked about Christopher getting his knickers in a knot, Priya might have asked Christopher if he was alright after noticing that he sat back and stopped contributing to the meeting. Christopher would have said, 'I'm fine'. But everyone in the room would know he wasn't fine if they noticed his body language.

It's hard to tell which is the greater of two evils – the fact that we use body language to qualify our communication, believing that it adds to a congruent message; or the fact that we think our interpretation of someone else's body language is right! But again, once we understand the challenges of language and how we are programmed to cut communication short, especially in families where we know each other so well, we can push more constructively towards shared meaning and agreement – which can, in turn, remove another chunk of complexity and uncertainty.

Let's go back to the Jacksons' incredibly short marketing meeting. Isaac is lucky he's already read this book, so as soon as John says, 'Let's just do everything we did for Pavilion' and the others agree he immediately knows that one word has conveyed an entire strategy to the others. But he doesn't know what 'Pavilion' is or what strategy it infers. Isaac points this out to the others: 'It's clear that you all know what "Pavilion" is and what that means for the strategy, but I wasn't in the company at that point – so can you explain that project to me so that I can then execute the strategy?' This is the moment when Isaac begins to 'learn the Jacksons' language'. Of course, if Isaac is really switched on he may go even further by saying, 'I understand Pavilion is useful as a guide, but before we drive forward, can we please do a reality check to ensure that all that was learnt and demonstrated by what you call "Pavilion" is in fact relevant for this project?'

CHAPTER 7

We Can't Be Subjective and Objective at the Same Time

The project development team is meeting about a problem. The certifier has made an error and construction has been suspended. A submission to the local council is expensive but may be the only way forward. The danger is that more issues may then be uncovered. It's the project development team's issue to solve and everyone around the table knows it. But they are confused and stuck as to what to do about it, or even where to start. Their concern is evident. What happened?

SOLVING A PROBLEM REQUIRES TWO SEPARATE MIND STATES.
WE CANNOT BE BOTH 'IN' IT AND 'ON' IT SIMULTANEOUSLY.
OUR BRAIN CANNOT FUNCTION AT ITS PEAK IF IT ATTEMPTS TO
BE BOTH EXPERT AT UNDERSTANDING THE PROBLEM,
AND EXPERT AT CONSTRUCTING THE SOLUTION.

What happened is that no one in the room realised the significance of the fifth limitation – we can't be subjective and objective at the same time. Solving a problem requires two separate mind states. We cannot be both 'in' it and 'on' it simultaneously. Our brain cannot function at its peak if it attempts to be both expert at understanding the problem, and expert at constructing the solution.

When it comes to problem solving, including family business problem solving, we usually go along with the concept that the 'answers lie within'. And they do. There is little doubt that the members of G1, G2, G3 and beyond who are working in the business will know more about the business than those who do not. Unfortunately, they can't always access those answers because human beings find it impossible to be objective and subjective at the same time. Of course, this is often made worse by other limitations such as default settings and emotion. We may think we are being logical, rational and objective about a family business challenge but the presence of family members in the discussion means default settings have almost certainly been triggered – and that means we are being subjective, not objective. On top of this, our emotional reaction to that default trigger means that any last vestige of objectivity that we may have been able to cling on to will have been torched.

The problem is: for our thinking to function to its potential, the *information* needs to be retrieved in a manner that serves the *conclusion* – not in a manner that serves our *personal* attachment to various *pieces* of information, or that is based on convenient conclusions we arrived at before the information was known. And this requires the one thing we can't give ourselves – objectivity. This is why the business I described in chapter 6 – led by three brothers, one of whom referred to non-family employees as 'strangers' – was able to get a significantly better outcome to its problem than the solution its members arrived at while stuck in their subjective mindsets. By hiring some objectivity, they saved $3 million.

Let's take a look at some *Macquarie Dictionary* definitions (my emphases are underlined):

Ob-jec-tive. n. **1.** an end towards which efforts are directed. -adj. **2.** Gram. denoting the object of transitive verbs. **3.** <u>unbiased</u>. **4.** of or pertaining to objects. – objectivity, n

Sub-jec-tive. adj. <u>belonging to the thinking person rather than to the object of thought</u> (opposed to objective).

Unbiased objectivity may occasionally be possible in business (although I would argue it's rarer than we might imagine). But it is next to impossible in a family business. Every interaction, every discussion and every decision are tainted by the endless family dynamics.

Have you ever faced a challenge, and no matter how many times you go at it, you just can't find a solution? Then from nowhere something external triggers a whole new thought process and the solution emerges? What actually happened was your brain was telling you, in the only way it could, that it was not able to do what you wanted it to do. It took the external trigger to remove the log jam. When you're stuck on a problem, sometimes all it takes is someone asking you a bunch of questions about it to remove the log jam around the problem. You know the best solution, but you need someone else's objectivity in that moment to help you access it.

There are two things required to produce your best thinking – *context*, which is how you think; and *content*, which is the thoughts themselves. Context over content is what sets the entrepreneur apart. Here's how they are different:

- Context is imagining how people might use the next iteration of an iPhone.
  - Content is looking for a way to make a better BlackBerry.
- Context is imagining all your music in your pocket.
  - Content is finding a better medium for recording and listening to music.

- Context is working out ways to make the PC operate so people find it easy to use.
  - Content is working out ways to help people understand how to operate a PC.

Entrepreneurs see what doesn't already exist; they are not tweaking what already exists. As such they are usually able to see the world with a degree of elegant simplicity. Successful founders almost always have this ability – they are proficient in context. I remember working with one very successful restaurateur. He could look at a plate of food and work out the gross profit (context), whereas everyone else saw a beautiful dish (content). He wasn't blind to content and could certainly tell if a dish looked and tasted good, but to the frustration of his chefs he could also look at a plate and say, 'That's not 34 percent.' What he meant was there was no way the business was making 34 percent gross profit on what they had just put down in front of him.

Understanding how people see things, or how they buy things, or how they might more easily embrace things is a crucial ingredient in success. Creating owner or shareholder value typically requires contextual thinking. However, keeping the wealth it creates is loaded with content: right structure, right investment, right people, right risk mitigation. And certainly, if the ego builds the wealth, the alter ego is needed to protect it.

IF THE EGO BUILDS THE WEALTH, THE ALTER EGO IS NEEDED TO PROTECT IT.

Perhaps the difference between objectivity and subjectivity explains why marriage guidance counsellors get divorced? They can't give themselves the one thing they can give their clients, and that is the umpire's impartial (objective) perspective. When we visit a psychologist or a counsellor, they provide context – we provide content. But when a founder is trying to find a path through the various family business challenges, they're trying to provide both content and context.

Any business, especially a family business that creates a strategic or operational plan from within the family, is committing itself to an outcome that is less than it is truly capable of. The rest is only possible when objectivity is systematically applied to the challenge. This objectivity separates thoughts from thinking, unplugs the default settings, defuses emotional reactions and communicates thoroughly, transparently and effectively. This objectivity is achieved through the application of scaffolding which instils engineered objectivity; or the application of a proven formula that serves to illuminate solutions to any family business challenge. My whole career has been dedicated to the facilitation of engineered objectivity – and the creation of a set of questions that, when answered, deliver the best strategic plan, personal plan, Family Charter and Family Retreat, which allows the four voices to be heard. My way is not the only way, but engineered objectivity *is* the only way. When assessing those that may help you on this journey, you need to look for evidence of engineered objectivity. Is there a process? Is there a systematic and ordered way to expose all the elements that are impacting any situation and work through those towards resolution and agreement? If there is, the proposed solution probably includes engineered objectivity. If not, you are speaking to a consultant. Consultants are notorious for bringing their black box subjective solution to the party before they even know the problem.

ENGINEERED OBJECTIVITY APPLIES SCAFFOLDING OR A PROVEN FORMULA THAT SERVES TO ILLUMINATE SOLUTIONS TO ANY FAMILY BUSINESS CHALLENGE.

To achieve high-quality thinking, two contributions must happen concurrently: subjective skill, knowledge and experience matched with objective, dispassionate, uninvolved questioning. The more dispassionate and uninvolved (the very definition of objectivity) the purer the thinking, and the more powerful the outcome.

Let's imagine John Jackson has been at a conference out of state and he's flying back home. He gets talking to the guy sitting next to him and discovers he is also in business. The stranger asks John some questions about his business. John considers the questions carefully and answers honestly, and finds some of his responses surprising and insightful. That unfiltered and unchecked engagement gives John some new context, which triggers useful new thoughts about how best to tackle a number of issues he's wrestling with.

We've all experienced this from time to time. Perhaps we go out with friends and share a problem we've been struggling with. The conversation that follows includes a number of possible solutions, some of which we have already thought of. But there are a couple of ideas that offer a fresh perspective. Our friends are able to bring some new context and unbiased objectivity to the challenge, which helps us to solve it. This can sometimes happen when we are forced to put a problem out of our mind because we can't solve it, and then halfway through a spin class or during a completely unrelated conversation the solution will pop into view. In this instance the space can help to provide objectivity. But it is always easier (and quicker) with a second brain involved.

Another word for objectivity applied to oneself is 'hindsight'. Hindsight is a list of *answers* that were not given the benefit of *questions* that could have been asked with foresight! And the great news is that you don't need to be a psychic to *know* the questions.

HINDSIGHT IS A LIST OF *ANSWERS* THAT WERE NOT GIVEN THE BENEFIT OF *QUESTIONS* THAT COULD HAVE BEEN ASKED WITH FORESIGHT!

Let's go back to John's trip home from the conference. Now imagine that Christopher also goes to the conference. Even if the stranger is still present and asks John the same questions, John won't answer them in the same free and liberated way, because his son is sitting next to him. Now imagine there is no objective stranger but instead Christopher asks his dad the exact same questions. Would John answer differently again? Absolutely he would, because he's no longer just listening to the questions and searching for the most accurate answer – he's trying to work out why Christopher is asking him these questions. He's also assessing how much he should say, as well as determining how much of what he will say will get back to Christopher's siblings and how they might then interpret what Christopher tells them about his 'chat with Dad'.

Subjectivity and objectivity are essential for the best possible out-come, but they don't happen automatically and it's next to impossible to provide both at the same time. Without genuine external, unbiased objectivity it's impossible for John to answer questions about the business honestly without suspicion, resentment, irritation or fear of creating unintended additional consequences in the family.

Part III of this book explains how to nullify all five of the human limitations I've spoken of in part I by instilling governance – engineered objectivity. Governance can vastly improve results in any business, especially a family business where the limitations are amplified because of the complex family dynamics. If governance is facilitated by a trusted advisor (that second brain), the results can also be faster and more effective.

The governance formulae together with an external advisor provides the scaffolding around a family business that can dial down our human drive to survive which, while helpful, need not be front and centre in every situation, conversation or discussion. Our world is not the constant threat it once was. We need to chill out and put our human limitations in perspective so that they don't cause unnecessary chaos and dysfunction. This scaffolding then allows the family business to implement and apply governance which, in turn, allows the business to thrive, all the while preserving love, loyalty and wealth.

Remember: wisdom arrives at the moment you are guided by your thoughts and governed by your thinking. Wisdom departs when you are governed by your thoughts. We have much more control over our thoughts than we imagine, but we have to take control. As Viktor Frankl once said, 'Between stimulus and response there is a space. In that space is our power to choose our response. In our response lies our growth and our freedom.'

So, let's go back to the problem meeting and the anxious participants.

John walks in and can tell everyone is anxious. Showing some wisdom, he asks a series of questions: 'So, what exactly is the problem? When did it start? Who found out about it? What did we do when we first found out? What result did that bring us? What do we think our options are? Which of those options do you think we should try first? What makes you confident that could work?', and so on.

The team members answer all the questions, immediately feel better and a best next step becomes evident, allowing them to work towards a solution. The four nervous, unsure and anxious people in the room when John arrived are four confident and focused people when he leaves.

Subjectivity (content) was sitting in the room, and objectivity (context), in this case John, arrived. Had the members of the project development team read this book, they would realise that no one can be subjective and objective at the same time. But as the holders of the content, they could pre-empt the questions that would elicit objectivity which, in turn, could help to facilitate an answer – in effect, an agenda made up of questions, not headings.

PART II

By the time I meet the individual members of a family business, issues will already have started to arise, or there will be a recognition that problems are gathering on the horizon. Often these family businesses are extremely successful and have generated significant wealth. When I listen to these families, they are always wrestling with the juxtaposition of two distinct things – the *family* and the *business* – and how to make both work without damaging either. This is not easy. Often, they are seeking to measure, monitor or better understand the impact the business and its resulting wealth is having on the family and its ongoing connectedness. In other words, the founder is increasingly aware that the business – it's size and/or complexity together with the resulting wealth – is causing issues or will cause issues that they didn't anticipate when they started the business. I encourage them to consider two things – what they have, and how they and everyone else in the family feels.

What we have is easy to measure as it is a simple mathematical calculation, but how we feel is not. How we feel often comes down to how happy we are. Happiness, certainly in a family business context, often comes down to the ability of the family to stay connected as well as feeling individually and collectively supported whether inside or outside the business.

The irony is that contrary to popular belief, wealth can make happiness less likely in this scenario. When faced with this uncomfortable reality, founders find it surprising, confusing, frustrating, irritating and alarming. That isn't how it's supposed to be!

Part II explains why this happens so we can better navigate the traps and create long-lasting solutions that support the happiness and connectedness of the family *and* the ongoing success of the business.

> *Happiness cannot be found; it must be chosen.*
> – Eddie Jaku

CHAPTER 8

Wealth ≠ Happiness

When asked what we want most in life, many of us would say that we want to be happy. But it seems that we are not very good at achieving this universal goal. Too often we attach certain rules, parameters or milestones to happiness as though we have to be, do or have something specific in order to be happy. As a result, happiness remains elusive. There are, of course, several reasons for this.

For years the theory was that happiness is genetic – we are either born optimists or pessimists and there isn't much we could do about this 'cortical lottery'.[40] Thanks to researchers such as Abraham Maslow, Aaron Antonovsky, James W Pennebaker, Tal Ben-Shahar, Dean Ornish, Martin Seligman and Mihaly Csikszentmihalyi, we now understand that our emotional outlook is not fixed as a permanent set point; rather, each of us has a 'range' that we can constructively move along.

This knowledge implies that we can choose happiness if we want to. But in order to do that we must also accept that happiness is not a permanent state of being. It is by nature transitory. We will never miraculously wake up one day to find we have finally arrived at our destination of 'happy' and blissfully remain there for eternity. That isn't how it works. In fact, without the periodic absence of happiness we could never know it in our lives.

Happiness is a conscious journey. During that journey there will be moments of recognised happiness when things go well in our lives – our football team wins, we secure a business deal, we become a parent or we enjoy a night out with friends (specific happiness). There are also recognised moments of unhappiness when we might break our ankle, fall out with a partner or be involved in a car accident (again, specific unhappiness). The determination of our level of happiness in any moment is focused around or linked to a positive or negative event or situation. And yet, these ups and downs of life are inevitable for all of us regardless of our situation or circumstance. This is just part of the human experience.

Part of the reason happiness remains so elusive is because we confuse these specific happiness-triggering or unhappiness-triggering events with general happiness or unhappiness. We need to view happiness in much more general terms. Let me ask you right now, 'All things considered, are you happy?' This broader vantage point allows us to appreciate that it is possible to experience especially good or bad days and moments and still consider ourselves happy.

Another reason that our goal of happiness fails to materialise is that we are looking in the wrong place.

For decades the focus of psychology and psychiatry was dysfunction – what was wrong with people and why they were miserable. No one was looking in the opposite direction at happiness and high function. In fact, it was largely viewed as academically irrelevant to research happiness or elevated performance.

However, the field of positive psychology started to change all that. We now appreciate the importance of emotional wellbeing and happiness and how that can influence everything from our health to the quality of our relationships to our working lives.

The quest was on to identify what it was that would make people happy. One of the primary targets was money. Surely, if we had more money, we would be happier. Certainly, for someone struggling on minimum wage, more money would undoubtedly make life easier which could, in turn, make them happier. But I meet extremely wealthy families all the time whose members are anything but happy.

Remember what Cornelius Vanderbilt's grandson said? 'Inherited wealth is a real handicap to happiness. It is as certain a death to ambition as cocaine is to morality.'

So, what is going on with wealth? Is it the panacea we all imagine or have we missed something?

Using Gallup data from almost half a million Americans, researchers from Princeton University demonstrated that while there is correlation between happiness and money the correlation stops at a surprisingly low level – US$75,000.[41] In other words, happiness will rise with income up to US$75,000 but once that income level is reached there is no corresponding uplift in happiness beyond that point.[42] This is intriguing and has been borne out by many other studies, including one by Elizabeth Dunn and Michael Norton. They took a national sample of Americans who earned around $25,000 to gauge their happiness levels. Everyone reported that they thought that their satisfaction with life would double if they made $55,000. To test this hypothesis the researchers took another national sample of people who already earned $55,000 and found that they were actually only 9 percent happier than those who made $25,000.[43]

Contrary to popular myth, money does not equal happiness.

In fact, it can be quite the opposite. Ever since the days of Émile Durkheim – a prominent French sociologist in the late 1800s – sociologists have documented how depression and suicide rates fluctuate with economic trends. Durkheim himself showed that suicide rates tend to increase not only during financial hard times but financial good times, too! This is both unexpected and expected at the same time. During times of dramatic personal prosperity, the rules change. The expectation is that life will become easier now that we are wealthy.

We think our problems will disappear – and of course they don't. This can be devastating. It's why lottery winners so frequently end up broke and report being happier before the money.

For those who don't have money, there is always a glimmer of hope – hope that tomorrow might be better, that they might get a break or a pay rise and the additional money will help solve their problems and make them happier. When that wealth arrives, but the expected happiness doesn't follow, the hope often disappears. Given time these people realise the adage is true – money doesn't buy happiness at all. The transformation from unhappy to happy fails to materialise or is fleeting at best. As such, the depression or sadness that follows can be even more profound.

This is a revelation that the whole world should know about. It could reduce the angst for those who consider they don't have enough and are missing out on happiness as a result. And it could reduce the guilt and confusion for those who are wealthy but for whom happiness is still elusive. Without exception, the families I work with are at first genuinely confused by the situation they find themselves in – a successful business, healthy family, more money in the bank than they could ever spend and yet the founders, siblings or both are miserable or at the very least struggling with their situation in one way or another.

Clearly, we *are* missing something.

Study after study has repeatedly demonstrated that quality of life and happiness depend on two factors: how we experience work, and our relationships with others (our connectedness).[44]

Of course, how a G2 experiences work in a family business is often challenging. Too often they are not taken seriously by G1 or by other senior non-family members of the team; or they are never quite sure of their place – whether they should be there, or deserve to be there. The hit show *Succession*, supposedly influenced by the Murdoch family, or *Yellowstone*, starring Kevin Costner, are extreme glimpses into the various potential dysfunctions of family business at this level.

The relationships we have with friends and family are paramount when it comes to happiness, but those relationships are put under significantly more pressure in a family that also operates a business together. Author Johann Hari has suggested, backed by a great deal of evidence, that lack of connectedness is even the source of addiction.[45] I have witnessed evidence of this.

Psychologists Richard Ryan and Edward Deci proposed self-determination theory (SDT), which outlines what we need in order to feel motivated and happy – competence, autonomy and relatedness.[46] According to Ryan and Deci, people need to be able to demonstrate competence in their daily activities; they need to have some level of control and autonomy over their work and lives; and they need to feel connected to others they care about. Again, we are able to see the potential problems that arise in the peculiar hothouse of family business. And money, far from being a balm to such issues, becomes an accelerant.

If unmanaged or taken for granted, money can actually work against motivation and happiness. Having money doesn't always help people develop competence using it, because those with money are not forced to forge their own path and earn a living the way those from non-wealthy families are. In many cases people from wealthy families never really achieve autonomy because they always have the financial safety net of the family wealth, and may even be paid an allowance well into later life. I mentioned the TV show *Succession* earlier; if you have watched it, you will understand this reference. If not … spoiler alert! The show demonstrates how dysfunctional extreme wealth can be. The oldest son spends a fortune on various fancies such as funding a play for his girlfriend and running for President of the United States, both of which are hugely expensive follies. In the final show of the second series, he pulls his dad, Logan, aside on the family yacht to ask for a small injection of $100 million. Zero autonomy. And this is not fiction for many wealthy families. Also, children of wealthy families often suffer from a lack of relatedness because they are never really sure if others are interested in *them*, or in gaining access to their parents or their share of the family wealth.

Finally, the most compelling reason happiness remains so elusive is because we don't appreciate the twin forces that most actively diminish or prevent our general happiness.

There are two enemies of happiness that impact us all, regardless of our economic situation, how we experience work or even our connectedness – they are uncertainty and complexity. What is not understood or even really considered is that uncertainty and complexity are especially challenging at either extreme of the wealth continuum. In other words, uncertainty and complexity make happiness as elusive for the very poor as for the very rich. Uncertainty and complexity can also play havoc with how we experience work (autonomy and competence) *and* our connectedness, which is the real source of happiness and family longevity.

Competence, autonomy and relatedness are constructs. They are experienced as real phenomena but they are constructs nonetheless. Complexity and uncertainty impact biological, psychological, pre-ordained, inherited, evolved predispositions. They exist for everyone operating in the modern world but are especially relevant for the very poor and the very rich.

What I referred to earlier in the chapter as 'all things considered' happiness is deeply impacted by uncertainty and complexity. And while we can never make another person happy, we can draw the rational conclusion that 'all things considered' they ought to *be* happy. Understanding uncertainty and complexity allows us to do that.

COMPLEXITY AND UNCERTAINTY IMPACT BIOLOGICAL, PSYCHOLOGICAL, PRE-ORDAINED, INHERITED, EVOLVED PREDISPOSITIONS. THEY EXIST FOR EVERYONE OPERATING IN THE MODERN WORLD BUT ARE ESPECIALLY RELEVANT FOR THE VERY POOR AND THE VERY RICH.

There are, in my view, two 'planes' on which happiness exists, just like there are two 'planes' on which thinking exists – content and context. If my football team wins, I'm happy; if I break my ankle, I'm unhappy. This is content shaped by the events of that moment. The second and more important 'plane' of happiness is contextual. I am healthy. I have a roof over my head. I live in a safe country. I have a job and food on the table. My children have an education. I am 'all things considered' happy. Contextual happiness is much more important and significantly more meaningful. Why, then, do we find it so hard to choose a 'chemistry' to match that state?

We need to become much more sophisticated in our understanding of happiness so that we can, in turn, better manage it, foster it and make it part of our lives.

CHAPTER 9

The Twin Enemies of Happiness

The twin enemies of happiness are agnostic. We all experience uncertainty and complexity in our lives and together they conspire to foster unhappiness in all Homo sapiens. Universally the assumption is that wealth or more money will help to mitigate the issues created by uncertainty and complexity which could, in turn, lead to greater happiness. And as I will explain in this chapter, this idea is at least partly true. But wealth is not the healing balm so many of us assume. Indeed, the reverse is often true. Wealth, especially the type of wealth that is frequently created inside successful family business, is not a cure to unhappiness – it is an amplifier, an accelerant or a steroid. Wealth magnifies the impact of the brain's limitations because it tends to trigger additional fears and anxieties around equity and entitlement. It also massively increases the levels of uncertainty and complexity that must, somehow, be managed.

On Uncertainty

Human beings abhor uncertainty.

Why do you think we have old wives' tales or religion? Uncertainty is the reason there are so many simplistic yet vaguely plausible stories about how an apple a day keeps the doctor away and convoluted explanations of God's power, such as virgin births and turning water into wine. Since human beings emerged from the caves, we have used our modest creativity to come up with answers to deal with life's uncertainties. Whether an explanation for thunder and lightning, pink skies, why we are here or where grandma went when she died, these stories have been designed to allay uncertainty and the fear and doubt that naturally follows it. Remember our greatest default – *in the absence of information* (uncertainty) our brain will deliver thoughts that will instinctively default to the worst *probable* conclusion. These stories – many of which are, frankly, ridiculous – are meant to provide certainty in an uncertain world. In essence the Bible, the Quran or any other ancient novel is nothing more than a fairly unsophisticated effort to minimise uncertainty! (Essential detour: read the breakout box – The Bible as a Novel.)

The Bible as a Novel

What happened for you when I referred to the Holy Bible and the Quran as 'ancient novels'? If your frontal lobe (that's the clever part) is well developed, you probably had a bit of a smirk and moved on. All that happened was your front of mind recognised that I am probably a passionate atheist who, like you, is entitled to my own opinion. Your amygdala therefore remained in neutral.

If, on the other hand, your first six years of life involved being hardwired to the notion of God, you might have been deeply offended – incensed, even. However, somewhere in your front of mind is the crucial piece of information about God creating all things, which would mean he made me just as I am and therefore my expressed opinion is part of that 'all things' and could legitimately be viewed as part of your God. But your reaction doesn't come from your front of mind. Your back-of-mind amygdala is not in neutral. You can't now appreciate that what I think is irrelevant to your faith. My point of view has no impact on your God and the sanctity of your religion and, perhaps more crucially, it has no bearing on your appreciation of your God or your commitment to your religion. So, any amygdala-inspired reaction, yours or mine, in relation to God is completely irrelevant. And yet we can predict with supreme confidence that some amygdalas will have hijacked their respective fronts of mind to such an extent that their frontal lobes will never even read this caveat. As soon as I referred to the Bible as a novel, these amygdalas reacted and used that intense emotional reaction as evidence that the author is obviously an idiot, evil, or both – and they stopped reading the book. It's a big book, so I hope they didn't throw it at anyone – they might have needed stitches!

Of course, such a reaction is as nonsensical as the original statement. I believe that religion is silly, but making jibes about religion is equally silly! No well-fuelled neocortex would give either a second thought.

Ironically, people think there is certainty associated with wealth. In other words, the more money someone has the more certainty they have. They assume that the relationship is as represented by figure 9.1.

Figure 9.1: The Assumed Relationship between Wealth and Uncertainty

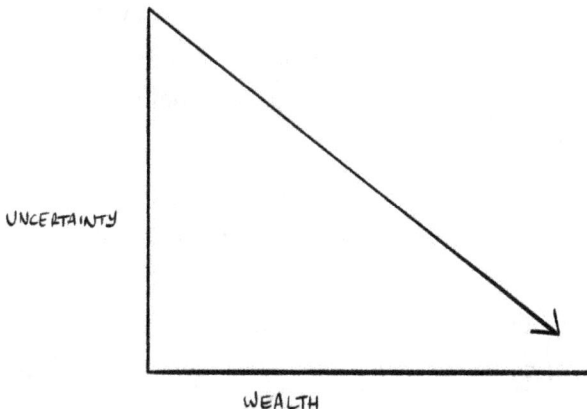

UNCERTAINTY

WEALTH

Although this assumption is logical – uncertainty is bound to be greatest when someone has no money – it is another example of Mencken's assertion that for every complex problem there is an answer that is clear, simple and wrong.

The real relationship between money and uncertainty is illustrated in figure 9.2.

Figure 9.2: The Real Relationship between
Wealth and Uncertainty

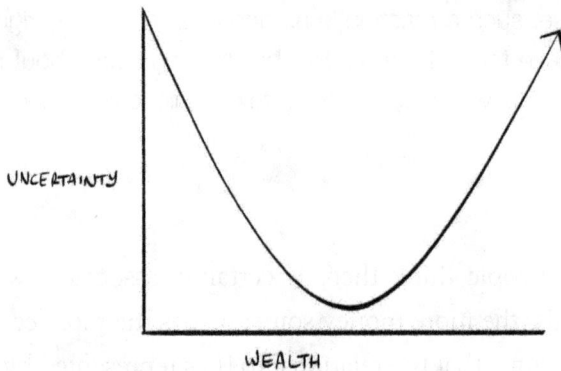

Having too little money definitely corresponds with uncertainty, which, in turn, impacts happiness – this is obvious. It's incredibly difficult to enjoy life when we don't know if we will be able to meet our commitments or keep a roof over our heads, or whether we will have to decide between heating or eating. There is nothing remotely enjoyable about struggling to pay bills, or being stuck in a poorly paying job or in a situation where we have to work several jobs just to be able to pay for groceries, electricity or rent. Uncertainty is a constant companion.

If knowing there is a tomorrow is evolution's gift to humanity, uncertainty is the price we pay for this gift. Uncertainty makes happiness harder to find. Uncertainty is the source of fear and doubt. If we are uncertain about our health, it rarely feels good. We are worried and concerned about what's wrong. This is why so many people feel relief at getting a diagnosis – the uncertainty is at least minimised and they can decide what to do about it. If we are uncertain about our job, we are rarely happy. Are we suitably qualified? Do we have the right skill set? What do others think about our level of contribution? Is our job safe? How else can we explain that the discovery of the body of a missing person actually elicits relief for their loved ones?

IF KNOWING THERE IS A TOMORROW IS EVOLUTION'S GIFT TO HUMANITY, UNCERTAINTY IS THE PRICE WE PAY FOR THIS GIFT.

Remember the Princeton study I referenced in chapter 8, which demonstrated that the correlation between happiness and money stops at US$75,000?[47] We see that it is actually the middle class – who have 'enough' money – who have the most certainty and therefore enjoy a consistent level of money-related happiness. Again, this is obvious. People in middle class experience two benefits: they are no longer uncertain about their ability to survive and meet their day-to-day obligations. Once the immediate threat of poverty is removed and they have enough money to cover their bills with a little left over, the fear and doubt of uncertainty disappears, or at least reduces significantly. Their complexity is also minimised because although they enjoy 'enough' money they don't have so much as to bring endless additional decision-making. As a result, those in the middle class have less uncertainty and, by definition, less complexity.

The reason so many of us are confused as to why our happiness doesn't increase as a result of additional money past a certain point is that we don't appreciate the role that uncertainty plays. And, perhaps more importantly, we don't appreciate that uncertainty roars back into play once wealth – especially serious wealth – is achieved. Hence the angst in successful family businesses.

Wealth breeds uncertainty – it doesn't minimise it.

For a lower- or middle-class child there is very little uncertainty about what they need to do in life in order to thrive financially. If they want to live a good life with a nice home and few money worries, they must choose an in-demand profession and get trained in that area – thus, exercising some autonomy and developing the competence Deci and Ryan identified as essential for happiness.[48] Children of families in extreme poverty or extreme wealth don't have that luxury. Those who are very poor are too busy just surviving day to day. They have limited access to the routes and opportunities that even the middle class have to design their future. They are also often not brought up in environments that actively encourage or even consider education as a legitimate route out of poverty, because survival is the only goal. It's also very hard to study when hungry.

At the other end of the spectrum, children of the very rich are equally uncertain, albeit in a different way. For the rich child money has never been an issue. Imagine if your financial future depended on your ability to choose the right hobby? Often, by the time children are old enough to remember, they have experienced wealth on a daily basis. The wealth is an integral part of their life. They have zero understanding of how other people who don't enjoy their level of wealth live and they certainly don't appreciate what it takes to make the sort of money they now take for granted. Their innate drive to strive for better is hampered by the fact that they already have 'better' and are therefore not necessarily encouraged to consider how they might make their own money or plot their own destiny.

And that is true whether there is wealth plus an operating business or a balance sheet without an operating business. Where there is a family business the uncertainty is often around the child's role in that business and parental expectations, as well as their rights and access to that wealth. For those where wealth exists without an operating business, the uncertainty is focused on the wealth. Why should I work at all? Why can't I have my share now? Why is mum or dad's lawyer or accountant controlling my money? Without the need to find their own way, pay their own way and work, descendants of wealth have even less chance of experiencing the autonomy and competence that are so needed for happiness and fulfilment. Without the need to support themselves they can easily become dabblers. There is a great sketch by Billy Connolly called 'Dinner Party' where he tells the story of going to a very fancy Christmas lunch at a huge house in Yorkshire – 'One of those houses that when you go in the gate you've got half an hour to go to get to the house.' Once at the house Billy was getting to know people and asked one guy what he did for a living. The man, clearly extremely wealthy, answered, 'Toboggin'. Billy says, 'And that's the difference between them and us. They think it's alright to be a tobogganist!' Clearly, those with wealth live a charmed and privileged life and we need not feel too sorry for them, but to assume that being a child of a wealthy family is a free pass, one-way ticket to happiness is pure fiction. In many ways, wealth removes the scaffolding that most of us are forced to build to create our adult life – the byproduct of which can be happiness and contentment. And this is why creating a personal plan is so vital in giving each individual member of the family a voice – it encourages everyone to step back from the assumptions or privilege and really think about what they want to do, create or achieve in their lives, regardless of the money they may or may not currently have access to. That voice, when spoken and heard by the founder and other family members, can be exciting and hugely liberating.

Learnings from the Field: Conditioned Career Choice

Without exception, G1 believes that their children were free to choose whatever career they wanted. Most are adamant that they did not expect their children to come and work in the business or pursue a profession they approved of. Most G2s, on hearing this belief, laugh. This is no one's fault. It is the product of conditioning.

In his brilliant book, *Sapiens*, Yuval Noah Harari states, 'Humans emerge from the womb like molten glass from a furnace. They can be spun, stretched and shaped with a surprising degree of freedom. This is why today we can educate our children to become Christian or Buddhist, capitalist or socialist, warlike or peace-loving.'[49]

When someone is brought up in a family business their life is dominated by the business. Conversation at the dinner table is about the business. The children are recruited as free labour from an early age and they are immersed into that life. They learn the industry vocabulary without even trying. They are spun, stretched and shaped into the business whether anyone is doing so deliberately or not.

As a result, most G2s believe they did *not* have a choice.

Often all the children are employed in the business. The business name of one family business I worked in was even created as a combination of the children's first names! Sons David and Paul inspired the creation of Daul Haulage. They were four and six years of age at the time. How were they not going to work in that business?

In another instance, while asking a G2 about why they went into medicine and became a surgeon, G2 wasn't immediately sure. After some thought she clearly remembered an incident and on recalling this incident also appreciated the insanity of what she was about to say. Before answering she qualified her answer: 'Obviously this isn't the reason why I became a surgeon but I do remember overhearing a conversation between Dad and a family friend. The family friend asked what Dad thought we [his children] would do for a living. Dad said that I wanted to be a surgeon. The family friend sounded encouraging and thought that sounded like an interesting career path for me. But Dad's response was, "Oh, she hasn't got the stomach for it."' What dawned on this G2 in that moment was that her entire career path and choice beyond that point was driven by her desire to prove her father wrong.

The problem lies here. If dad is a run-of-the-mill accountant, the daughter may have simply thought, 'What would Dad know about being a surgeon?' and the exchange may not even have stayed in mind. But if dad is regarded by all as 'wealthy' and 'successful' then his daughter becomes hyperalert to his view, because so many others are too. Average or less well-off dads and mums have opinions. Wealthy parents have instructions, even if they are not expressed as such.

It is a complete myth to imagine that G2 and onwards have the type of freedom of choice when it comes to careers as the children of non-wealthy families have. Yes, there is also an inherent safety net for those children in pursuing a career in the family business, but it is definitely not the easy ride non-employed family often assume. In addition, the children of wealthy families often have no sense of what is going to be expected of them or what options are genuinely on the table in terms of their role or possible role in the family business.

This is often very different to the experience of the founder, who probably enjoyed the freedom of a lower- to middle-class upbringing. Often it was the financial struggle in their early lives that drove them towards 'something better'. When they left school and ventured out on their own, they walked out their parental home, down the front path and could choose to go in any direction they wanted. And they did – they started the business. By the time *their* children come along and are old enough to play a role in the fledgling dynasty, the founder has already built a four-lane highway and the children are influenced by that one way or another. G2 does not have the same freedom or options – regardless of what G1 might imagine.

Every parent wants their child to have a better life than they did. This is universally true of all caring parents. But parents too easily forget that the things that made them successful in the first place were born out of necessity, resilience and determination – which came more often than not from financial hardship. Wealthy parents, in their rush to provide a 'better life', undervalue the difficulties they experienced themselves as children and their own children are raised in ways that are light years from their own upbringing. The question is no longer, 'What can I give my children?' It becomes, 'How can I raise my children so that they still grow up and access all the anchors and touch points that gave me my character and context?' – the character, context and drive that created the business in the first place.

The children of wealthy parents may enjoy a huge bounty of benefits, privileges and experiences that children from lower- to middle-class families will never comprehend, but they also often lose the autonomy and responsibility to define their own path and develop competence in an area that genuinely interests them.

G2s of wealthy business owners suffer from the Goldilocks effect. Like the porridge in the fairytale their life is not too hot and not too cold, it's 'just right'. They are warm and comfortable, and they find it hard to make decisions – especially those that may negatively impact that 'just right' environment. As a result, their personal momentum stalls. If they are in the business their professional momentum can also stall because they don't have the internal will to strive for better – because they already have better. This mindset is exacerbated by the fact that they have spent every school holidays overseas in a luxury resort being spoilt, and they have no reference point that is self-propelling. These are, of course, generalisations and there are always exceptions, but the Goldilocks effect is a very real challenge for wealthy G2s and beyond.

Back to the Jacksons

Let's revisit the Jacksons. Of the four children, Christopher and Priya still remember their first home: a three-bedroom house in Glebe. Nathan and Anika only remember the six-bedroom house with manicured garden and pool in Bellevue Hill. Every evening meal was peppered with discussions about John's business; the children – particularly the two boys – were expected to help in their spare time if needed. Both Christopher and Priya earned pocket money by working in the business after school and on weekends. Nathan would go with his dad on weekends, but he also played sport so he was given an allowance. By the time Anika came along, money was not an issue so she received an allowance without any exchange of chores or helping out. It was this reality that was also triggering Christopher, Priya and Nathan's default settings and emotional reactions to Anika receiving money from her parents for her restaurant. In the siblings' eyes – especially the two older children – this was just typical. They had to work for everything and Anika and to a lesser extent Nathan just got given stuff.

At the point we meet the Jacksons, everyone in the business is experiencing a huge amount of uncertainty. John knows he has to make some decisions but there is no heir apparent. He's also reluctant to step back because he is uncertain about whether any of his children have the ability to take the business to the next level. Ayesha is also uncertain about whether she will ever get John to step back so they can enjoy the wealth they have created together and pass the mantel on to their children. What's the point in creating wealth if everyone is too strung out to enjoy any of it?! The children are, of course, no longer children. All in their late 20s and 30s, they are as uncertain now about what their dad plans to do with the business as they ever were. Their lack of certainty and corresponding lack of information activates their innate pessimism and they all, to one extent or another, imagine the worst probable outcome.

Christopher has done an architecture degree which he enjoyed, and while he works in the business he also works with other firms on other projects. He doesn't know if he wants to work with John full time or even if that is an option, as Nathan has positioned himself as John's 2IC. And there is no way Christopher is working for Nathan! Priya did an engineering degree, although she sometimes wonders why she bothered. John still doesn't really ask for her input – but she does have a project management and business development role in the business. Like her elder brother she is pretty sure her role would be more significant if she was more like John and Nathan – or even just male. Nathan went straight into the business from school, starting as a labourer and moving around the business from there. As such, his levels of specialised competence are lower than both Christopher and Priya and he has a big fat chip on his shoulder to prove it. He's not 'qualified' but neither was John so he still feels he's best placed to take over – but he has no idea whether that will actually happen. This is a worry for him because his lack of qualifications means his other options are more limited than either Christopher or Priya. And finally, Anika trained at a French culinary school and has opened her own restaurant with the help of a loan from her parents. It's a very uncertain industry and she's missed a few repayments to her parents, and is worried that if her siblings find out it will cause problems in the connectedness of the family. They have all grown up inside the bubble of the business and benefited from the wealth that business has created, but the uncertainty around whether they should be, could be or want to be in the business has robbed them of genuine autonomy and consequently direction, drive and happiness. They are uncertain and the options are complex. They are confused about the wealth, which further amplifies the pessimism. They know there is money but do they have access to it? Are they entitled to it? What are the rules? What are the expectations? For the most part, they have no idea. And that uncertainty in the G2s is creating tension in their own families. It is leading to arguments with their own partners and their siblings which further strains the connectedness and diminishes happiness.

Intended and Unintended Consequences

When I've worked with well-functioning family businesses with happy and healthy G2s, there is at least one G1 who has seriously and authentically imposed on G2 the responsibility to chart their own course (autonomy). They have ensured that each of their children has a voice and has been able to express that voice in the family. This is often facilitated by some sort of personal plan. As much as possible G1 has also removed some of the uncertainty by either spelling out that there will be a role in the family business for them should they want it and do the necessary work to earn it (competence), or made it crystal clear that no such opportunity will ever exist. The worst-case scenario is when there is lack of governance and lack of clarity and the children of wealthy families are left wondering what their role is, where they fit, if they have to fit or want to fit – all while knowing that there is probably a financial safety net which, while comforting, can be debilitating and demotivating because it diminishes both autonomy and the journey towards competence. The fact that this safety net is almost never explained or made clear simply serves to further amplify the uncertainty which, in turn, impacts the connectedness of the siblings and family members, eroding happiness still further.

Without conscious intervention to prevent it, two things commonly happen to children of wealth. They end up being spoilt, which fosters a sense of entitlement. Often the 'spoiling' of these children is a method applied by the founder/parent to avoid or delay the challenge of guiding G2 towards a meaningful relationship with the business and the wealth. As a result, they never find a passion or a profession so they don't access the first prong of happiness – the experience of work. They may end up experimenting with lots of different work activities, never really putting their shoulder to the wheel on any of them. Consequently, they don't experience autonomy or a sense of growing competence and instead rely on their allowance or mum and dad to fund their lifestyle. They are never taken seriously so they don't take themselves seriously. This is a recipe for disaster not just for the business but the individuals involved, their sense of worth and ultimately their wellbeing and happiness.

The other common outcome is that children of wealthy parents end up feeling guilty or resentful about the wealth, which is equally destructive. Where the children of wealthy families think they are just lucky to be born into that family, they often don't feel connected to the underlying causes of that wealth. This is why giving the family community a voice is so crucial, because it demystifies how the wealth was created. And this is equally relevant for spouses or partners of G2 and all the generations that follow – they were not there. They don't know how the wealth was created. Without that understanding and connection to the journey, the wealth can be misunderstood as simply luck. Luck is winning the lotto. Luck is when something happens that we have no control over. We certainly don't have any control over the family we are born into (or even marry into) so this thinking is logical. But it's also potentially destructive.

Instead, I have found it useful to encourage G2s and beyond to consider themselves *fortunate* instead of *lucky*. Fortune is when good things happen as a result of circumstances where we applied influence. Children of wealthy parents are fortunate, and they certainly shouldn't or can't take any credit for that fortune – but they still have responsibilities towards themselves, their parents and that wealth.

One of the most important distinctions any parent can teach their child is the difference between need and want. This is an especially critical lesson in wealthy families.

I remember when I was about seven years old saying to my father that I needed a Batman utility belt. Throughout my childhood my dad maintained that if I could prove to him that I needed something then, being my parent, he was *obligated* to get it for me. If I simply *wanted* it, and was honest about that, he might only be *inclined* to get it for me. I didn't get the belt. My lesson was simple. Need and want are two very different things and at seven years old I should have known the difference! This difference is frequently mixed up in all families but especially wealthy families, because 'No, sorry, we can't afford it' is not a valid excuse.

Learnings from the Field: G2 at Sea

The youngest son of a wealthy G1 was not able to connect with the family wealth at all. He did everything himself and refused to leverage it in any way. He was also dyslexic so left school as soon as he could and took on massive challenges, teaching himself various skills in tough conditions, including learning how to sail and captain yachts. At 32 he hadn't really found his place. While competent, his competencies lay outside the business arena and wouldn't necessarily allow him to make a comfortable living. He wouldn't take advantage of his family wealth because he didn't feel it was right to, just because he'd been 'luckier' than most to be born into wealth. In truth, he was fortunate not lucky and it would be a misfortune if he didn't apply his parents' good fortune.

He respected his parents' wealth and that was important. He, like his siblings, had the view that the wealth wasn't his – but the fact that it wasn't his didn't mean he wasn't responsible for it. Each child had two choices: the moment the parents died, they could give it all away to a charity of their choice. Or, they could recognise their good fortune and make sure they did good things with it, ensuring that the wealth would grow for future generations to also have the opportunity to do good things with it. And in doing those good things they would be entitled to live a lifestyle that afforded them what they *needed*. Not everything they *wanted* – everything that they *needed*.

Uncertain = Unhappy

It's very hard to be happy if there are important things in or around our lives that are shrouded in mystery, about which we feel uncertainty. It may appear counterintuitive, especially to those without wealth, but appreciating the role of uncertainty can help us understand why wealth *can* and often *does* create unhappiness.

Wealth brings with it a whole new level of uncertainty about whether it will be looked after, who will get it, when everyone will get it, how much will they get, what the responsibilities and obligations to the wealth are – the uncertainty is endless. And, of course, this uncertainty is fertiliser for the default settings we explored earlier.

The minute a family accumulates significant wealth, a new level of uncertainty is created. I've worked with a number of G2s who are unable to commit to a career path or develop the autonomy and competence so essential for happiness because of that uncertainty. They believe that sooner or later whatever path they chose will be disrupted or compromised by the need to manage wealth or the expectation that they manage wealth. In other words, they may want to work outside the family business and become a lawyer but they know that even if they invest their time in that pursuit and are 'allowed' to become a lawyer there will come a time where they will be tapped on the shoulder and expected to return to the family business in whatever way necessary. This wouldn't be so destructive if they were able to be a lawyer in the business – but this is not always the case. Conversely, I've met a lot of

G2s who are not prepared to commit to a career path because their true desire is to be responsible for managing the wealth, but there is no clear pathway to that outcome or certainty that a role even exists for them. G2s are often stuck in a limbo situation where they know there are some expectations and obligations on them but are not clear about what those expectations and obligations are, or whether they even want them.

It's interesting to note that other words for certainty in family include *discipline* and *rules* (governance). There is a clear correlation between a happy kid and a kid who must abide by certain rules and who is certain of their limitations. Ironically, less well-off families tend to be better at tough love than their wealthier counterparts. They have to be: the children must pull their weight in the home for it to function. They are forced to learn the meaning of the word 'no' because money constraints demand it. To their detriment, wealthy families don't have the same constraints and consequently have fewer rules which, in turn, amplifies the uncertainty and helps to breed unhappiness.

I vividly remember being with the parent founders of a successful family business when they were reflecting on the fact that every single one of the holidays they had taken with their children for as long as they could remember had been a five-star overseas trip. They shared with me that when discussing the next family vacation one of the children said, 'Can't we just stay at home?' This revelation led to the couple asking themselves, for the first time, 'Are we doing the wrong thing by our children?'

Regardless of wealth, children's health and wellbeing is a function of governance and stewardship. And governance and stewardship may be *informed* by parenting, but it is *not* parenting:

- *Parenting* is about values and behaviours imposed.
- *Governance* is values and behaviours defined.
- *Stewardship* is values and behaviours demonstrated.

A detailed look at the latter two is ahead of us. The first, parenting, is best left to clinical psychologists and child health experts. I am not either.

On Complexity

Today we live in an incredibly complex and uncertain world. In business there is even a term for it – VUCA: volatile, uncertain, complex and ambiguous. This is the new normal. And it is having a profound impact on our emotional and mental health as well as our ability to achieve what we all say we want – happiness.

When it comes to complexity, we are also confused about its presence and impact. We assume that the relationship between complexity and wealth can be illustrated by figure 9.3.

Figure 9.3: The Assumed Relationship between Complexity and Wealth

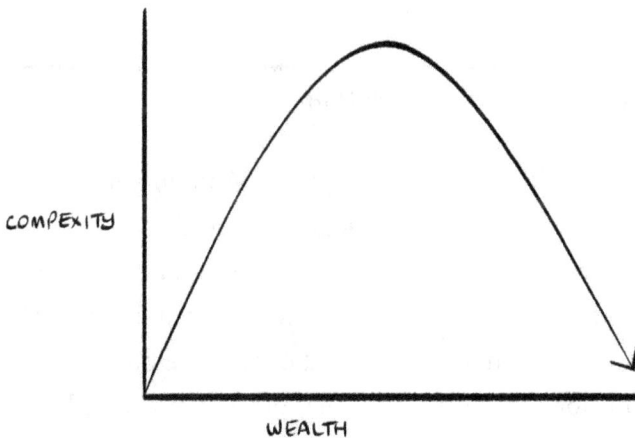

Sure, there is very little to no complexity when we have no money. Those who are struggling to survive are just struggling to survive. That is their sole focus. But once wealth grows so does complexity.

What do we do with it? How should it be invested? Where do we save it? Who has access to it? But we assume that past a certain point that complexity tails off again. Because serious wealth makes life so much easier – right?

Wrong.

The real relationship between complexity and wealth is illustrated by figure 9.4.

Figure 9.4: The Real Relationship between
Complexity and Wealth

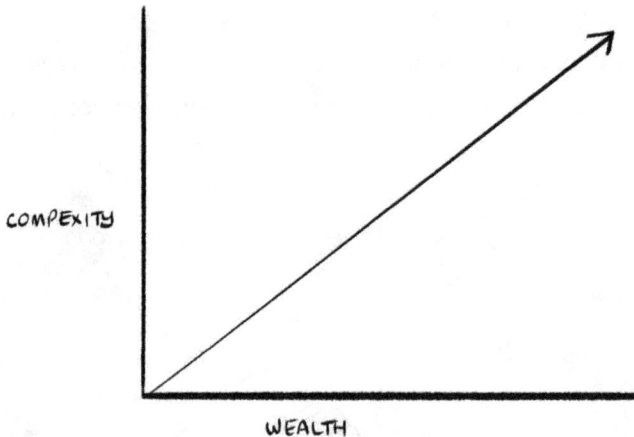

COMPEXITY

WEALTH

The more wealth, the more complexity. And unless wealthy families take constructive and conscious action to wrestle that complexity into some agreed rules and order the outcome is assured – shirt sleeves to shirt sleeves in three generations. It is inevitable and, frankly, deserved.

There are now so many things that complicate our lives, and yet we are not built for complexity. Our neurology is not wired for the level of complexity that we are currently experiencing. Remember our brain is pretty much the same as the brain of our hunter-gatherer ancestors and yet our experience of life is vastly different.

We live in a world of almost infinite choice and endless distractions. We find it impossible to think about more than one or two things at once and yet our lives demand we consider multiple things at the same time, constantly. This is what's difficult.

There is a huge difference between a decision, a judgement and a conclusion and yet we use them interchangeably without really thinking about the consequences:

- A *decision* is a course of action we've settled on when we don't consider all the relevant facts.
- A *judgement* is a course of action we've made when we don't have all the facts but we have all the facts that we are likely to get.
- A *conclusion* is a course of action we've chosen when we have all the relevant facts.

Because of the complexity in our lives, most of us are making decision after decision after decision with the occasional judgement. Very rarely do we draw conclusions. Why? Because conclusions take time, and we don't have the luxury of time in our complex world. We have stuff to do. As I said in the introduction, we have to make more decisions by breakfast than our ancestors made in a month! Add to that the fact that many of our decisions are not even decisions but triggered default settings and the complexity of the situation starts to become clear.

Complexity is deserving of a 'deep dive' to fully appreciate how it contributes to unhappiness for wealthy families. But the role of complexity is not just central to our ability to find happiness; these twin enemies also impact success in the family business. As such it's worth zooming into the three elements of family business to unpack just how complex they really are. Recognising this fact and coming to terms with it can have a profound impact on our willingness to take appropriate steps to navigate and mitigate the potentially toxic influence of complexity.

Let's now turn our attention to complexity. We'll explore family, business and wealth, and their impact on complexity.

CHAPTER 10

Family Is Complex

Family is challenging.

We may never see that on a Hallmark card but we all know it's true. Family, to borrow Kurt Vonnegut's reference to history, presents us with 'nothing more than a list of surprises [and] prepares [us] for nothing more than to be surprised yet again.'[50] I would go further and say that family relationships are the only relationships we have that can withstand these surprises without eventually breaking down.

Family is the constant audience in front of which we experience the ups and downs of our lives. Those experiences often complicate our family relationships. If we are lucky, family is also one of the most rewarding parts of life, offering us lifelong connectedness to people we care about. Our family circle represents our first 'tribe': our place of comfort and safety against the outside world. It is the place where we are loved no matter what – at least that's the theory. Our family members often know us better than we know ourselves, but there is a downside to that familiarity that can be infuriating.

Family is intimately and personally involved in the conditioning process that creates the default settings and reflex responses that define our thoughts as adults. Remember, most of our conditioning occurs before we are six years old. Who do we spend most of our time with before the age of six? Family – almost exclusively. Their influence on us is therefore profound.

Family is the universal safe haven for dysfunction.
– Steve Vamos

We already know that we are not in charge of our thoughts. Our thoughts are unconsciously bubbling up from long-forgotten events and associations that we created when our brain was developing and seeking to pick up as much information as possible about the world. But because the frontal lobe of the neocortex wasn't fully formed, we were not consciously assessing that information for relevance or accuracy. As a result, we are carrying around a ton of really useless information, much of which is just plain wrong – and yet we are using it, albeit unconsciously, to direct our decision-making and adult behaviour. This creates complexity. It can't *not* create complexity. It also facilitates uncertainty, because we don't ever really know where those thoughts came from or whether we should be actively thinking about them or not.

By the time we reach adulthood we have thousands of default settings that were facilitated by an overactive but fully functional amygdala. And the only part of the brain that could have made these defaults more accurate wasn't even functional yet, leaving us with default settings and reflex responses that play out on a near-daily basis. This is, of course, especially true in a family business setting because family members are often one of the markers or triggers for the default being unleashed in the first place. Family members direct our thoughts, our emotional responses to situations, our actions and our behaviour without our conscious awareness, which again adds to the complexity in a family business setting. Remember: thoughts fire emotions. They are two sides of the same coin. One never arises without the other.

Our over-reliance on emotion and our inability to accurately determine one emotion from another similar one or allow it to usefully inform our actions also exacerbates complexity. Family is a hotbed of emotion. Even in a typical family that is not connected by a business enterprise we feel the whole range of emotions from joy, love and compassion through to indifference, resentment, frustration and rage. Family is the place our emotions leak out the most. The familiarity we feel towards each other often means we say things to each other and react emotionally to each other in ways that we would never dream of in a different setting. Nathan would be far less likely to tell a non-family member that they shouldn't get their knickers in a knot, for example. We reserve such disdain for family, or in some cases close friends. Again, this adds to the complexity of these relationships. Many families have their own language, too (as we discussed in chapter 6), which can confuse things yet further, and we are certainly not able to be subjective and objective at the same time. In fact, everyone in business including family members will seek to find data or information that supports their pre-existing conclusions, and seek to present that to the rest of the group as objective fact. It's not. It's cherry-picking data so that they can present their entirely subjective opinion as objective fact.

Family Dynamics

Family dynamics have everything to do with individual family members and their respective personalities. Every family will have factions and cliques. Some siblings will like each other more than others. Just because a group of people is a family doesn't mean that everyone will like everyone else to the same degree. They may all love each other but chances are there will be alliances and friendships within the family group. That's just the nature of family.

The dynamics, however, also generate additional complexity. Things like the age gap between the children, gender difference, birth order, cultural differences in the parents, number of children, the presence of twins, second families and blended families all play a role. The presence of an 'outlier' in the family – for example, a gifted parent/sibling, whether academic, musical or athletic – can also add to the complexity.[51]

In my experience there are two easily observed tendencies amongst families. Those born first live their lives making decisions for themselves and their peers. And those born second must negotiate from the day they arrive. Do you know of a firstborn who is considered driven, and a second born who is considered a 'people person'? It is remarkably common.

As siblings arrive in the family, they tend to occupy the space left vacant by those before them. In other words, if the role of 'the serious one' is taken, the next child will find another role such as 'the black sheep' or 'the joker'. This is why families are so different, and you might hear comments such as, 'It's hard to imagine they are brother and sister, isn't it?' Of course, each child is just forging their own role or place in the family and must chose a role that isn't already taken by another sibling – or live in permanent, often aggressive, competition with their sibling(s).

Functional differences in the family dynamic also lead to additional complexity. Families come in myriad states and forms, including favourites and personal bias. These challenging dynamics don't even take into consideration each person's skills, knowledge or experience, or their personality or competencies. Each parent also brings their own family dynamics to the new family, along with their experiences and expectations of how the new family will be. One parent might be from a large family and the other an only child. One might like their family and the other be estranged. It is these family interactions that shape who we become as adults – not least because the bulk of the conditioning that created the default settings was created in the presence of or because of something that occurred in the family. Those individuals in our family, even when we love them and get on with them, become data points or markers that may trigger a default setting. This is why family events are often so fraught. Everyone in the room is triggering some form of default setting and pushing everyone's buttons. This provokes an emotional response instead of engaging the frontal lobes. Invariably any outbursts confirm that person's stereotypical role to the rest of the family: 'Geez, there she goes – my sister being her usual bossy self'; 'Oh my god, I can't believe my brother is bringing up the motorbike incident *again*'; 'Oh look, what a surprise, Mum's on to her second bottle of wine'; 'Where's Dad? Oh, that's about right, he's nicked off to walk the dog' (to avoid escalating tensions).

Let's go back to the Jacksons to illustrate this complexity. We've already established that the current family dynamic is causing confusion. No one really knows what to expect or what's expected of them and there are clearly favourites.

But imagine if Priya was the oldest child and John didn't have rigid gender stereotypes. How different would the business be? Even if Priya was the same person but born first it would change the dynamic. Imagine if John and Ayesha split up and John went on to marry again and have two more children. How would that add to the complexity of the business moving forward? What if he married someone who had children from a previous relationship who also wanted to be involved in the business? Would that create additional complexity? The iterations and possibilities are endless, but one thing that stays constant is the escalating complexity.

Universal Family Issues

Regardless of how the family is made up, whether the parents are separated or still married, how many children there are, and the genders, aspirations or age gaps, there appears to be universal family dramas that play out in a family business. In his book, *Stewardship in Your Family Enterprise*, author Dennis Jaffe shares what these universal dramas are.[52]

There is always conflict between the often larger-than-life founder and their children. This is true regardless of founder gender. The founder may say they want succession and may encourage their children's involvement in the business but the route towards that outcome is rarely smooth. As the founder gets older and the children become more confident in their own abilities and opinions, conflict is almost inevitable. Often vanity and ego mean the founder becomes reluctant to step aside. They end up undermining their children and plotting against them in an effort to hold on to power. They are often not even conscious of doing it.

Conversely the children might start plotting against the founder. This is especially common between sons and fathers. Freud explains this via the Oedipus myth. It can also be seen in various royal houses around the world where family members plot the king's demise. It can even be seen in old novels like the Bible with Cain and Abel or the story of Joseph and his brothers.

OFTEN VANITY AND EGO MEAN THE FOUNDER BECOMES RELUCTANT TO STEP ASIDE. THEY END UP UNDERMINING THEIR CHILDREN AND PLOTTING AGAINST THEM IN AN EFFORT TO HOLD ON TO POWER. THEY ARE OFTEN NOT EVEN CONSCIOUS OF DOING IT.

As Jaffe points out, 'Family business offers a grand stage for this mythic behaviour.' The larger-than-life founder builds the business through blood, sweat and tears. They experience the trappings of success professionally and personally and are in absolute control of that empire – and they like it that way. It is their baby. It is in their blood;

the business is running through their veins. Of course, they want their children to take over the legacy and move the business forward. They want their children to be successful – just not so successful that they end up making a better job of the business than the founder did. This sounds petty and a tad immature, but actually it's just human nature – and while few will admit this, even to themselves, it creates additional complexity. The founder may continually see problems in the child-successor, and use those problems, whether real or imagined, to delay transition. Henry Ford famously thwarted his son Edsel's efforts to take over the business, despite Edsel's competence. The misery this caused is thought to have contributed to Edsel's early death.

The children may know that they will inherit at some point but they are forced to wait in the wings, promised various enticements to keep them 'in play'. However, these enticements rarely materialise, which, in turn, fosters resentment and negatively impacts connectedness and relatedness. The children stay, but don't have any real power or authority and they know it (they have zero autonomy or ways of demonstrating the competence so essential for happiness). Plenty is talked about in terms of succession, but it never happens. Instead, the founder drags their heels until the day they drop dead and all hell breaks loose.

PLENTY IS TALKED ABOUT IN TERMS OF SUCCESSION, BUT IT NEVER HAPPENS. INSTEAD, THE FOUNDER DRAGS THEIR HEELS UNTIL THE DAY THEY DROP DEAD AND ALL HELL BREAKS LOOSE.

Business is all about making good decisions at the right time, but that is often very hard to do in a family business because of the emotion, default settings and legacy that exists amongst the group. They are family but they are also running a business and the two are not natural or easy bedfellows. This emotional complexity can't be ignored forever.

Learnings from the Field: Business as Cover

Imagine a scenario where G1 has supposedly passed a business on to G2, in this case the eldest son. But he's never really stepped back. G1 constantly talks about how it is G2's time, G2 is overdue. He talks about how the boys are empowered (his second son runs a different territory). He waxes lyrical about how he is looking forward to playing more golf. He probably means all of it, and yet he doesn't and won't step away.

No one can understand it, but the business gives him cover to do what he wants. Successful entrepreneurs usually have pretty healthy egos. The positive expression of that is the success of their business and the kudos that brings. They learn to love the lifestyle and the freedom. The negative expression of that success can be a sense of entitlement and untouchability that encourages them to do whatever they want, which might include excessive drinking, gambling or infidelity. This G1 in this case is effectively using the business to cover his negative expression. It's very easy to get away with a lot of extracurricular activity when the business provides the perfect cover. His desire to maintain that cover and maintain his lifestyle with its corresponding 'walking around money' is enough for him to subconsciously suppress G2 for a decade. Not only does that prove disastrous for G1, who suffers a major health event and is forced to step down anyway, but he does irreparable damage to the business and his family.

The irony is that when all is said and done both the founder and the children usually want the same thing. The founder wants a safe pair of hands into which they can place their business, knowing that it will prosper into the future. Most founders want to create a legacy and they don't want their business to be back to shirt sleeves in three generations. As for the children, for those who want to be part of that legacy they want a real place in the business, not a charity position. They want to use their abilities and talents to grow that legacy on their own terms and not be constantly compared to the founder or live in their shadow. Most children of successful founders are not looking for special treatment and are happy to learn on the job and progress on merit so that they can develop genuine competence and feel secure in their own abilities – ultimately finding their own identity within that family business. For those who choose not to be in the family business, they don't want to be made to feel guilty about it or that they have somehow turned their back on the family or walked away from their opportunity to enjoy the shared assets or inherit any of the wealth. Their choice is not rejecting the family, and the family can easily remain intact if these dichotomies are spelt out and proper financial provision is built into the governance framework.

There are many different family voices, often saying very different things with very different aspirations and intentions. This is why it's so imperative to step back from the hustle and bustle of the business to elicit all those family voices, not just the founder's, so they are all heard and acknowledged equally. This is made possible by instigating individual personal plans for the founder and each member of the family. But the voice of the family as a separate entity or unit is also imperative.

It is the Family Charter that expresses the shared voice of the family, whether the members are working in the business or not. By bringing individual voices together the charter is the mutually agreed expression of the vision, values and rules of engagement within the family, and between the family and the wealth. It answers all the questions around the business, opportunities and access to shared assets. The Family Retreat, designed to give the family community a voice, also cements that connection between all family members, born in or married in, across all generations. Everyone still feels involved and heard.

The Four Voices

Managing love, loyalty and family wealth successfully generation after generation comes down to your willingness and determination to allow four distinct voices to be heard:

1. The business (or balance sheet) must have a voice (achieved by the strategic plan).
2. The individuals (founder and family members) must have individual voices (achieved by the personal plans).
3. The family must have a collective voice (achieved by the Family Charter).
4. The family community (spouses and generations that follow) must have a voice (achieved by the Family Retreat).

One of the biggest mistakes I see in family business is the confusion around wealth and who is entitled to it. Too often G2 assume that they must work in the business to benefit from the wealth it generates. This is not accurate. All the children are equally entitled to inherit wealth from the parents, should that be G1's wish. Those who also want to work in the business should be paid a going-rate salary for their position, which is separate from the inheritance of wealth. Again, this is why the four voices are so powerful. When the business has a voice, what position is open to a family member becomes clear based on the needs of the business and the skills of the family member in question. The remuneration is also clear because, assuming the family member is suited to the role, the salary is the same as the salary the business would need to pay to secure a suitably qualified non-family member.

ALL THE CHILDREN ARE EQUALLY ENTITLED TO INHERIT WEALTH, SHOULD THAT BE G1'S WISH. THOSE WHO ALSO WANT TO WORK IN THE BUSINESS SHOULD ALSO BE PAID A GOING-RATE SALARY FOR THEIR POSITION.

Learnings from the Field: Work or Nothing

Imagine there is a business that has been passed equally to three sons (G1); they, in turn, are wrestling with the succession to G2. Initially the oldest G1's sons are involved in the business but various health challenges make this extremely hard and they step back. During a heart-wrenching meeting between the oldest G1 and one of his G2 sons, G2 says that he is fully aware that his dad wants him in the business, and he has taken on various roles but he simply can't be the person his dad wants him to be, largely due to his ongoing health challenges. According to his dad, however, this isn't the reason – it is because G2 hasn't received the right training or support, and this can be 'fixed'. (Imagine if your dad thought you could be 'fixed'!) G2 doesn't want it to be 'fixed' – at least not in the way his dad wants.

During a conversation I have with the two, it becomes apparent that G2 thinks that ownership and employment are the same thing – in other words, if he doesn't work in the business, he has no ownership rights to the business. He is confusing shareholding with employment – an extremely common mistake in family business. It's a bizarre conundrum that this distinction is obvious in business but not family business. It is perfectly possible to own shares in a company and receive a dividend but not work in that company; or to work in a company and get paid a salary but not own the company. And yet commonly those inside a family business believe that they must work in the business to own the business or benefit from the wealth it creates. Not only does this common misconception risk the wrong people being in senior roles, but it also puts an unnecessary burden on G2 and beyond to try to shoehorn themselves into roles they are simply not suited to, that don't use their talents and don't make them happy – as is the case with this G2.

The relief in the room when this G2 understands this distinction is palpable. The poor bloke had felt that if he didn't work for the company in some role or another his own young family would miss out on whatever benefit or wealth the business created. Clearly, this is not the case and should never be the case.

Going back to the Jacksons, there was a festering issue with Anika and her desire to open her own restaurant. She has never expressed a real interest in the business – not because she doesn't care about it, but because her interests lie elsewhere. There are also three siblings ahead of her all jockeying for position in the family business. But Anika has never really been sure what that means for her. She certainly doesn't want to ask. How do you ask your family if you are going to get any of the wealth that has accumulated without sounding grasping and entitled? It has never been clear what she and her fellow siblings have to do or are expected to do in regards to the business, and it certainly isn't clear if there is a route where they can follow their individual aspirations. It has never been clear that should those personal aspirations and strengths align with skills the business needs then there would be a route into the business so they could deploy those skills in the family business. Of course, there also hasn't been any discussion about what that means in terms of how the business will be passed to the next generation.

In place of clarity and governance, anxiety and assumption fill the void.

As a result, Anika thinks that her working elsewhere precludes her from inheriting anything while the other three wrestle for position, often working against each other to reposition themselves in their parents' minds as the worthy successor. None of them are paid market value for their contribution, based on the faulty logic that they are family so should sacrifice themselves.

As a result, they always have nagging doubts as to whether they are in their roles because they are family, rather than because they are qualified or suited. And that suspicion rubs off on non-family employees who often, in turn, assume nepotism instead of ability. It is a veritable landmine waiting to explode.

But it gets worse.

Did I mention that Anika is married? Her husband, Tom, is from what would be described as a 'typical' family. He is always encouraging Anika to speak up for herself because, surely, she's just as entitled as the other three to share in the wealth. Christopher and Nathan are also married. Christopher's wife, Rya, is also from a 'typical' family with no wealth; but she doesn't want anything to do with the wealth. She thinks it has corrupted them all and doesn't want her children anywhere near any of what she sees as 'spoilt entitled bullshit'. Nathan's wife, Georgia, is the daughter of a family friend and her father is actually even richer than the Jacksons. Her input is relentless – she suggests what Nathan should and shouldn't do to curry favour with his dad. Priya is engaged to Delvyn and he's not really that fussed. He's got a good business of his own. He worries about Priya a little because her uncertainty about what her role is gets her down. He knows she feels unappreciated and diminished in the family business and is encouraging her to step out on her own. Besides, she's really much more interested in design than building.

Thankfully for everyone, Anika is a smart woman and decided that an open and honest conversation with her parents was necessary, and they agreed on a loan to help her start the restaurant. But if she had not taken the initiative, or she had entered that meeting with her husband's words ringing in her ear, the outcome could have been very different.

Without guidance the complexity of family will almost always prove too great and the curse will materialise.

Introducing the Family Business Theorem

When I first came up with my family business theorem, I had been playing around with the relationships between family, business and wealth. I was sure there was a way to unite them and wondered if it might be possible to express it as an equation or theorem. A theorem is a non-self-evident statement that has been proven to be true.

A great thinker once said to me, 'Anything truly meaningful in the pursuit of knowledge can and should be expressed as an equation.' There is an elegance in equations or theorems that unites logician Kurt Gödel, artist MC Escher and composer Johann Sebastian Bach.[53] I am no peer of theirs; nor am I a peer of the great thinker and proponent of equations (my father). But the family business theorem allows us to understand the intricate impossibility that is the enduring, connected family business.

If n = complexity, family is the foundation complexity.

$$n = F$$

n = COMPLEXITY
F = FAMILY

The theorem will take shape over the following chapters.

CHAPTER 11

Business Is Complex

Considering the challenges of family, it's a relief to know that business is at least straightforward. Right? If only that were true! Of course, business is not straightforward. It is the antithesis of straightforward.

Human beings are designed to survive. We are not designed for business. Not only that, but the level of complexity inherent in business makes happiness in this context challenging at best. We may experience pockets of specific happiness in a business context – when we land a large order or the figures show an increase in market share or profit – but general happiness is much more elusive.

We assume that every human being comes to work as a functioning adult. But we already know that while we may look like adults on the outside, the presence of certain people or markers – whether emotional, environmental or situational – causes us to stop thinking, triggering long-forgotten default settings, reflex responses and habitual behaviour. We may look like an adult but we act like a small child.[54] Tantrums in the boardroom and 'toys out of the pram' episodes in meetings serve as an example. If there was ever an environment that required genuine consideration and rational thought it's business – and yet we march off to work in the morning convinced that we are making decisions and ploughing through 'to-do lists', attending meetings and getting stuff done based on intelligent thought, assessment and constructive adult intervention. We are not. At least not at often as we would like to believe.

From time to time, we are all prone to the sort of 'Uncle Marvin Moments' we talked about in chapter 2 – moments where we react to something in the present even though the reaction was triggered from the past, and we don't even realise it. For example, say a perfectly suitable new recruit is not offered the job. We may explain our reaction or default setting as 'gut instinct', 'intuition' or 'business experience' but the reality is, the new recruit reminded us of Uncle Marvin. We don't like Uncle Marvin so we immediately don't like the new recruit! A presentation that didn't go according to plan is blamed on a wardrobe choice, when the real source of the failure was a 'matches incident' when we were a child!

This can all seem ridiculous, but only if we hold on to the illusion that we are in charge of our thoughts and that just because we see an adult in the mirror that adult is calling the shots. In many situations in life, especially business where there are so many other people, our behaviour, decisions and actions can jump from one default setting to the next. We could, on a particularly bad day, fail to engage our frontal lobes even once.

We already know that our central nervous system is only capable of processing a tiny fraction of what it could be aware of via the five senses. Not only are we not aware of a vast amount of information that could be pertinent to business and help us make better choices, but because of conditioning and our early programming, any one of the 11 million bits of data could trigger a reflex response. A response that, in turn, alters our behaviour or decision-making without us even knowing about it. We retrospectively justify the decision or behaviour with information to hand and move on.

Unless we realise that we are susceptible to this illusion and take steps to call it out and bring genuine rigour to business practice, behaviour and decisions, it becomes virtually impossible to distinguish between real external data and potentially erroneous data. This erroneous data comes courtesy of our default settings and outdated reflex responses.

Business is not the open plains of the savannah. It holds its own dangers, but for the most part we are able to get through each day without facing mortal danger. As a result, our amygdala is almost certainly overreacting in this environment and alerting us to dangers that simply do not exist, which ironically leaves us even more exposed to the dangers that do exist!

BUSINESS IS NOT THE OPEN PLAINS OF THE SAVANNAH.
IT HOLDS ITS OWN DANGERS, BUT FOR THE MOST PART
WE ARE ABLE TO GET THROUGH EACH DAY WITHOUT
FACING MORTAL DANGER. AS A RESULT, OUR AMYGDALA IS
ALMOST CERTAINLY OVERREACTING IN THIS ENVIRONMENT
AND ALERTING US TO DANGERS THAT SIMPLY DO NOT
EXIST, WHICH IRONICALLY LEAVES US EVEN MORE EXPOSED
TO THE DANGERS THAT DO EXIST!

As I mentioned in chapter 2, precision decision-making is the domain of the frontal lobes of the neocortex, but the poor old frontal lobes don't stand a chance against the lightening-quick amygdala. The connections made when the frontal lobes weren't even fully developed or engaged are now alerting us to danger around every boardroom door and in every staff meeting. If this is unhelpful in life it's especially challenging in business because there are so many moving parts and so many people involved in the delivery of an outcome – each with their own default settings and reflex responses. Frankly it's a wonder anyone gets anything done in business!

There is an endless list of complex issues to deal with: staffing, marketing, business models, markets, publicity and image management, logistics, and customers and how to reach them. In the course of my work, I help businesses unpack, assess and where necessary rebuild their businesses for optimum efficiency and operational excellence. Invariably each workgroup has a set of core functions – there are anywhere between 270 and 330 tasks that make up these core functions. Curiously, where the workgroup is between 13 to 16 people – the size of the average workgroup – these numbers rarely vary regardless of the type of business. What also doesn't vary is the number of those tasks that a workgroup believes are done 'as well as could be expected' – it's always in the vicinity of 15 percent of the overall number of tasks. This means that 85 percent of tasks are *not* seen as being done as well as could be expected – something that surprises everyone. Thankfully, it is also true that people know how to fix the problems and obstacles preventing those tasks from being done well about 80 percent of the time.[55] (If you would like to explore the dataset on this, it's available at fourvoicesadvisory.com.)

The economic environment and political leadership will also play a role in business, whether the prevailing conditions for business are positive or negative. Laws and regulations add another layer and they are never static. The advance of technology is also changing business in every way from customer engagement to business models.

Back in 1981 when there was no internet, no personal computers, no satellite TV or digital technology and no smart anything – phones, TVs, tablets, nappies or sensors (yes, you really can buy smart nappies!), futurist Buckminster Fuller predicted the 'knowledge doubling curve'. He noticed that the more knowledge that was accumulated the faster more knowledge was created. At the very end of the 19th century human knowledge doubled every 100 years or so. By the end of World War II the complete knowledge of mankind doubled every 25 years. In 2013, IBM predicted knowledge would soon double every 12 hours. It seems this calculation has become too complex for any researcher to attempt defining the figure today.[56]

Whoever is right and whatever the precise rates are doesn't really matter – it's a staggering amount of knowledge and information. Granted, a lot of it is nonsense in the form of social media feeds and videos of cats playing the piano, but even that data holds value. Everything creates data in a constant 'datafication' that goes way beyond words, numbers and images. Everything is a potential data point that can be collected and analysed for commercial insight. Potentially, at least, this datafication is changing the nature of business underfoot at an unprecedented rate.

Sensors capable of collecting data that was simply impossible a few years ago are now fitted as standard to cars and aircraft engines. Rolls Royce has used sensor technology to transform its business model from aircraft engine manufacturer to service provider.[57] Instead of just selling engines to airlines, Rolls Royce monitors the performance of its 3,700 or so jet engines via thousands of built-in sensors. The information from the sensors increases efficiency and safety. In the pre-sensor days when a plane was hit by lightning it would have to be fully inspected on arrival before it was cleared for onward travel. This took time and would often cause delays and irritate passengers. Now, sensors monitor the engine constantly so the impact of a lightning strike can be assessed before the plane even lands. We are also seeing a flood of sensors into health care and beyond that are also changing business models.

Increased data storage and processing power means we can use that data much more effectively to predict behaviour. Enter the world of 'big data' and analytics. The premise behind big data is that everything we do, say, write, visit or buy is leaving a digital footprint or soon will be. And that data can then be analysed. We are entering a new world where hypothesis will give way to probability. US retailer Target got into hot water over big data algorithms when a father complained at the inappropriate discount coupons for baby products sent to his school-age daughter. Target apologised profusely, assuming a glitch in the algorithm, only the father discovered a few days later that his daughter was pregnant![58]

This explosion in technological capability is disrupting just about every industry and adding levels of complexity that were simply not part of the business mix when the business was started. In his seminal essay 'The Law of Accelerating Returns' US inventor and futurist Ray Kurzweil states, 'There's even exponential growth in the rate of exponential growth. Within a few decades, machine intelligence will surpass human intelligence, leading to The Singularity – technological change so rapid and profound it represents a rupture in the fabric of human history.'[59]

This technological advance and escalating complexity is upending established business models and pushing many industries towards zero marginal cost. In other words, the cost of producing each additional unit once the fixed costs are covered is nearly zero.

What happens to established businesses and well-worn business models when the goods and services they offer are free or nearly free? What is going on in the world when the home-sharing company Airbnb is valued at more than the Hilton Hotel Group and yet doesn't own a single property? The same could be said for Uber – a hugely profitable transport company that doesn't own a single vehicle. Production costs are becoming so low due to technological advances, reduction in labour costs and industry consolidation that there are no longer any barriers to entry into some markets.

We are already seeing this in green energy where the cost to install your own power supply has plummeted. 3D printing is changing the face of manufacturing. There are free or nearly free courses offered by prestigious universities.

Today, it is almost impossible to know what our industry will be like in five years' time, never mind 10 years or more. The digital disruption we have seen in the information industries is now moving into the real economy of physical things. Fast-moving consumer goods and retail are experiencing major disruption.

Take voice technology as an example. Voice is almost certainly going to be a game changer. For generations business has made a product and sought to differentiate that product from similar offerings through advertising. If they were successful, they were able to build a strong brand and reap the rewards of elevated margins. This approach worked for everything from cars to shampoo to computers.

Then voice arrived.

According to Scott Galloway, Professor of Marketing at NYU Stern School of Business, 'Voice is the Grim Reaper of brands.' The number of people who can name their favourite brand has declined between 20 and 40 percent. Everything is being turned back into a commodity again. Imagine you've just been to the bathroom, you use the last of the toilet paper, look in the cupboard and realise there is none left. You wouldn't add it to a list like your mother or grandmother would have; instead, you walk into the living room and say, 'Alexa buy toilet paper'.

You get your toilet paper a few days later but meanwhile Kleenex, Quilton and Sorbent are having a meltdown. You didn't say, 'Alexa buy Kleenex long roll complete clean 12 rolls', you said, 'Alexa buy toilet paper'. So, Amazon chooses what toilet paper to send you. This type of disruption, accelerated by Covid-19, is impacting all industries and escalating complexity.

And on top of that, we must operate efficiently in a commercial environment while managing political, economic, social, technical, legal and environmental (PESTLE) issues just to remain competitive and relevant. All of this is real. It is bringing significant disruption to every industry and yet it is only the neocortex that can understand it. Only the front of mind can plan for it and capitalise on it. The amygdala is useless. Remember, the amygdala is a threat alert system. These disruptions are threats – make no mistake. But they are also opportunities if we engage the front of mind and nullify the back.

Business is not just about registering a business name, hiring some staff and selling some stuff – there is a raft of complexity that comes with even the simplest businesses. There is regulatory complexity, supply chain complexity, financial management complexity, product testing and evidencing complexity and tax complexity to name just a few. And we must deal with all of it while managing productivity and seeking to get the best out of our people day in, day out.

Even the most forward thinking, technologically savvy founder in any industry today, with all their know-how and expertise, will not even recognise their business 20 years from now. To assume that the founder has all the answers for G2 and G3 is therefore stupidity of the highest order – simply because the change that is occurring across business in almost all sectors is so rapid and so far-reaching to render business as normal obsolete in one generation, never mind across multiple generations. G2 will need to know things that G1 never even knew. Expecting an out-of-touch school system and obsolete curriculum to plug the gaps is foolhardy at best.

Family business is in a unique position. Family is complex in its own right. Business is clearly increasingly complex in its own right. Put them together and they provide a multiplier effect.

If we look for a moment at John and Ayesha Jackson's construction business. The business itself would be challenging enough because of all the things that need to be considered and actioned. All the supplier relationships, and the relationship with the bank which can and does change with the prevailing economic conditions. Property ownership is also something that politics gets involved with; policy affects who can buy and invest in property in Australia. This can and does change depending on which political party is in office. This changes the demand in the market which diminishes profitability and alters the viability of development projects. The pipeline needs to be managed very closely to ensure that enough money is being made by the business, the projects are progressing on time and on budget, and the people employed by the business are doing their jobs to the highest standard. If something falls through the cracks additional pressure comes to bear. Deadlines and supplier issues can cause delays and budget blowouts. Lawyers get involved – complexity on steroids all by itself.

Now throw family into the mix and the scope for complexity increases 100-fold. Long-serving, loyal employees who have helped to build the business can very easily get their noses pushed out of joint if one of the children is introduced as the CEO's new sidekick. It doesn't matter that Christopher and Priya studied relevant degrees at university or that Nathan worked his way up the business. There will always be people who say they are only there because of their surname. Even if they do a great job, they will always be resented by some. G2s can rarely win in business. They are either unprepared, so employees resent it, or they are forced into the job, so they resent it. Even if they are prepared, want the job and do it brilliantly, some employees will *still* resent them.

As mentioned in the introduction, it's impossible to inherit a job or role. Apart from family business this fact is so obvious that it doesn't even need to be said. The adult child of the local dentist is not expected to fill the position and perform root canal surgery when their dad dies in a car accident or decides to retire early. The idea is preposterous and yet G1 almost always believes that their son or daughter should 'inherit' their position.

THERE WILL ALWAYS BE PEOPLE WHO SAY THEY ARE ONLY THERE BECAUSE OF THEIR SURNAME. EVEN IF THEY DO A GREAT JOB, THEY WILL ALWAYS BE RESENTED BY SOME. G2S CAN RARELY WIN IN BUSINESS. THEY ARE EITHER UNPREPARED, SO EMPLOYEES RESENT IT, OR THEY ARE FORCED INTO THE JOB, SO THEY RESENT IT. EVEN IF THEY ARE PREPARED, WANT THE JOB AND DO IT BRILLIANTLY, SOME EMPLOYEES WILL *STILL* RESENT THEM.

As for the children, they are still as confused as ever by the family and business complexity. What's expected of me? If I want to take over, will I be allowed to? Who is going to take the role? What, if any, will my role be? And worse, often these types of crucial discussions just don't happen. They will be ignored until something happens to John and they simply can't be ignored any longer. But, by then, the damage caused by the ongoing complexity will already have been done. Plus, without John at the helm to steady the succession ship it can be devastating to the business and the family. Imagine the additional complexity if John and Ayesha got divorced. What would happen if John needed to buy Ayesha out?

Families can be wonderful and make events, occasions and normal everyday life so much better, but put them inside a commercial enterprise and the challenges that emerge can cause havoc. Let's revisit the theorem.

The Family Business Theorem Continued

When thinking about the potential existence of a theorem, first, I considered the relationship between family and business, in terms of complexity. Was family a multiplier to the complexity of business or was it accretive? In other words, should family complexity simply be added to business complexity or was family complexity a multiplier of business complexity? It was immediately obvious that family was a multiplier of business complexity. At the time I was reminded of a family business that had a vacancy to be filled. If a vacancy is in a typical business with no family element, the person in charge of the department will simply outline exactly what skills they need, create a job description to explain exactly what the individual will be expected to do, advertise the position and hire the best candidate.

However, if the vacancy is in a business where multiple family members across multiple generations work in the business and the person in charge of the department discovers that one of them is interested in that job, a couple of things happen. First, the number of people consulted or involved in that appointment explodes. Everyone in the family, even those not in the business, will have an opinion about that possible appointment. Those closest to the prospective appointee may very well think that the family member should be given the role automatically and will often lobby hard on their behalf. The family member themselves will also often have a view as to whether or not they should automatically be given that role.

In addition, everybody employed in the company is going to be affected by the appointment of that family member because it will trigger their own survival fears, which will, in turn, trigger their own default settings. Remember, in the absence of information the mind defaults to the worst probable conclusion. So, unless the entire search process and the method for decision-making is broadly published and transparent, the rest of the employees will presume that the family member got the job because they're family, not because they're capable. And in some situations that may pose a direct threat to a non-family employee who may feel pushed out or marginalised.

Think of the complexity if you are joining a company and there's no family tie – you just happen to be the successful candidate. You have a two-dimensional challenge which is to demonstrate your professional capabilities and build meaningful relationships with your colleagues. Now, imagine the complexity if you also carry the founder's surname and receive the job ahead of other candidates. You are no longer dealing with colleagues who simply need to see your professionalism evidenced; you are probably dealing with colleagues who want their view on that decision evidenced. Often, they will actively want you to fail because your failure will prove them right – that you were only hired because you are family (ethnomethodology again!). It sounds mean-spirited but it's just human nature.

Family makes *every* situation more complex for everybody and more uncertain for some. This is obvious and yet it is dismissed with monotonous regularity in family business. Think of the uncertainty that your employees feel when they are in a job based on a certain level of capability. A vacancy comes up for a similar role and is filled by a less-than-qualified or capable family member. How does that make the existing employee feel about their perceived value or about their own job security?

There are other challenges. One idea that I find particularly entertaining is when successful G1s presume that the people that report to them and who have their interests at heart will automatically want to help their children enter the business and succeed in that environment. It may seem logical, and it may be a fair enough expectation or assumption, but it's almost universally wrong. Let's remember that first and foremost, we are Homo sapiens. Think about that reality and the corresponding real-world behaviour of the key employees. Now it's perfectly understandable that these individuals usually don't help the children. If you are a non-family employee and you've spent years building up a strong and constructive relationship with the founder, you are not going to smooth the path to succession for a family member. You know that the longer the son or daughter takes to get up to speed and ready for that role the longer you can extract value from the relationship that you've built. And all this occurs, almost exclusively, below awareness. People in this sort of situation are not bad people; they are not mean or vindictive – they are simply trying to survive and prolong that survival. The very best that most G1s can hope for is acceptance and no active sabotage.

In the course of my work, I can say that in 35 years I have seen only two non-family employees in the above position who have actively and positively taken that family member under their wing and done the very best they could to prepare that individual for success and later succession. I can literally count on one hand the number of times I've had a conversation with those trusted employees, and I have lost count of the times where the opposite is true. Most of the time employees will exaggerate G2's weaknesses and develop resentment that will fester over time and magnify those perceived weaknesses still further. G2 is rarely given a fair go, even if they deserve one.

Family is therefore definitely a multiplier of complexity.

$$n = F \times B$$

n = COMPLEXITY
F = FAMILY
B = BUSINESS

CHAPTER 12

Wealth Is Complex

By now, I'm sure it will come as a huge relief to you to arrive at a topic that is *less* complex – wealth. Sure, family is complex. So is business, but at least wealth is straightforward. Right?

Of course, whether you are reading this as a millionaire or an aspiring millionaire everyone knows money is complex. Groucho Marx once said, 'While money can't buy happiness, it certainly lets you choose your own form of misery.' Wealth may be the universal yardstick of success; it may be what we go into business to create; but once the business starts to generate significant wealth, that wealth invites additional complexity. It may solve some problems but it also creates even more new ones, many of which are anything but easy.

As discussed in chapter 8, in terms of the correlation between money and happiness, studies have shown that the magic number is US$75,000 or its equivalent. More than that simply adds complexity. Significant wealth brings significant complexity, not least around how that money should be managed, maximised and distributed.

Where should it be invested? Clearly, there needs to be a strategy, but who decides the strategy? What is the optimal investment mix for the portfolio? Are we investing in property, managed funds, index funds, bonds, gold? Are we investing in our own market or diversifying risk across geographies as well as investment type? Who should invest it? Do we trust them? What happens and who is responsible if those investments don't work? How do we know that the advice we are getting is good-quality advice? Prevailing economic conditions also impact return on wealth, interest rates and risk. No wonder those with a track record for managing it well are deified. (Think of Buffett and the many other 'Investment Brand Names'.)

But when that wealth is generated inside a family business the complexity goes through the roof because of a whole new set of issues. What are the rules for distribution? Is there a G2 who is best placed to manage the money? Does that person have the necessary qualifications and experience? How comfortable do the other members of the family feel about that? What is that person's risk profile in relation to the risk profile of the other members of the family whose wealth that person is managing? Each person has a natural disposition towards risk that can radically alter opinion – not only inside the business and what the business should be focused on, but also in terms of wealth management. In a wealthy family business, there are often pools of money being governed and yet even something as simple as risk profile creates an infinite number of possible portfolio allocation strategies. I have met many families where the root cause of many of their internal business and family issues was a difference in risk profile between the family members in the business. Unless recognised and addressed this difference can be extremely destructive.

Learnings from the Field: the Danger of Risk

I once joined a G1 founding couple of a successful family business for breakfast. Let's call them Harry and Hilary. The story they shared was not unique. There were three sons (G2) – let's call them Josh, Steven and Lance. The relationship between the first and second born (Josh and Steven) had completely broken down. It was toxic, aggressive and debilitating for everyone. Their individual and collective happiness and quality of life was being consumed by it. Not only did Josh and Steven refuse to work together but they could barely be in the same room together.

Part of the solution I proposed was an assessment of their individual business philosophies, which highlighted fundamentally different risk profiles between Josh and Steven. Josh had inherited Harry's cavalier entrepreneurial spirit, while Steven had inherited Harry's mature recognition of 'enough'. Harry is a rare entrepreneur: humble, kind and unlike many G1s I meet he is also fully aware that the wealth he has created is more than enough for any family. He isn't constantly searching for more and is a more rounded and contented person as a result. Steven is still entrepreneurial but he believes that some of the family wealth should be locked away as an unexposed stake and the business move forward from that basis.

In many ways it wasn't the difference in risk profile that caused the problem. It was the fact that these differences were handled in a totally default, birth-order way. Josh couldn't understand why Steven couldn't just embrace his genius, while Steven couldn't understand why a three-year age gap gave Josh the right to put the family wealth at risk (in his eyes) – so they fought like children over it. Knowing their respective risk profiles helped the brothers better understand each other and more importantly helped find a business model that empowered each of them to manage their portfolio according to their risk profile.

The following Christmas Josh and Steven sent a photograph to Hilary of them together, arms around each other, smiling as they enjoyed a skiing trip together. As far as the parents were concerned it was the best Christmas present ever. The fractured relationship that was causing so much angst and upset was healed. When we separated the business voice from the individual voice and from the family voice, everyone began to wonder what the argument was even about. It was so easy to solve – yet they had hated each other over it.

Every generation has a different attitude to risk, and every generation understands different categories of investment on different levels. Even if you go back to 2006, which isn't that long ago, the five largest companies by market capitalisation were ExxonMobil ($540 billion), GE ($463 billion), Microsoft ($355 billion), Citigroup ($331 billion) and Bank of America ($290 billion). In 2018, Microsoft was the only one still left in the top five. The new winners were Apple ($888 billion), Alphabet ($773 billion), Amazon ($748 billion), Microsoft ($723 billion) and Facebook ($539 billion).[60] They are all tech companies. Covid-19 recalibrated this list almost overnight. The big winners were Amazon and Netflix. In fact, as the world was in lockdown, not driving their cars and looking for something to watch, Netflix's value reached $196 billion, overtaking ExxonMobil![61]

An exponential shift is happening in society. As author Yuval Noah Harari points out, if you died in 1800 and were miraculously brought back to life in 1900, you'd just go about your business – nothing much would have changed, not even the knowledge. But if you died in 1945 and came back in the 2020s, you would be deeply confused. Everything would have changed and the knowledge available to man-kind would be exponentially greater than it was in 1945.[62] While the scale and complexity of the challenges we face are changing, the timing seems oddly predictable. There are those who say we couldn't have foreseen Covid-19. If we lay aside the fact that there are scientists and epidemiologists who have said such a pandemic has and always will be an existential threat to our species, we may not always know what is coming but we do know that *something* is coming. In my own lifetime that something is remarkably consistent: 1987 stock market crash, 1990s property crash, Dot-com crash of early 2000s, 2008 global financial crisis and 2019 Covid-19, which might make the rest of them look like a walk in the park.

These issues cause even more complexity because the generation that has the most influence in a family business (G1) usually has the most intuitive understanding of the changes, but the least experience with the true lifestyle impacts they bring about. G1 may be able to tell G2 what is happening and why but won't listen when G2 tells G1 what that means. G2 may be talking a language G1 understands but G1 is coming from a dictionary and encyclopaedia of experience that G2 has never had, and that can and does cause problems. This is not to say that G1s can't do their homework – many do – but it's G2 and G3 that are often living the shift. Considering many of the shifts that happen today are tech shifts, not least the tech shift caused by Covid-19, G2 and beyond have never lived in a world without tech. G2 understand it, its possibilities and ramifications, in ways that G1 will never understand, and yet their input is frequently dismissed. There is a world of difference between doing your research and wrapping your head around the changes, and living those changes.

And these changes have a profound impact on wealth. The tertiary qualifications required just to look after wealth are complex. Those qualifications also usually only relate to one wealth category, and those categories are changing all the time. Just think about the rise of cryptocurrency as an example. Not only does the person managing wealth need to stay abreast of the various investment categories, understand them deeply and be aware of the trends in that investment type, but they also need to stay on top of the new opportunities that are emerging – which adds another level of complexity to wealth and the management of wealth.

In family wealth the usual stereotypes and default settings also come into play. How would Christopher, Priya and Nathan feel if John and Ayesha decided to involve Anika more in the business and assigned her, 'the baby', the role of managing the family wealth? It's not her passion and a qualification from a French culinary school isn't going to cut it, regardless of her surname. Each generation will also almost certainly feel differently about the various types of investments. John, for example, has no interest in exploring what he views as riskier investment in cryptocurrency while Nathan believes it's worth a punt. Of course, Nathan's disagreement with John started much earlier. We all know the story. Nathan's friend Mike would come around to the house to visit and would hang off John's every word, soaking up any advice the successful John could offer. But Nathan wasn't interested in Dad's 'outdated thinking' – often even before he heard it. It's the alpha male jostling for position that happens in every family between men and their sons. First the father is the hero (up until the son is about 10 years old) and then the father is the enemy who must be beaten, bested and ultimately overthrown. Oh, the joy of family drama.

Needless to say, as the wealth grows so too does the philanthropic pressure to do something good with at least some of the excess. Not only does this have significant tax advantages but it also offers a family an opportunity to develop a legacy outside the business and give back to causes that unite them.

There are essentially eight issues that escalate complexity in family business wealth, summed up by figure 12.1.

Figure 12.1: Wealth: A Model of Family Business Wealth Complexity

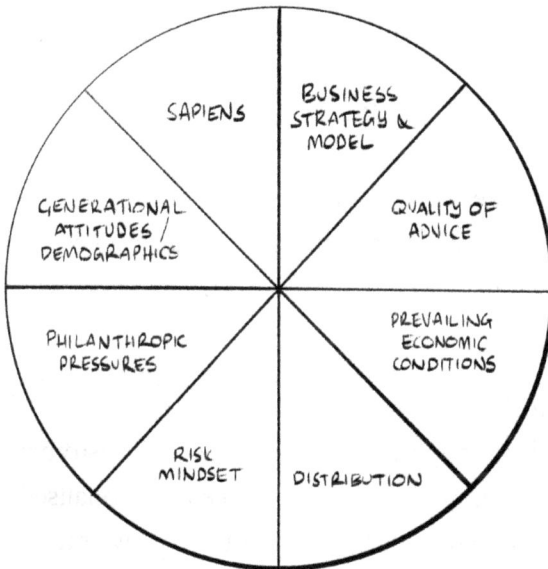

Below are just some of the questions that might arise in each category – further amplifying the complexity of wealth.

Business Strategy and Model

- What is our operating model?
- What is our point of difference?
- What impact will new regulation have on our offer?
- How do we scale the business?
- What emerging technology will influence us?

- Is our offer responding to demographic change?
- What's our risk framework and mitigation strategy?

Quality of Advice

- What's the advisor's track record?
- Who has judged them on that track record?
- Is that track record relevant for our experience and our portfolio and balance sheet?
- Do they understand the personality of our family and what's important to us?
- What experience do they have managing a family dynamic?

Prevailing Economic Conditions

- What global trends will impact the supply of money?
- Will interest rates hold, drop or rise?
- Will any geo-political problems impact our markets?
- What will happen to commodity prices?

Distribution

- What will technology do to our supply chain?
- What will demographic trends do to the way customers buy?
- How will the supply chain marketplace be rationalised?
- How will automation and AI impact the way we buy?
- What traditional methods of consumption will become redundant?

Risk Mindset

- How much is enough?
- What's our baseline holding target?
- What investment options do we have an advantage in understanding?
- What exposure do we have, or will we allow, to banks?
- How do we become our own bank?
- Do we invest in family members' commercial endeavours?

Philanthropic Pressures

- What do we want to support?
- What's the political consequence of our choices?
- How do we make sure our money gets properly used?
- How do we know the benefactors are genuinely motivated?
- How do we know they're capable of delivering the promises?
- How do we know we won't be poorly judged by our selection?

Generational Attitudes/Demographics

- What is the consumer confidence level?
- What are the prevailing political and social issues?
- Do these issues impact our decision-making?
- What sectors benefit from prevailing sentiment?
- What impact will Covid-19 have, short, medium and long term?

Sapiens

- How will the tech revolution impact our health – mental and physical?
- What does the life experience of the cloud native individual look like?
- How will this drive sector performance?
- When does the experience of the founding generation 'flip' from asset to liability?

Of course, all of these factors are amplified by our human limitations. Money can do very strange things to people, largely because it triggers the survival response and people can become selfish, scared or demanding. People with level three generational wealth can very easily lose their sense of reality. There are now whole industries dedicated to helping the wealthy part with their cash via outrageous gifts and experiences – everything from gold cars to famous footballers showing up for a kid's birthday party. Wealth is complex.

But, put that wealth in a family and it rachets up the level of complexity still further. How much is there? Will I receive any? If so, how much? What will I need to do to be entitled to that? Does my surname entitle me to some of it without effort or involvement in the business? Should the distribution be the same for those involved in the business and those not? Who decides? Money creates tensions and causes arguments. And of course, it's considered impolite in most societies to talk about money so the conversations that are so needed about wealth either never happen or happen too late. This lack of knowledge triggers the greatest default of all, being that everyone jumps to the worst probable conclusion. Emotion enters the picture as everyone wants to know but is scared to ask. Worries emerge about whether distribution is fair or equitable. If one sibling gets something do all the siblings get the same? When it comes to money family members employed in, by, or as a consequence of the family business are certainly not in charge of their thoughts.

Learnings from the Field: Ludicrous Entitlement

Imagine a family where four siblings can't work together. Part of the issue is that the firstborn G2 has always assumed that she is the heir apparent, which gives her the right to influence G1s decisions, especially around wealth. Again, this is not uncommon. If no one talks about succession or transition and sets out a plan, G2s will make assumptions based on birth order, skill set, gender or simply force of personality. Indeed, if these issues are not addressed, one G2 will almost always push forward and become even more aggressive than even they want to be. The firstborn G2 is doing what countless firstborns do – assuming the business is primarily hers (or would be) and therefore she has a duty to protect it and ensure fairness and equality. Plus, because it is all assumption, she feels it necessary to stamp her authority on everything – even on issues that have very little to do with her. In truth, the stamping is even more robust because she is a woman and she is aware of the company-wide assumption that her younger brother is better suited to the CEO role, just by dint of his gender.

Nowhere is this steamrolling mindset more clearly revealed than during an intense disagreement about what to do when her youngest brother splits up from his first wife. His ex-wife decides to live independently with their daughter – G2's daughter and G1's granddaughter. G1 decide to make a financial contribution to their ex-daughter-in-law to ensure that the transition is smooth and their granddaughter can live in a healthy and positive environment. The firstborn is incensed by this decision to essentially 'help the younger brother out' and feels that the contribution should be paid for by her younger brother.

The youngest son is, meanwhile, incensed that his big sister is seeking to influence their parents' decision. The tension is so great that G1 are going to cave to their daughter's demands. The whole idea that they would be taking any advice or guidance from any G2 in relation to how they (G1) would support G2 or beyond financially is preposterous.

Whatever motivation G1 have to invest in solving the problem is primarily a function of G3 – the desire to make sure their granddaughter's life wasn't made any harder by the separation of her parents. It has nothing to do with G2. G1 always have a right to do with their money what they choose to do for *their* beneficiaries in whatever form that beneficiary has a need and they want to support.

In the end, through the coaching and governance process the oldest daughter came to recognise how ludicrous her original demands had been and apologised to G1 and G2.

Back to the Jacksons

Let's take a look at the Jacksons again to illuminate the complexity of wealth and perceived inequality.

John is looking to retire or at least step back a bit from the business. Both Christopher and Nathan work in the business. Nathan enthusiastically, Christopher less so.

Nathan believes (although he doesn't voice his belief) that he does most of the work and has for all intents and purposes taken over the top job from his dad. He doesn't believe he is being paid fairly. His irritation stems from the fact that both he and Christopher earn the same but Christopher, who is a qualified architect, only works part-time in the family business. Christopher has his own business too. Nathan is sure that a good architect could be found for half the price.

Christopher on the other hand believes that the work he does for the family business is worth considerably more than he is paid in his role. Christopher believes his firm bills the family business at a heavy discount – especially as he does all the family work and doesn't delegate it to his junior staff. (An important reality that

Nathan was not aware of until, as we will discover in part V, the business got its voice through the Jackson Developments & Construction Strategic Plan.) The amount Christopher charges his clients is much more than he is paid for the same work in the family business, and he is becoming increasingly resentful of this fact.

Priya also works in the business but in a project management and business development role, which doesn't really use her engineering degree or experience. She is aware of her father's gender bias and believes that at least if she is in the business, she can perhaps show her worth over time. She doesn't make anywhere near what her brothers make which disappoints her no end – especially as she finds the opportunities that contribute to the stellar profit. Priya is thinking it may be time to leave.

Anika doesn't really pay that much attention, although she is aware of the family wealth after something was said in passing at last year's Christmas gathering that made her realise the extent of that wealth. Now she is increasingly worried that her lack of attention will prevent her from benefiting from it, and to add to her woes she feels guilty for having those thoughts. She has recently opened her own restaurant with the help of her parents but what she has been given is a loan, with interest payable! She assumed that her siblings realised that, but it was only once her mum and dad spelt it out to her siblings that the simmering hostility she was feeling from them dissipated again and connectedness was restored.

For their part **John and Ayesha** have tried to keep the true value of the business and the assets they own independently away from the children. They are aware that it could cause issues, but don't know how to raise it. The wealth pool of the business

and owned assets is significant – $150 million at last assessment. And they have no idea how to extract what they need for a comfortable retirement while also being fair to their children and their relevant contributions to the business and honour the fact that regardless of input they are all their children and should all benefit.

These concerns, coupled with his desire to retire, have resulted in John taking a more reserved approach in business which Christopher, Nathan and Priya notice and yet he can't really explain. As we all do, John has rationalised his change of tack as a consequence of his getting older and wanting to pursue a more cautious approach. Again, this is an example of ethnomethodology where stuff happens to us and then we rationalise it and explain it to ourselves so that 'it' makes sense.[63] John's response is a classic example of this. In chapter 6 we discussed the recent large-scale project, Pavilion, which went exceptionally well and coincided with a steep property boom, resulting in a significant uplift in business value. Once the euphoria wore off, anxiety crept in although John would never admit it. That anxiety stemmed from a recognition that his plans of the business being worth $250 million in five years' time had already been realised. So, the decisions he had planned to make in five years' time really needed to be made now. Only he isn't ready now and the size of the challenge ahead in terms of succession and making sure he makes the right choices weighs heavy on his mind. He's not even that aware of this thinking so he rationalises this new, more cautious approach in a way that makes more sense to him. That might include pointing to his friend David who is also extremely successful but for whom there is no such thing as rich enough. John tells his children that they don't need to be like David and it's about sustainability. And those sentiments may be true and they may be noble but they are not what is really driving the caution. He knows that he has to make some succession choices for the continued success of the business but he doesn't really know what to do. So, he's pulling back as an instinctive response to the uncertainty he feels about the big decisions he has to make.

Behavioural science has also demonstrated another quirk that could have a bearing – loss aversion, which is where losses loom larger than gains. In other words, we fear losing something we already have more than we are willing to risk achieving additional gains. In John's case, the reminder of what was at stake shifted his focus, albeit unconsciously, to protecting that wealth rather than building on that wealth.[64] This quirk is a survival-based adaptation – if we treat threats more urgently than opportunities, we are more likely to survive. This makes sense if we are being chased by a brown bear, but it doesn't make sense in business. Another useful reminder that we are not in charge of our thoughts.

The truth is this: family is complex, business is complex but put a family inside that business and it's a multiplier. Add wealth to the mix, especially significant category three or generational wealth, and the complexity increases exponentially. And yet our minds are not built to handle complexity.

When someone makes the observation, 'Wow, that family really screwed things up!' no one should be surprised. The only correct response to such an observation is, 'Of course they did – they were human beings trying to build a skyscraper without scaffolding. It's amazing more people were not hurt!'

WHEN SOMEONE MAKES THE OBSERVATION,
'WOW, THAT FAMILY REALLY SCREWED THINGS UP!'
NO ONE SHOULD BE SURPRISED. THE ONLY CORRECT
RESPONSE TO SUCH AN OBSERVATION IS, 'OF COURSE
THEY DID – THEY WERE HUMAN BEINGS TRYING TO BUILD
A SKYSCRAPER WITHOUT SCAFFOLDING. IT'S AMAZING
MORE PEOPLE WERE NOT HURT!'

We should not be surprised when the scaffolding of the family business takes the form of the founder. The founder dies and the scaffolding evaporates immediately as the rest of the family are halfway through building level 15 and the whole thing implodes. Made worse by the fact that the scaffolding is not the only thing to evaporate with the founder's death – the strategy often dies with them.

This constantly escalating pressure of complexity should lead us to the conclusion that we ought not be surprised when success and wealth becomes the undoing of a family. We ought not to be shocked by the curse of shirt sleeves to shirt sleeves in just three generations. It is a law of nature.

In fact, we should be utterly stunned and amazed when a family is able to navigate business and wealth, *and* stay connected, as a family.

What impact does wealth have on 'n', our variable for complexity? Let's revisit the theorem.

The Family Business Theorem Continued

Again, thinking about the relationships between family, business and wealth I considered this question – does wealth influence complexity and uncertainty? Is it $F \times B \times W$? Is it $F \times B + W$? Or is it $F \times B$ to the power of W? One way to consider this is through the lens of good and evil. How much good can someone do with no money? Well, they can volunteer their time and offer their knowledge, skills and experience but their impact is limited without money. How much good can someone do with money? The possibilities to effect real positive change are immense.

The opposite is also true. How much harm can someone do without money? One on one – quite a lot, but their impact is still relatively limited. If you are an unpleasant or mean person you can do some damage, but if you are rich and unpleasant the possibilities are endless. Just look at the global financial crisis as evidence of that. By some accounts the global financial crisis, which devastated millions of lives and brought the global economy to its knees, was caused by as few as

50 individuals.[65] Feel free to watch the film *The Big Short* to determine whether any of them are unpleasant!

Wealth is like injecting a steroid into complexity. Part of that reality comes from the escalation of choice.

When I was a kid, my brothers and sister and I would be asked around the kitchen table where we would like to go on holiday. We would ask what the options were and we would be given maybe three or four choices. At the time they sounded varied and we felt as though we had a good range of options. We didn't realise at the time that they were all dictated by the length of time both my parents could tolerate four children in a car. The options were therefore all within a day's drive.

As children we felt as though we had some choice but not too much and that worked for us. We could make a decision collectively. Now imagine that same scenario if my family were wealthy. The nanny would be looking after us in economy class while my parents travelled business (unless G1 had lost the plot and we were all in business class). We could go anywhere, do anything – there was no limitation. Anywhere was possible and consequently the choice was overwhelming. Wealth explodes choice and with it, complexity and uncertainty – the twin enemies of happiness.

It was clear that wealth compounded any situation and since the impact is felt on both family and the business, we bracket (F × B) and we apply W.

$$n = \frac{(F \times B)^{\omega}}{}$$

n = COMPLEXITY
F = FAMILY
B = BUSINESS
ω = WEALTH

191

Wealth makes *everything* more complex. It magnifies the challenges that family and business must solve. In fact, the impact is so profound, it is exponential.

Basic mathematics tells us that the result produces a significant quantum of complexity. It further tells us that the only way to reduce this 'quantum' is to introduce a denominator: something below the line.

If we look at family businesses that have successfully navigated their way through this extreme complexity – functionally, operationally, financially and emotionally – where the business is thriving and the family are 'all things considered' happy and still connected, they all have two things in common:

Governance and stewardship.

They are the denominators, and we will explore them in part III.

PART III

Part I and part II have thoroughly unpacked the problems we face – our brain limitations and the problems caused by uncertainty and complexity. I also introduced you to a theorem relating to family business and the complexity that's created by such entities.

Everything above the line, the numerator in the theorem, is the problem.

Part III outlines everything below the line, the denominator – the solution.

Namely, governance and stewardship. Trying to manage the succession of wealth without governance and stewardship is like trying to build a skyscraper without scaffolding.

CHAPTER 13

Governance

What is governance? Governance is about answering the question, 'How do we make decisions?' Governance is engineered objectivity. It is an agreed set of rules about how decisions will be made and how issues will be resolved that binds the family together.

Remember the three domains we explored earlier that create complexity: family, business and wealth. Those same domains convert, not by accident, into a well-accepted, well-tested family governance theory called the three-circle model (see figure 13.1).

Figure 13.1: The Three-Circle Model

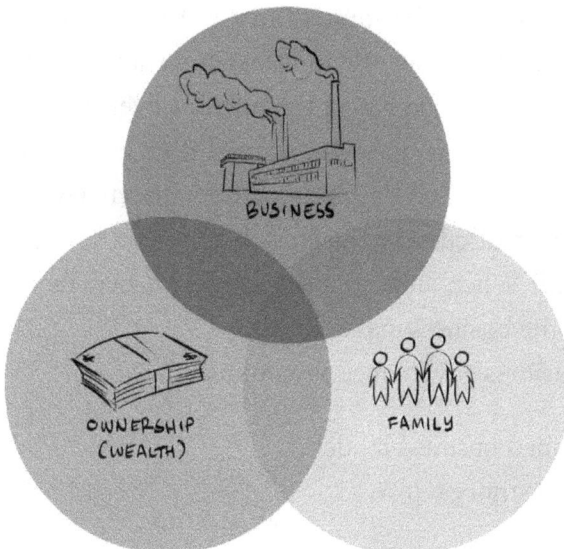

The best way to counter complexity is with clarity. Think of these domains as tennis balls and you as a juggler. One tennis ball and it's not very complex and isn't really juggling! Two is a little more complicated and certainly needs more concentration. Three is much harder. By purposefully separating the three domains, you immediately make things clearer and easier to manage. Family decisions are family decisions; business decisions are business decisions; wealth management decisions ... and so on.

So, let's break these down.

Business

If you look at a business that's successful in the absence of its founder you will find strategy, operational plans, standard operating procedures, performance contracts and so on. There is almost always a clear governance framework. Without it, business rarely succeeds beyond the founder.

Think about your own business right now or a business you work in ... Do you know how decisions are made and why? Who makes strategic decisions? Financial decisions? Where are those decisions made? For example, is there a forum that comes together to debate the big issues or does the founder or CEO make them alone? Does the founding partner make them? Does the way decisions are made change depending on the day of the week or over time? Is there consistency of treatment or does it appear ad hoc? Is the effectiveness of decision-making assessed or questioned retrospectively? Are decisions made in sidebar discussions or are lobbying and back-room discussions involved? When viewed in this context it may be that you have no idea how the business makes decisions.

Robust business governance should include:

- a well-defined business model
- a published strategic plan

- an organisational design that matches the strategy
- performance contracts that spell out the expectations on individuals
- KPIs so those expectations can be measured
- financial reporting
- performance management to give employees useful feedback on contribution and where they can improve
- standard operating procedures that define how things are done
- a skills matrix to ensure the right people are employed.

Governance provides much-needed objectivity. The resulting answers to the questions, or formulation of the agreed process, provides the subjectivity. Remember: we can't be objective and subjective at the same time. Governance – systematically created after mutual discussion and agreement, across every aspect of the business – applies that objectivity to the business moving forward. The bullet points above are essentially engineered objectivity. Get the objective part right and a business can successfully nullify a great deal of the subjective tension and angst that can and often does bloom in family enterprise.

We often believe that governance will be bureaucratic and make the business less responsive or flexible but the opposite is true. It liberates those involved in the business to just get on with their jobs rather than worrying about who is making decisions, why, where, when and how. They know how all types of financial decisions are made because it's already been agreed by all parties. Everyone also knows where they are made and when they are made. Governance provides clarity and direction so that everyone in the business knows what they are trying to achieve.

Governance is a bit like buying a jigsaw puzzle with the picture on the box versus buying a jigsaw puzzle in a plastic bag from a charity shop. The picture on the cover provides context and allows you to better understand how best to complete the puzzle. The puzzle in the plastic bag provides none of that. You are flying blind – just like a business without governance.

Successful businesses always have an agreement and set of rules about how decisions will be made and how issues will be resolved that bind everyone in the business together.

GOVERNANCE IS A BIT LIKE BUYING A JIGSAW PUZZLE WITH THE PICTURE ON THE BOX VERSUS BUYING A JIGSAW PUZZLE IN A PLASTIC BAG FROM A CHARITY SHOP.

Ownership (Wealth)

So, what about ownership? Does governance exist in this domain?

Absolutely. It's called the law. There is a huge amount of governance that provides agreement and a set of rules about ownership and wealth.

Robust wealth and ownership governance should include:

- share certificates
- trusts
- wills and estates
- right of ownership – contractual and equitable
- intellectual property
- shareholder agreements.

The entire legal system is almost exclusively focused on the governance of ownership. Imagine trying to govern wealth and ownership without it – it would be anarchy.

Imagine if there were no method of resolving whether somebody owns copyright or not, or no method to resolve whether somebody's stolen an idea or not, or no method to resolve whether somebody owns shares in a business or not, or no method to resolve whether the transfer of those shares was legal and enforceable.

The law is therefore the governance of wealth and ownership.

Family

Now, let's take a moment to consider family. Is there any governance in a family?

No. At least not beyond some vague notions of how we are expected to treat each other or some rules about bedtime when the children are small.

'But a family doesn't need governance!' I hear you cry.

Perhaps this is true when there is nothing *but* family.

However, if you add either business or wealth, I promise you it does need governance. A family without wealth doesn't have to worry about the influence of one generation on the next, other than personalities and preferences. But when wealth is introduced, the influence of one generation on the next and the next and the one after becomes meaningful and unavoidable.

Just think about it. What makes family different from all the other relationships we have? Beyond the biology the only real difference is psychological; namely, levels of tolerance. If we shock and surprise a stranger, they won't engage with us. If we surprise a friend, they may tolerate it. If we shock them, it can and eventually will hurt the relationship. Family are the only people who will typically recover from shock. They tend to forgive. But too many surprises and too much shock and even a family will fracture.

A FAMILY WITHOUT WEALTH DOESN'T HAVE TO WORRY
ABOUT THE INFLUENCE OF ONE GENERATION ON THE NEXT,
OTHER THAN PERSONALITIES AND PREFERENCES.
BUT WHEN WEALTH IS INTRODUCED, THE INFLUENCE OF
ONE GENERATION ON THE NEXT AND THE NEXT AND THE
ONE AFTER BECOMES MEANINGFUL AND UNAVOIDABLE.

Nothing has the capacity to surprise and shock like the addition of wealth. As a result, family is placed in an exceptionally precarious position without governance to prevent, mitigate and avoid those shocks in the first place. We mistakenly believe that the other difference, biology, will be enough to endure these shocks. It's not.

It has to be governed, just like a good business is governed. Just like ownership is governed. Just like our laws themselves provide governance; a prosperous family needs to be governed. And this is especially true if that wealth comes from a business that generations beyond the founders may be involved in. Otherwise, a whole bunch of questions go unanswered, or even worse, unasked which can and will fester to cause tension, distress and disconnection. Those questions might include:

- Who gets the money?
- Can I use the holiday home in Aspen at Christmas?
- Can I get a job in the business?
- If so, what qualifications do I need or is my surname enough?
- What level will I join the business at?
- Do all my siblings also get a job?
- What experience do we need?
- What will we be paid?
- What if I don't want to work for the family business? What do I get then?
- Who's going to take over from Mum and Dad?
- Who's going to look after our balance sheet?
- Whose advice are we going to listen to as a family?
- How are going to choose our advisor?

Robust family governance should therefore include:

1. the legal ownership
2. the management of the business

3. the relationship between the family and the business
4. the relationship between the family and the wealth.

When these are all in place, a family is properly governed.

It is also worth pointing out that if you want to know about legal ownership there are mountains of law books. If you want to know more about business management there are thousands of books, some of which are useful. (You could start with mine – *Elephants and the Business Laws of Nature.*[66]) And this book is dedicated to the relationship between the family and the business and the wealth and the *governance* of those relationships.

Family governance is not about taking the humanity out of relationships or creating some type of sterile turnkey family culture. It's about instituting mutually agreed rules so that everyone feels heard and listened to and understands the road ahead. Everyone has a voice – the business, the individuals (founder and individual family members), the family and the family community (spouses and the generations that follow). Do that, and you nullify the situations and ecosystem that would normally allow the five brain limitations to flourish and cause havoc. The outcome of such effort means everyone can engage their front of mind and leave their back of mind to worry only about how to cross the road safely.

Family Business

Genuine governance is rare in business and it's exceptionally rare in family business. This is both ironic and understandable. Ironic because governance is even more critical in family business, because of all we learnt in part I, and the nature of the family dynamics within the business. Understandable because in family business it's often acutely obvious to everyone who works in the business, family or otherwise, who decides – the founder. This is the reason the business works under the leadership of a founder – the governance is clear. It might not be perceived as governance but functionally the founder decides every-thing, so everyone is clear about their role and remit. The founder *is* the governance. Of course, this immediately stops working as soon as that founder dies, gets ill or wants to step back. Then all hell breaks loose as people lament the fact that it worked fine when Dad was in charge, or the business was humming when Mum was alive.

Founders lead by dint of their position – they started the business, it's their baby and everyone is expected to fall in line behind. Fair enough. But what about G2, G3 and beyond? How are decisions made then? Who decides who decides? Businesses transition successfully to the next generation, or survive beyond the founder, when the founder makes a genuine and concerted effort to establish governance and pre-side over their own succession.

Once the strong founder is no longer at the helm it can be next to impossible to know how and where the decisions are being made, and this will amplify the uncertainty and complexity and foster tension and discord amongst family members and the wider business.

BUSINESSES TRANSITION SUCCESSFULLY TO THE NEXT GENERATION, OR SURVIVE BEYOND THE FOUNDER, WHEN THE FOUNDER MAKES A GENUINE AND CONCERTED EFFORT TO ESTABLISH GOVERNANCE AND PRESIDE OVER THEIR OWN SUCCESSION.

It's useful to think of governance in business as the institution of corporate democracy following the inevitable corporate autocracy of the founder or monarchy of a husband-and-wife founding couple.

The concept of democracy is usually associated with the efforts of the ancient Greeks and Romans, who were themselves considered the founders of Western civilisation. Eighteenth-century intellec-tuals attempted to leverage these early democratic experiments into a new template for post-monarchical political organisation. But it was the end of World War II that really put democracy on the map. Modern political democracies attempt to bridge the gap between the Hobbesian 'state of nature' – the hypothetical life of people before societies came into existence – and the grip of authoritarianism such as the type demonstrated by Hitler and Mussolini. Social contracts sought to enshrine the rights of the citizens, curtail the power of the state, and grant agency through the right to vote. Eventually all autocrats and monarchies lose their relevance and effectiveness. This same phenomenon can frequently be seen in family business where the founder or founding partnership is the autocracy (or monarchy) and thus the decision-maker on *everything*.

Commercial Benefits of Governance

Governance is the recognition that while that might work for a time, possibly even several decades, it will not work once that powerful leader or leadership team is no longer present. And a member of G2 cannot simply inherit that power role due to birth order and little else. Governance brings much-needed rules, systems and procedures into the business, proposed and agreed on by all the family members so that the founder is replaced by a decision-making framework – not a new authoritarian decision-maker. As a result, all the family members and the business can prosper and remain connected.

Governance is the only tool to reduce uncertainty and complexity, increasing the chance of continued happiness and connectedness in the family as well as business success. It also deflates many of the default settings and reflex responses that derail rational thought. Moreover, it paves the way for autonomy and competence where those in the business know they are in their role because they are the best person for that role and not because of their surname. This improves self-esteem and bolsters confidence. If every family member in the business is in the same position this fosters an environment where continued connectedness is more likely. Governance provides everyone in the business with a series of detailed and robust mechanisms and processes which are thoroughly understood and consistently implemented across the business. Not only does governance continuously improve organisational efficiency and the quality of decision-making on complex issues but it clarifies accountabilities and increases executive alignment. As such effective governance also reduces pressure in the system because it facilitates answers to key questions that very often stay unanswered or even unasked prior to governance. These unanswered and unasked questions are landmines in family business.

The only way to successfully manage the inevitable complexity of family business is through the relatively new field of multigenerational family governance. Let's revisit the theorem once again.

The Family Business Theorem Continued

Clearly, the possibilities for things to go wrong are immense in family business. When that business achieves a level of success that delivers significant wealth an already challenging situation is made exponentially so. Family, business and wealth are all, therefore, numerators – they add to the complexity.

So, is there anything we can do to reduce the complexity and uncertainty? Is there any way that we can systematically nullify the default settings and disconnect the reflex responses so that the hypersensitive, hyperalert amygdala can work on things that really do threaten our survival, such as initiating extra driving vigilance on icy roads? In other words, is there a denominator?

Thankfully there is. Governance is the denominator and it reduces complexity and uncertainty every time it's applied in every situation. No exceptions.

Instituting agreed-before-relevant rules, systems and procedures into a family with wealth allows the autocratic or monarchy governance system of the founder to influence the business without destroying the family. While such a decision-making system might have worked when the founder was building the business, it is a recipe for disaster when it comes to successful succession and the continuing connectedness of the family from generation to generation.

If we think about what we face inside a family business, it can also be helpful to think about it through the lens of survival:

- **Physiological survival** – this is purely unconscious, the domain of objective consciousness. It is all the stuff our brain and body does, to keep us alive and functioning. We are not aware and have no control over any of this.
- **Physical survival** – this is the domain of those default settings and reflex responses, designed to move us out of the path of physical danger. They are primarily focused on our physical protection and frequently triggered by an overly cautious hypervigilant amygdala. Although blunt and excessive, they do work.
- **Intellectual survival** – this is the domain of governance. Governance is the only way to ensure intellectual survival because it tempers our powerful subconscious drivers, fosters safety, dials down complexity and reduces uncertainty. In doing so it forces all the frontal cortexes in the room to engage rather than allowing our human limitations to run the show. Thus, the very thing that makes us human, the frontal lobe, is finally allowed to shine.

Governance requires conscious activity that allows everyone in the family to have their voice heard, establish their position and achieve success, on their terms, in the social and commercial infrastructure. So ...

$$\eta = \frac{(F \times B)^{\omega}}{G}$$

η = COMPLEXITY
F = FAMILY
B = BUSINESS
W = WEALTH
G = GOVERNANCE

Governance can be extremely powerful in family business success, but even governance can be accelerated. Governance, to be useful, requires one more 'variable'.

If petrol is an accelerant to fire, stewardship is an accelerant to governance. With poor stewardship, the fire won't light. With good stewardship, the fire will establish itself. With great stewardship, the power of governance is fully unleashed.

IF PETROL IS AN ACCELERANT TO FIRE, STEWARDSHIP
IS AN ACCELERANT TO GOVERNANCE. WITH POOR
STEWARDSHIP, THE FIRE WON'T LIGHT. WITH GOOD
STEWARDSHIP, THE FIRE WILL ESTABLISH ITSELF.
WITH GREAT STEWARDSHIP, THE POWER OF
GOVERNANCE IS FULLY UNLEASHED.

CHAPTER 14

Stewardship

The single most important ingredient necessary for governance to take root and facilitate its considerable benefits for the family, the business and the wealth is stewardship. As I said in the previous chapter, stewardship is an accelerator for governance.

But what is stewardship?

Again, the three-circle model can help (see figure 14.1).

Figure 14.1: The Three-Circle Model

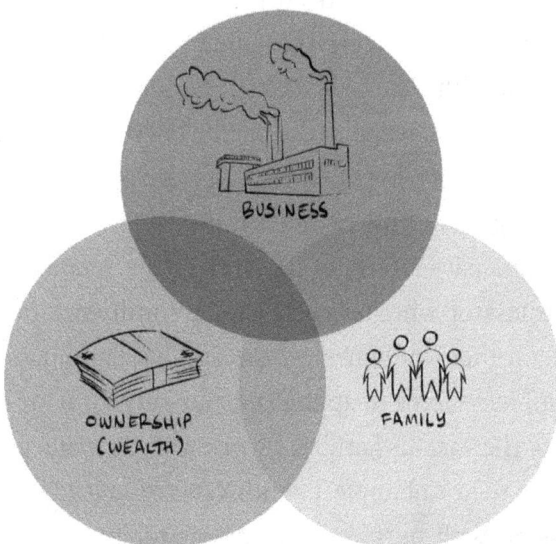

How do we make business work properly? Leadership makes a business work. The leader takes control of the formation and articulation of the strategy. The team makes a meaningful, formative contribution to the strategy. The leader then ensures the team is encouraged, enthused and empowered to deliver the strategy.

How do we make the domain of ownership and wealth work properly? There are police officers, lawyers, the Australian Securities and Investments Commission (ASIC) and various law enforcement bureaus that ensure that the governance of the ownership domain is adhered to. They make the laws work.

Neither a leader nor a police officer works in a family. You cannot run a family like an enforcer and you cannot run a family like a chief executive. Founders might get away with a benevolent dictatorship for a while but that benevolent dictatorship will die the minute the business transitions from them to G2. And, by definition, G2 might have five dictators and that's never going to work.

You have to run a family, with shared interests, like a steward. And a steward is different. A steward is somebody who's less interested about where we're going and more interested about everyone getting there together. A steward knows and ensures that appropriately qualified people are in place to provide the guidance and advice needed on matters such as wealth.

A steward knows and respects the person chosen to lead the business and takes responsibility for ensuring they are properly qualified, as opposed to telling them how to do their job.

And a steward pays attention to every single member of a family. Because regardless of whether each person's influence on the wealth is large or small, their influence on the family's happiness and health is equal. What I have come to appreciate, not only from my own life but also the lives of the various families I work with, is that a parent is only ever as happy as their unhappiest child. Whereas a leader might ignore that and press on with business objectives, and an enforcer might try to bulldoze their way through a situation, a steward is focused on taking everyone on the journey – whether everyone is in the business or not. Stewardship is the only place where 'We are family' is a relevant and important statement. We are family and above all else that's what matters the most.

Stewardship is essential in the transition from one generation to the next, and yet it is a way of leading the business and the family that is often alien to those actually in charge of the business. The only reason there is a successful company worthy of succession or transition in the first place is almost always down to a dominant, headstrong and determined leader who has driven the business to its current success through sheer hard work and bloody-minded determination.

STEWARDSHIP IS THE ONLY PLACE WHERE 'WE ARE FAMILY' IS A RELEVANT AND IMPORTANT STATEMENT. WE ARE FAMILY AND ABOVE ALL ELSE THAT'S WHAT MATTERS THE MOST.

They are the leader. Often, they have spent a lifetime being the leader. They see themselves as the leader and everyone around them agrees.

But it's not enough if they want to create an enduring legacy AND protect the integrity and health of the business and every family member.

At an individual level, stewardship focuses on promoting wellbeing for each family member. One of the many ways to promote this wellbeing is to ensure that each individual is generally happy in his or her working environment. Remember in chapter 8 when I introduced self-determination theory (SDT) proposed by Edward Deci and Richard Ryan? Deci and Ryan explored human need in relation to happiness and argued that we have three innate psychological needs – competence, autonomy and relatedness.[67] When those needs are met, we are motivated, productive and happy. When they are thwarted, our motivation, productivity and happiness plummet. It doesn't take a genius to see how these needs can be seriously thwarted in a family business. The inference is often that employed family members are only in the business because of their surname. Even if they are competent this is frequently overlooked by the founder or dismissed by non-family employees who may be unhappy with what they view as nepotism. The individual is never quite sure if they are there because they are good at their job or because of their family connection. Autonomy is also a thorny subject in family business. Employed family members may appear to have control or autonomy but everyone knows that actually the founder is in charge. Even those G2s that break out of the business know that there may come a day when they are asked to come back into the fold. Autonomy is largely an illusion. And relatedness also has the potential to become an issue as the limitations rear up to pollute the family dynamic and cause rifts and disagreements between family members, thereby reducing relatedness. G2, especially those with generational wealth, are also never quite sure if others like them or simply like the family wealth and potential connections. This too can cause havoc with relatedness.

In the course of my work, I've seen countless situations where one family member is marginalised and one or more of these needs is thwarted. They are viewed by the other siblings as the black sheep or in some way diminished – not least because of all the default settings that spring up around that individual, constantly pigeonholing them as 'the whinger' or 'the awkward one'.

In the transition from leadership to stewardship, the role of an independent advisor can be useful. They can act as an 'interim independent' steward for the family business until the role is fully understood and embraced by the family. Once the concept of stewardship is understood and embedded in the culture, a steward can often be found within the ranks.

Learnings from the Field: Everyone Has a Voice

Imagine the fourth child of a successful company founder was regarded with frustration by his other three siblings. Everyone was impatient with him, which impacted his perception of his own competence and negatively affected his relatedness to his siblings. In meetings he would often struggle to get his point across and because of the other siblings' default settings they didn't have the patience or willingness to stop and try to understand his point of view. Of course, the siblings took their cue from the founder whose impatience proved highly infectious. The fourth child was immediately dismissed or ridiculed by the rest of the family with entirely predictable results.

Working with him individually to allow him the time to slow his thinking down and consider what he wanted in the business gave him more control and autonomy. Instead of constantly focusing on what he didn't want he became better at speaking up to advocate on his own behalf, expressing himself clearly. He stopped getting so nervous, wasn't so easily triggered by his siblings' reactions, and his language skills and his self-confidence improved. In a remarkably short period of time, he emerged as a peer.

During a conversation I had with his sister, it dawned on her that most of her angst and irritation was not about *what* her brother actually said but the *way* he said it. Being aware of his immediate reflex response to his siblings allowed her to consciously dismiss her initial irritation and move past it. Her compassion increased as she started to appreciate that in some situations, he just struggled to say what he meant.

Once the older siblings stopped the judgement and irritation and simply supported their brother, allowing him to be himself, their relatedness increased and the once-ignored sibling became a source of insights and ideas that were clearly equal to the other family members.

It is difficult to make these types of breakthroughs from a leadership position because there is always a place to be or goal to be achieved. The only plan a steward has is to ensure that the family arrives at whatever destination they collectively decide on – together. The leader is constantly focused on where they are going – and what they need to do to get there. The steward is only concerned with how the family gets there, together, and it's only possible to build a picture of that destination by talking to everybody and involving everyone and every entity. Hence the four voices: business, individuals (founder and family members), family collective and wider family community (spouses and the generations that follow).

The G1 formula for success often requires the leader to become a steward. But this is hard to pull off because the modus operandi is different. Being a steward requires a leader to radically change the way they behave and think. Where a leader has a plan for the business, a steward has a plan of engagement with everyone. They have a different focus – helping all family members across generations to meet their needs in a way that suits them, either inside or outside the business.

Whereas leadership is a temporary role that is outlasted by the life-span of an organisation, stewardship is the process of actively preparing for an organisation's future vitality. It is about holding something in trust for another. Stewardship allows a family relationship with the business to continually develop and adjust to an ever-changing commercial environment within that context.

This is why independence can become vitally important at the family governance table and why the steward may need to be an external, independent advisor, at least at the start. Often, the character of stewardship is just not present in the business! However, if the founder or another family member is willing to develop that character, has a full understanding of the three circles, and participates in the family governance framework, it is possible for a founder or family member to be an effective steward.

The key to success is for the leader and the steward to fully appreciate the crucial differences between stewardship and leadership. For a leader to get people to understand the destination, they have to explain their position, tolerate challenges and be patient with the responses. Ultimately, they dispense with the negativity and focus on the journey. They encourage others to follow, or persuade them if necessary. A steward can't begin the journey until they are cognisant of everybody's individual point of view. Again, this is why the four voices are so crucial. The steward's job is to help the family define a destination that everyone can get behind, and that will take the whole family on the journey together while valuing each family member. The steward therefore helps articulate what the destination must look like – not in the sense of dictating what the destination is, but influencing the manner in which the family heads towards the collectively agreed-upon destination. The direction of travel and that the family stays intact during that journey is much more important to the steward than the eventual destination. In fact, the family staying together IS the destination. Ideally everyone stays on the bus. However, it might be that the majority are heading in a direction and a minority can't be convinced, in which case it's the steward's job to make sure that the minority volunteers out of the *business journey*, or even the *governance framework*, in such a way that ensures that they don't also volunteer out of the *family*. That's the key.

IT'S THE STEWARD'S JOB TO MAKE SURE THAT THE MINORITY VOLUNTEERS OUT OF THE *BUSINESS JOURNEY*, OR EVEN THE *GOVERNANCE FRAMEWORK*, IN SUCH A WAY THAT ENSURES THAT THEY DON'T ALSO VOLUNTEER OUT OF THE *FAMILY*. THAT'S THE KEY.

Stewardship therefore begins with ensuring individual wellbeing; transitions into a focus on team effectiveness; and ultimately leads to a need for larger family business considerations such as ensuring that family values and missions remain well articulated and intact.

This suggests a need for a culturally competent set of family values, agreed through the Family Charter, that are implemented as an institution throughout the family.

Stewardship puts a family in a position where they can say:

- 'We're well governed.'
- 'We're connected as a family.'
- 'We're not defined by our wealth but we manage our wealth efficiently.'
- 'We're confident the business, our wealth and the family will endure for generations to come.'
- 'Each of us understands and respects our relationship with the business and the wealth.'

If not all family members can say any or all of those things, it's a clear indication that the family doesn't have governance. And if they want to change that situation, they will not achieve it without governance *and* stewardship.

The steward of the 'family circle' is responsible for getting the family to their chosen destination – safely and in one piece. It is a role that is focused on the people and the relationships that the family members have with one another as a team, where they are each playing the right role alongside the two other 'circles' – ownership and business.

If there are many influential members of a family, the business leader's job is to secure buy-in to the business plan by everybody in the family. The steward's job is to keep the family together, understand the scope of everyone's expectations and take them forward. And from that implement a governance framework that delivers the most benefits to the greatest number of people in the family to ensure ongoing connectedness.

The leader should read and reread Patrick Lencioni's *The Five Dysfunctions of a Team* or anything from Michael Gerber or Simon Sinek. The steward should instead read and reread the earlier chapters of this book (on the five limitations of the mind) or anything from Steven Pinker, Richard Dawkins or Eric Berne. Whereas the leader is mission driven, the steward is relationship driven. Both are needed, and they are rare to find in the same person. This is the biggest challenge because whether this dual role can be performed by one person depends on the maturity of the individual in question and the quality of the governance.

If the steward's 'value' is zero, governance is lost. If the steward understands and applies themselves to the task, the value of governance is impacted exponentially. Let's revisit the theorem one last time.

The Complete Family Business Theorem

Initially I thought that governance was the end of the theorem, but it became clear to me that governance alone didn't always fully solve the issues I was seeing in the families I was working with. Although powerful and certainly capable of removing a huge amount of the angst in the business, the mindset of the founder or leader was also instrumental in how that governance landed. The complexity of family business is profoundly reduced by governance to the power of stewardship. Stewardship is the difference between leadership for the good of the many and leadership for the good of the leader.

Great stewardship endures beyond the life of any one steward. Poor stewardship reduces governance to zero, leaving a numerator divided by zero which equals infinity. Infinite complexity. Stewardship therefore exponentially improves the value of governance.

The final theorem is therefore:

$$n = \frac{(F \times B)^w}{G^s}$$

$$n = \text{COMPLEXITY}$$
$$F = \text{FAMILY}$$
$$B = \text{BUSINESS}$$
$$w = \text{WEALTH}$$
$$G = \text{GOVERNANCE}$$
$$S = \text{STEWARDSHIP}$$

It's easy to say that business or family or even wealth is complex. It's a little like saying the sky is blue. So what? Those involved already know this and wrestle with it on a daily basis. Complexity will come as no surprise. But what the theorem does is break that complexity down so we better understand its component parts and characteristics.

We can't avoid it, but we can understand it and nullify most of its jagged edges. If we don't, failure is the probable and likely result.

It is heartbreaking to sit with a founding couple who have successfully built an $80 million plus business and have them recount the dysfunction in their family and business. How they can no longer gather as a family or how one sibling despises another. I have lost count of the number of times a parent has broken down in tears and I've heard some version of, 'This is not worth it. If we'd have known that it was going to come to this, we'd never have started the business in the first place.' It is distressing to witness and worse to experience. Each one believes their situation is unusual and has therefore formed the belief that they have failed in some way. They fail to grasp that families collectively governing wealth, whether a business or a balance sheet, is a near impossible challenge. I hope this theorem reminds you of that. It's just not possible for it to work the way we think or assume it's going to work or should work. The complexities make that impossible without governance and stewardship.

As for the situation being unique, it's not. And part IV is designed to prove that. There are, in reality, a handful of scenarios that occur in family business time and time again. We will explore them now so that everyone inside a family business can finally realise that there is nothing unique or unusual about their problems. And, more importantly, that there is a solution, which is tested, proven and always, *always* works.

John is an Australian migrant having arrived from England when he was five years old. Making Australia his home, John got into construction straight out of school and started Jackson Developments & Construction with his wife Ayesha in 1983.

The business has seen some changes over the years but it's been very successful. John could easily sell it and live a life of luxury but he's a grafter. He wants to stick around and dabble and more than anything he wants to create a legacy. Typical of G1s with children, John can't make up his mind what he should do in regard to his business. If he's honest he's not sure which, if any, of his children are up to the task. None seem to have his all-around experience or insight.

John is stuck. He wants to step back but doesn't know how or when to do that and he's not comfortable in making that lifestyle change until he feels confident the business is in good hands.

Ayesha is also a migrant, arriving from Sri Lanka as a child in the mid-1960s. Like John's parents, Ayesha's carved out a life and a home in Australia through sheer hard work and determination. Australia has always been home for both Ayesha and John.

Ayesha and John were married when she was 20 and he was 24. Christopher was born in 1985. Priya followed a year later, then Nathan and Anika. Ayesha continued to work with John after Christopher was born but stopped once Priya arrived. By the time Christopher arrived, John had progressed his foray into building property. When the children were in school Ayesha went back to work for the business and stayed involved for many years.

Ayesha can see John's hesitation around succession. He's old school so doesn't really believe that Priya, as a woman, can manage the business. Ayesha works hard to dispel that myth but she's not convinced she's making any headway. She knows he recognises parts of his sons are positive for the business but those positive parts are not in the same son! Nathan has his qualities and his drawbacks as does Christopher, so there is no logical or clear choice to take over.

Ayesha has always worried about Christopher and Nathan as they have never seen eye to eye or been friends. They love each other but don't necessarily like each other and she can't see how that would work in a business where one would need to be in charge.

Ayesha is stuck because she can see what the situation is doing to John *and* their children.

Christopher as the oldest son has always felt the burden of succession even though he is also acutely aware that his dad isn't all in on the idea. Christopher is sure that he would have preferred that Nathan be the eldest son and then it would be easier. John is traditional so the eldest son idea still holds sway with him. Christopher and John are very different people. John is a grafter, hands-on. He built the business up from nothing and did everything in the business onsite and off. Christopher is a thinker. He's always been happier in an office working on the creative side of the business rather than being knee deep in dirt on the site. This is why he studied architecture. If he was being honest with himself, he would probably have preferred graphic design but he decided that architecture was a good compromise that might keep his dad happy. He's not sure it has.

In many ways Christopher is trying to find his own path but keep onside with the family business at the same time. He loves John and doesn't want to disappoint him but he dislikes Nathan a lot and has zero interest in working under him or over him. Nathan is more like John, and Christopher often feels diminished because of it – as though they are both in on some private joke that he doesn't understand. And yet he does enjoy being involved in the family business – he's just not sure he wants to get involved in all the parts of the business, which being CEO would demand.

Christopher is stuck living a half life trying to keep his father happy but keep himself happy too.

JOHN 63

CHRISTOPHER 35

RYA

PRIYA 34

DELVYN
(ENGAGED)

MILLY-8

DAVID 6

AYESHA 59

NATHAN 32

GEORGIA

ANIKA 29

TOM

LIA 6

LUCY 6

BEN 2

Priya is the smartest of the four children, at least academically. Certainly, smarter than Nathan who appears to be the one most likely to take over the family firm. Priya is closer to Christopher and can see how he is struggling to find his place.

She is too. Despite having proven herself over and over again in the business, and gaining an engineering degree, she is still seen first and foremost as the boss's daughter. Not *child* but *daughter*. She's irritated that she doesn't make anywhere near what her brothers make despite doing equally important work.

Like Christopher she has limited interest in working in the business if Nathan takes over and as much as she believes he has talents and is valuable in the business she doesn't feel he has the nuance or brains to run it. Priya is thinking it may be time to leave.

Priya is also stuck because she can't get her dad to take her seriously but if she leaves the business, she might never get back in.

Nathan worked his way up in the business from school. He's had experience in most departments and understands the processes of building very well. As such, he believes (although he doesn't voice his belief) that he does most of the work and has for all intents and purposes taken over the top job from his dad.

In personality, looks and nature Nathan is most like John and he knows it. Nathan uses the difference between John and Christopher to stir up trouble and mock Christopher at pretty much every opportunity. He is also savvy enough to work that similarity with John in his favour – hence his belief that he will get the top job. He also believes that John connects with him in a way he doesn't with his other children, largely because John worked his way up in the building industry too. This isn't really true; John is proud of all his kids for different reasons.

Needless to say, Nathan doesn't believe he is being paid fairly. His irritation stems from the fact that both he and Christopher earn the same but Christopher, who is a qualified architect, only works part-time in the family business. He has his own business too. Nathan is sure that a good architect could be found for half the price. He's been told many times that Christopher bills the family business at a significant discount but he doesn't really believe that.

Nathan is also stuck because he doesn't have any qualifications to fall back on, unlike Priya, Christopher and Anika. He's not ready to set up on his own so his only options would be to work for a competitor and that doesn't feel right. He's also stuck because he believes he's entitled to take over the business now because he just is and besides, he sees himself as the favourite.

Anika never really paid that much attention to the family business. As the youngest there were already too many siblings vying for attention in that regard. She knew pretty early on that she needed to forge her own path outside the business. But she is aware of the family wealth after something was said in passing at a Christmas gathering that made her realise the extent of that wealth. Now she is increasingly worried that her lack of attention will prevent her from benefiting from it, and to add to her woes she feels guilty for having those thoughts. She has recently opened her own restaurant with the help of her parents but it has already caused friction in her relationship with her brothers and sister. This was only cleared up when they found out that the money was a loan and not a gift.

Anika is stuck too because she is as much part of the family as her siblings; and yet, if she benefits in any way from the wealth the business has created, she is made to feel guilty. She is also a mum and is concerned that her own children will miss out on a better life because she didn't get involved in the family business. She knows this is ridiculous and that she has followed her heart but she still worries that she's done the wrong thing.

PART IV

Part IV begins your governance journey. We'll use the hypothetical Jackson family as an example of a family business going from ungoverned to governed. We'll look at how that comes about and how governance is the answer regardless of the question.

CHAPTER 15

Ungoverned to Governed

When a family shares their story with me, as much as it is important to listen to the words they say (the content), what is more important is listening for clues (context) regarding the founder profile, the next generation profile, the family dynamics and the trusted advisor framework. In other words, the answers to just four questions:

1. Is the founder motivated to find a solution? (Yes or no.)
2. Is the next generation ready? (Ready and impatient, ready and patient or not ready.)
3. What is the level of family hostility or dysfunction? (Normal levels of family dysfunction or hostile.)
4. Does the family have a history of employing trusted advisors when needed? (Yes or no.)

The answers to these four questions tells me pretty much everything I need to know to figure out the governance sequence best suited to that family and bring about the biggest wins in the shortest time.

Throughout the book I have introduced you to a fictitious family – the Jacksons. The Jacksons are stuck. In terms of the above questions, John is motivated, albeit a little reluctant to step fully away. The next generation are ready and impatient but are unclear of their roles or career progression and opportunities. The level of family dysfunction is pretty normal – the brain limitations cause a typical level of angst. On the bright side, they can all be in the same room as each other without breaking into a cold sweat. The family is used to employing trusted advisors from time to time although they are more familiar with employing a lawyer or accountant rather than a governance advisor. Surprise, surprise: John Jackson 'hates' consultants. On the whole, the Jackson family business is functional but largely ungoverned. There is no formal governance. And what *that* means is that everything will probably tick along pretty well until John dies. If there is no governance in place before that happens then chaos and dysfunction are almost inevitable.

Thankfully, John is smart enough to recognise that he needs some objectivity. The one thing that every family business is always woefully short on is objectivity. So, he decides to take the bull by the horns and ask a trusted advisor to meet with him and Ayesha. He recognises the challenges on the horizon. To be honest many of the challenges are in the here and now. But he wants to know that the trusted advisor has a plan and isn't just going to bamboozle him with industry jargon. Is there a proven process or road map so the whole family can move on together? Is there a way to become unstuck?

Over coffee in the Jackson Developments & Construction boardroom the advisor opens the discussion with John and Ayesha by reminding them that when it comes to family business there are three domains or circles. The advisor draws the three-circle model from chapter 13.

What follows is the conversation between John, Ayesha and the advisor …

'Right now, the Jacksons' three circles of family, business and owner-ship (wealth) are virtually indistinguishable from each other …' says the advisor as he draws the circles in figure 15.1 on the whiteboard.

Figure 15.1: Current Jackson Reality

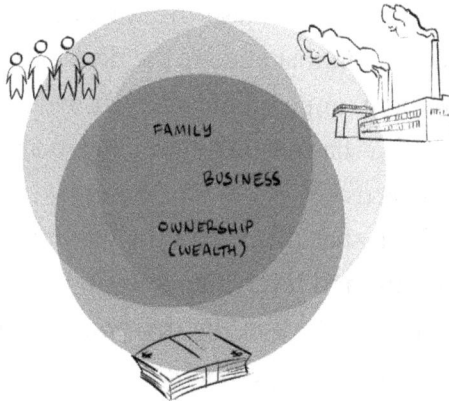

'Your goal is to separate those circles consciously and deliberately using governance and stewardship', the advisor says, as he draws fig-ure 15.2 on the whiteboard.

Figure 15.2: Optimal Jackson Reality

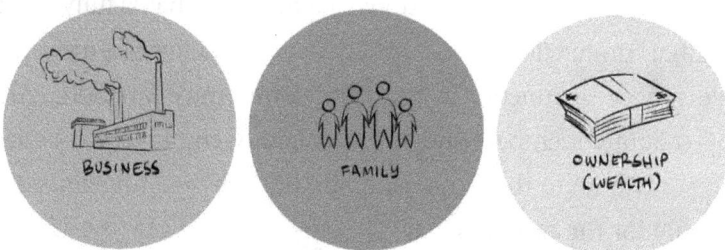

John and Ayesha are interested, but wonder, 'Is there a system to achieve this?'

'Let me explain,' says the trusted advisor. 'First you need to separate the business circle.'

Establishing the Business Circle

'In order to begin the process of separating the business from the family and the ownership or wealth, Jackson Developments & Construction must be given a personality independent of the two of you as cofounders. Up to this point you are the business. The name of the business is your name. You are also the walking-talking governance system of your business in that you are the decision-making protocol. Engineered by you both, imposed in large part by John.'

John laughs and Ayesha rolls her eyes. They both know that what the advisor is saying is true.

'So, I'm right about that then!' says the advisor. 'John, you make all the key decisions and everyone knows it. You may include Christopher, Nathan and Priya in the decision-making process along with key non-family staff, but you have the final say and everyone is clear about that. And hey – that's totally understandable, and probably works pretty well.

'But, for the business to take on its own identity it must be separated from your identity. This is achieved via the preparation of a strategic plan.[68] The strategic plan speaks for the business. It's not the ambitions of the individuals in the business, in this case you, Christopher, Nathan and Priya. It is the ambitions of a business that is fully realising its potential, understands the marketplace and delivers a meaningful, credible service or function within that community for profit. All the employed family members and key non-family employees are encouraged to contribute to that strategic plan, but the resulting agreed plan speaks only for the business.'

'We have a strategic plan, we're not that backward!' says John, a little indignantly.

'I'm sure you do, but does your strategic plan go into enough detail to allow you to assess the agreed direction against the current capability in the business?' the advisor asks. John doesn't answer.

Further investigation uncovers that the 'strategic plan' John is confident he has is a mental spreadsheet that defines scale, profitability, preferred markets and strengths to play to. It is clearly written – in his head. It is the expression of his experience, largely undocumented, and his learnt capabilities. Having avoided the discipline of documenting the corporate (his own) memory, John retains the mystery around his genius. It hardwires the rocky road ahead without governance.

Remember, the degree of pain endured by a wealthy family in the absence of the founder reflects the founder's failure to respond to the consequences of having been successful. It is not a reflection on the family.

The advisor continues, 'Without a clear and rigorous strategy, it's really hard to determine whether you have the right people in the business to deliver on that strategy. Instead, you rely on filling gaps or moving people sideways to cover shortfalls or try to shoehorn family members into those gaps. This strategic assessment will include employed family members and non-family members alike and is seeking to answer the question, "Does the business currently have the experience, capability and skill set necessary to deliver on the strategy?" With a well-articulated strategy that considers the landscape inside and outside the business, it becomes possible to assess family members' employed relationships with the business.

'One of the reasons that you are stuck is because you are probably unsure if any of your children should or could take over the business. From what you've told me they each have their own strengths and weaknesses, making that decision difficult. Is that right?'

'Well, yes,' says John. 'Christopher is the oldest and if he was more interested in the actual building side of things, rather than just the design, he would be the logical choice, but I just don't think his heart is in it. Plus, he and Nathan don't get on. Priya is smart as a whip but construction is no place for a woman. Ayesha disagrees with me on this but I've been on building sites. I don't want her having to deal with that nonsense. And Nathan is gung-ho and really enthusiastic but he leads with his gut. He's not got the brains of the other two to step back and see the bigger picture. His decision-making is too rash for the top job – certainly just now.'

'Okay, I totally understand that,' says the advisor. 'But remember, this is your impression. You don't actually know. And without a detailed strategy the business is revolving around your skills, knowledge and experience. It does not have a voice of its own. You talk of Nathan leading with his gut – does that remind you of anyone? To what extent is that the characteristic that has brought the business to this point? What's useful is an objective measure of capabilities assessed against what is needed in the business now as opposed to what was needed at start-up. To deliver on the Jackson Developments & Construction strategy, does the business need the types of skills and experience that Christopher, Nathan and Priya have? Only when the strategic plan is clearly spelt out can that question be asked and answered. If they do have the needed skills, then the next stage would be to define the commercial relationship between each family member who is employed in the business, and the business itself.

'I'm wondering, how do you currently pay Christopher, Nathan and Priya?' asks the advisor.

'They get a decent salary. Chris's architecture practice bills me the same amount as I pay Nathan, and Priya gets about $10,000 less, but they are potentially owners so ...'

'So what?' enquires the advisor. 'Are you saying you pay them less than you would someone else doing a similar role because they are your children and will, presumably, inherit the business?'

'Well, yes, but there's more to it than that,' stresses John.

'You're not going to like this, John, but there is no justification for paying your children less than what they are worth as a cost saving in lieu of future returns. Having this type of family subsidy and continuing it for as long as possible is a common mistake in family business. Senior leaders with the family surname are routinely underpaid based on the assumption that they are also owners and will eventually inherit the business. So, what? Are you saying that Christopher, a qualified architect, Nathan, a grafter who has worked his way up through the business, and Priya, a qualified engineer, should be happy to compromise their immediate real-world human value for some hypothetical future world value – just to subsidise Jackson Developments & Construction? Surely, you see that's nonsense – right? It's dangerous and it has to stop at the first opportunity. As soon as any business can afford to pay employed family members a commercial going-rate salary, the sooner that family can steer its way out of the murky waters of uneven or unfair distribution.'

'And,' adds the advisor, 'this professional commercialisation of the employment contract between employed family members and the business can now be done accurately because their activities form a part of the structure, which supports the strategy. The strategy is in turn endorsed by the shareholders, who fund it. In other words, having clear strategic objectives for the business allows each employed family member the opportunity to see if and how their current skill set fits into that strategic vision. And of course, it also gives you the same clarity.

'When the strategy is done it will be independent of you or any other employed member of the Jackson family. It will be the independent voice of Jackson Developments & Construction, and that business will finally be able to enter into an arrangement whereby the relationships it has with each employed member of the family and non-family employees is a function of their respective capabilities, skills, knowledge and evidenced performance – rather than their surname. Nothing else is relevant.

'This role clarity and definition is achieved through purposefully and well-drafted position descriptions.[69] The institution of position or job descriptions commercialises the relationship between family members and the business. Commercialising the relationship is done by answering the question, "What would it cost us to employ somebody with this skillset?" There are two forces that need to be governed regarding the commercialisation of each position. First is the evidence test, which is, broadly, "What salary does a person with that experience typically command in this industry?" And the second is the unique test, which is, "Does that individual have any special characteristics that would entitle them to a different compensation arrangement?" And, just to be clear, having 'Jackson' as a surname is not a special characteristic. But Christopher having a separate business with access to a larger team of architects and design professionals might be.

'Once the strategic plan and performance contracts are complete, Jackson Developments & Construction has its own voice, separate from you. It is articulated by the collectively agreed strategic plan. Any family members in the business are now in a role that is needed to achieve that strategic plan, and they are in that role not because they are family members but because they have already demonstrated the capability, experience and skill set to deliver their part towards that strategic objective – or they have used that clarity to make a different choice.

'How do your children feel right now?' asks the advisor.

'They are confused,' says Ayesha. 'Especially Priya. She knows John doesn't believe construction is a suitable profession for women. He's never said it, of course, but he doesn't need to. I think Christopher feels guilty and is trying to make everyone happy, and Nathan is irritated because he thinks he's most "qualified", and that he is "doing all the work"'.

'Exactly,' says the advisor. 'They don't know what's possible or what they want, so they are in this weird limbo waiting for you to make a decision. It may very well be that a great deal of your confusion will disappear when their confusion disappears. The strategic plan is the first part of that puzzle and the personal plans are the second. I'll explain that in more detail in a moment, but in short the personal plans allow everyone in the business to engage with their own capabilities and aspirations. That process may illuminate for Priya that she actually doesn't want to be in the business, and you have one less problem. But, if your children do decide to stay in the business, there must be a genuine role for them – one that supports the strategy and in which they are paid the going market rate for their respective positions. That salary must not be altered in any way (up or down) as a result of their familial connection to you.

'This disregard of familial relationships to position or compensation puts your children on a solid commercial and professional footing that then separates the business circle from the family and ownership or wealth circles. Christopher, Priya and Nathan may still be employed by the family business but if they are, they are treated the same as any other key non-family employee. Their surname becomes irrelevant in the context of the business and working towards the strategic objective. This allows each sibling, including Anika who is not employed in the business, to arrive at the beneficiary or ownership table as an equal. Plus, Nathan can't claim that Christopher is making more because his business is billing Jackson Developments & Construction, and Christopher and Priya can't be irritated because their qualifications aren't being recognised or compensated for. By taking these crucial governance steps, you put an end to any real or perceived family subsidising.

'And, perhaps more importantly, the Jackson business circle has been successfully separated from the family circle and the ownership circle. Does that make sense?'

Both John and Ayesha nod. Finally, there seems to be a glimmer of hope that all is not lost and that something might be able to be done to help the business and the family.

Establishing the Family Circle

'Okay,' continues the advisor. 'Now we need to separate the family circle. To do that you need to understand what the family wants. What are Christopher's personal dreams and aspirations? Do you know what Priya really wants to achieve in life? Do you have any idea what Nathan is aiming for? And what about Anika? Do you know what your children want? Forget the business for a moment – as individual human beings, what do your children dream of?'

'I don't know, we don't talk about that sort of stuff,' says John. 'I know Anika wants to create a successful restaurant, but beyond that they don't talk much.'

'Don't feel bad about it,' says the advisor. 'Most people haven't got a clue. The solution is a personal plan. These personal plans ensure that each family member, regardless of whether they are currently employed in the business or not, is charged with the responsibility of clearly and openly declaring the future they want for themselves.[70] It's worth pointing out that personal plans are not compulsory – until a family has a business or shared wealth. Even then, it is okay for an individual to step away from the business, family or wealth and divine a private pathway. However, if that individual is to govern their wealth, and if family members intend to influence that wealth, they must declare their hand, otherwise the family is governed by default settings. The resulting plan, which covers personal and professional aspirations, describes what success looks like for each member of the family over a set period of time. Too often these questions are left unasked and unanswered so no one knows what the others want. Personal plans bring those aspirations out into the open so that you can say, as parents, founders and life partners, "This is our plan for our future. It provides a clear basis for understanding what drives our point of view about both the business circle and the ownership circle." Your children no longer have to wonder; instead, they can figure out if they want to fit into that picture via the business or not. They can then make their aspiration clear to you. You can then guide and support your children on how best to make those aspirations a reality within the strategic direction of the business, or outside the business. Remember, this knowledge of aspirations led to your support of Anika. But that only happened because Anika was clear about what she wanted. Personal plans give that opportunity to your other children, too.

'Once that work is completed, everyone can sit at the table – business or kitchen – with the personality differences between each family member moderated. There is always a louder voice in every family. Sometimes that louder voice might come from the oldest or most domineering child, who is then the most likely to win an argument simply because everyone else gives up or others don't have the ability to put their case forward with clarity. In your family, who has the loudest voice?'

'Oh, that's easy!' laughs Ayesha. 'John. If John isn't there, Nathan. The oldest, Christopher, has always struggled to get his point across without Nathan undermining him or making fun of him. The girls can and do stand up for themselves but they tend to pick their battles.'

'Makes sense', says the advisor. 'The great thing about personal plans is they help nullify these typical family dysfunctions by giving each individual family member a voice while also helping them to gain clarity about what they want in their own future, either inside or outside the business. Never underestimate the influence you both have had on the career choices and life paths of your children. The name of the business is Jackson Developments & Construction. Every conversation at the dinner table for the first 20 or so years of their lives involved Jackson Developments & Construction. Every Saturday job was at Jackson Developments & Construction. Whether deliberate or not you have influenced the path or perceived path for your family. Personal planning presses the pause button on that influence and encourages each of your children to really consider all their options.

What is it they really want? This clarity allows each family member to step into their own journey with authenticity and ensure that they get to the negotiating table equally. This isn't about equal weight of each voice in relation to the business, however; should your voice have any more influence on the lives of your adult children than their own? Only you can decide your shared future. And the same is true for Christopher, Priya, Nathan and Anika along with their partners.

'This process also creates a rational and logical opportunity to include their partners. Again, the mistake that is frequently made in family business is that it's just too complicated to involve the second generation's partners. It's not. Each of your children have one vote. If they are in a relationship, they still have one vote, only now that single vote is shared with their partner 50/50. Assuming they have a rational and reasonable partner, 50 percent of their vote then belongs to their partner. That partner's voice is therefore heard in the preparation of the personal ambition of each of your children.

'For example, when Christopher prepares his personal plan, he will do so with his wife Rya. They might talk about where they want to live, where they want their children to grow up, what schools they want their children to go to and what opportunities they want their children to have, what career path Christopher wants for himself and what career path Rya wants. These are likely to be issues they have already discussed, and all of them can be accounted for and taken into consideration when thinking about the future pathways for them both. The same is true for each sibling. Their plan will include their partner and their partner will have shared influence regarding anything that impacts their unique family.

'Once this work is complete all four children are well represented. Instead of waiting and wondering if or how they might fit into the family business at some point in the future, they step back and assess what they really want to achieve individually. Those aspirations may or may not involve the business and they may or may not be possible, but at least the individual is setting the agenda. They have stepped out of the shadow of the business, if only for an afternoon, to genuinely consider their own future and what they want that future to entail. That clarity can be liberating and energising for both the individuals themselves and likewise for you as the founders of the business.

'Each family member has their own voice irrespective of their role in the business and their partner's voice is represented in that plan. And each of your children knows what they want to achieve in the years ahead and has a plan to deliver that outcome.

'It's important to reiterate at this point that the personal plans are personal. They are used to empower the planner, the individual. When each person presents their personal plans to the family, they do not share the information verbatim. They don't include any judgements or comments they have made about other family members. This means that, instead of hearing, "This is what I think of you all", the family hears, "This is what is important to me, what I want to achieve, and how I intend to go about it."

'The next step in the process to separate the family from the business and wealth is to create a structure around the way Jackson Developments & Construction makes decisions moving forward. John, you've said you want to step back, but you're worried that if you do, Christopher and Nathan will just argue endlessly. The personal planning process will allow you to see a way forward for the first time. The information from these personal plans allows you to be cognisant of everybody's individual points of view which, in turn, allows you to move away from the founder role to a stewardship role. As steward your role is to help the family define a destination that everyone can get behind, which will take the whole family on the journey together where each family member feels valued. The direction of travel and making sure the family stays intact during that journey is much more important than the eventual destination. Stewardship therefore begins with individual wellbeing; transitions into team effectiveness; and ultimately leads to larger family business considerations such as ensuring that family values and missions remain relevant and contemporary.'

Augmenting Governance through a Family Charter

The advisor continues: 'John, if you, as the current walking-talking governance framework, are to step back effectively and with confidence, a replacement governance framework needs to be installed so that everyone in the business, family member or non-family member, knows how decisions are made: by whom, when and in what forum. What belongs at the dinner table, what belongs at the board table and so on. These decisions might include things like how you endorse the strategy of the business, which family members might be appointed to hold board seats and what to do with the shared family assets. These and countless other decisions will be documented in a Family Charter. The Family Charter also affords the whole family an opportunity to create a culturally competent set of family values that are agreed and implemented as an institution through the family and the business, that will live on through the charter to inspire generations to come.'

STEWARDSHIP THEREFORE BEGINS WITH INDIVIDUAL
WELLBEING; TRANSITIONS INTO TEAM EFFECTIVENESS;
AND ULTIMATELY LEADS TO LARGER FAMILY BUSINESS
CONSIDERATIONS SUCH AS ENSURING THAT FAMILY VALUES
AND MISSIONS REMAIN RELEVANT AND CONTEMPORARY.

'So, hang on, the Family Charter is different from the personal plans?' asks Ayesha.

'Yes,' says the advisor. 'Think of the strategic plan as giving the business a voice, the personal plans as giving individuals a voice, and the Family Charter as giving the family a voice. All are necessary to separate the circles. A Family Charter needs to be authored to document values and how the family makes decisions. This will include how the Jacksons make decisions about personal assets and the expectations your children may place on those assets while you are both alive and after you're gone. Sorry to be so blunt. For example, I understand you own a ski lodge. Do you have any expectations or hopes around that asset?'

'Well, yes actually,' says John. 'We have always had such great family holidays there, so we would like that property to be the place the family comes together at least once a year to ski and enjoy each other's company – no shop talk.'

'Okay, well, that would go in the charter. You are not saying the family must do that after you die, but right now, as the asset exists, you would like this wish to be known to the family. Without this knowledge and its formal expression, the question "what should we do with the lodge?" can become a trigger for default settings.

'The charter should also set out how the family makes decisions about endorsement of the trading business's strategy, and about the career pathways or migration of non-employed family into the business or into and out of positions of influence.

'The Family Council is then the body that "governs" the charter and ensures it is contemporary and remains relevant. A Family Council includes representation of all generations that have reached the age of majority.

'If the business is being discussed, the Family Charter or the Family Council decides whether to invite non-family employed representatives into the meeting to advocate or speak for the business so that a family member's position is not compromised. This ensures family members are not expected to wear two hats at once. The role of the CEO of the business may be laid out together with performance expectations of that role and what will happen if that person decides to step down or doesn't meet the required standards. The Family Charter is a comprehensive document that covers a vast range of possible future scenarios and how they will be dealt with and decided upon. And the Family Charter is created and agreed collectively and reviewed periodically. This document is crucial in the separation of the family circle from the business and ownership circles.'

The advisor continues, 'In addition, family matters must be systematically removed from the business. Every family business starts life in a place where the family, the business and the wealth are indistinguishable from each other – we talked about that right at the start. This marks the start of a journey. The only question is whether you are going to elegantly and purposefully separate the family, the business and the wealth (the three circles) or wait for the inevitable catastrophe that will rip them apart. The removal of family affairs from the business is part of the process and represents a shift to mature and disciplined administration of family affairs.

THE ONLY QUESTION IS WHETHER YOU ARE GOING TO ELEGANTLY AND PURPOSEFULLY SEPARATE THE FAMILY, THE BUSINESS AND THE WEALTH (THE THREE CIRCLES) OR WAIT FOR THE INEVITABLE CATASTROPHE THAT WILL RIP THEM APART.

'Typically, this is known as a "family office" but I know this is a terrible term. The idea of family office causes nothing but grief because it triggers a whole bunch of default settings about bureaucracy as well as waves of really intense emotional reaction from anger through to stonewalling. While the term is dangerous and unproductive, the idea is not.

'Do you find that you are asking people in your business to do things that are related to the family?' asked the advisor.

'I try not to, but it's impossible to avoid at times,' admits John.

The advisor continues: 'Looking at your balance sheet and recognising the size of the business I can assure you that the time has now passed where it is appropriate to ask a member of staff if they could pick up your grandchildren from school, and it probably feels bizarre to be asking a PA to organise travel arrangements for the family to your Hamilton Island holiday home, while also organising John's birthday bash. As Jackson Developments & Construction has grown and employed more and more people across different locations, the family's personal or non-business affairs have almost certainly become a burden on the business. It's time for the two to be separated. How that is done will depend on you and how you choose to answer the question, "What is a better or different way to manage the family's personal, non-business affairs?"

'Those personal and non-business affairs might be investment advice for the children, or how to manage the family's recreation assets and provide equitable access to them. It might include organising the family rhythm or meeting agenda, the calendar of family events, the funding, booking or organisation of family events as well as travel, managing frequent flyer points, or the funding and investment in education for your children and future generations.

'My guess is that you have certainly reached the point where your personal affairs are more than an executive assistant can or is willing to handle, and it's time for change. Even the use of a PA for personal matters is increasingly frowned on.'

'Yes, I am aware of that and I'm conscious we need a different solution,' admits John.

'The tipping point where separation becomes essential is that moment where your family's affairs, personal and non-business, are of a magnitude or dimension that, to continue to have the business manage them, causes many negative outcomes.

'There are a number of practical and financial considerations that make the separate management of personal matters effective. First, employed members of the business must no longer be asked to do things that are prone to misunderstanding, appear demeaning or, worse, appear to be seen by others as a means to "infiltrate" the family. Your staff must not be put in awkward situations that have no bearing on their job description. The other benefit is that this entity, whatever it is called, now contains most of your joint personal assets that have no bearing on or relevance to the business. It will include the holiday home and the ski lodge as well any other properties or assets you have. Creating such an entity therefore shifts the dynamic between you and your children as their relationship with the family's shared wealth is through this entity rather than through you personally. Your grandchildren might request a small stipend to assist them through university, for example, but that request, outlined and agreed as possible in the Family Charter, would be made to this entity – not to you directly as "granny and grandad". And whatever arrangement is agreed in the Family Charter would be available to all your grandchildren equally should they seek assistance through university.

'Once the work on the Family Charter is complete, the business and family circles are largely separated. The business has a voice and the family has a voice. Can you see how this process will make your life so much easier, minimise disputes and allow you to know the business is in safe hands and the family is still connected and happy?'

'Absolutely,' says Ayesha. 'This seems like a formula for sustainability, allowing our wealth to be a catalyst for family togetherness, rather than a wedge.' John then replies, 'Yes, we don't want to end up like the …' and proceeds to rattle off the names of several wealthy friends whose families have imploded due to their wealth.

Establishing the Ownership or Wealth Circle

'Okay, fantastic', says the advisor. 'Now there's just one more circle to disentangle from the current family arrangements, business and all.

'Clearly, Jackson Developments & Construction has been extremely successful and the business has created significant wealth. That wealth should be governed by shares, titles, trusts and registered interests. As such, at least in theory, it is the easiest to define. The relationship between the family and the wealth should be outlined in the Family Charter. Beyond that, do you hope to pass both the wealth and potentially the business on to your children in some form or another?'

'Well, yes, of course,' reply John and Ayesha in unison.

'Again, the rules and decision-making protocols regarding the wealth will be spelt out in the Family Charter.'

Transition of Wealth or Wealth Plus Business

When we talk about love, loyalty and wealth, we're not talking about the compulsory inclusion of a trading business. Our examples all revolve around the transition of wealth and a trading business because that's the most complex. If you've got a balance sheet without a trading business, that still needs to be managed. You may appoint investment advisors to ensure the family wealth is governed properly but there's less complexity. That said, a balance sheet still needs a similar governance framework, individuals being able to speak for themselves together with clear decision-making rules around the balance sheet.

Finding a home for Philanthropy

'The last piece of governance is around philanthropy. Like many other families with wealth, you are expected to use at least some of that wealth for the greater good. This adds even more complexity and uncertainty about whether your gifting is well placed. I know you are especially concerned about this Ayesha. You're not sure if your gifting is achieving what you intend. Most jurisdictions provide legal instruments to facilitate philanthropic governance. In Australia it's called a private ancillary fund (PAF) and it has useful tax incentives. There are lots of rules around the use of PAFs but they are well governed.

What's especially useful about PAFs is that they can only invest in things that are properly endorsed and evidenced to be community focused. They can't be used as a family slush fund. The institution of a Jackson PAF might be useful to aid in the separation of the circles.

'It's also worth noting that, whether you like it or not, you've created sustainable wealth. This means that there are problems brewing that subsequent generations will face if you don't face them. How to manage wealth and how to best navigate the legislative frameworks around the wealth will almost certainly change. The world is changing, the divide between rich and poor is widening and there will be a reckoning. There has to be. Add a Covid-19 global economic slump and the cries for high wealth taxation and greater equality are inevitable. A changed regulatory environment that puts limits on how much wealth an individual can retain and control is not out of the question. Ensuring future generations are equipped to deal with these changes and actively engage in philanthropy to use that wealth for the greater good is important.

'Once this work has been done, you will have a full and comprehensive governance framework. You will no longer be stuck. The circles will have been purposefully and respectfully separated and a great deal of the complexity and uncertainty will have been removed from the family and the business.'

'Great!' says Ayesha. 'So how do we start?'

'Well, we might begin by letting the appropriately qualified professionals provide the right advice on the ownership circle. What is owned? How it is owned? And how does it transition to the next generation under the auspices of the state law, trust law or contract law? Then you have the business circle. It's now governed under the auspices of the strategic plan. The strategy defines the structure and the structure then defines the possible employment paths that Christopher, Priya and Nathan can pursue based on properly specified roles that have meaning and value. Should Anika ever want to join the family business the same process will apply and she will only be given a job that is required to deliver on the strategic plan and that she is qualified for.

'Later, should any of the family members leave the business and want to re-join the same process will apply and they will only be given a job that is required to deliver on the strategic plan and that they are qualified for.

'Each family member must then demonstrate their capabilities and subject themselves to the same rigour and discipline as any other employed person in the business, including annual reviews, skills assessments and appropriate training and development.

'As a result, when all four siblings are sitting with you enjoying a family dinner, Anika – who is not paid a salary because she doesn't work in the business – no longer has to worry whether she has the right to access the family ski lodge or holiday home. There is no inference, real or perceived, that she is at the back of the queue because she is not employed by the business. Why? Because the family, business and ownership or wealth circles have been separated through governance. The only debate is who wants to visit the lodge and when. If Priya and Nathan would like to visit on the same week then the family applies the tie break that appears in the Family Charter. Anika can expect the same as her siblings who are employed in the business in terms of distribution of wealth or access to family assets. And should Christopher, Nathan or Priya want to borrow money from you in the same way Anika did for her restaurant they can expect the same repayment terms. But all such decisions are clearly laid out in the Family Charter. Whether the siblings are employed by the business or not is irrelevant to distribution. Those that are employed are paid a proper commercial salary for their contribution and have equal rights to the ownership or wealth as those who have chosen to pursue a different path or career. If you are interested in equal distribution, then you'll consider all siblings equally regardless of their relationship with the family business. No one will be worried about whether it was fair or not because the employed siblings are already compensated for their work via a salary.

'The only touch point between the family as a family and the business is the family's right and obligation as shareholder influencers to endorse the strategic plan of the business, or to provide family constraints to the trading business. For example, the trading business might have restrictions on investment or trading with industries that the family believes are unethical or unsustainable. Everything else is left to the business and its management and leadership which, where that involves family members, is outlined in the Family Charter.

'At the family table, you will now have a governance framework that is driven by each individual being able to properly represent themselves. You will both be properly representing your ambitions for succession. And the children will be properly representing their ambitions for the future. They are each then able to sit at the table and engage in the Family Charter conversation and properly represent their views at the charter table. And through that process, you'll also have dealt fairly and equitably with your children's life partners because each partner has 50 percent of their family's one vote, however that is represented at the table.

'If you action this plan as steward, John, you will have successfully put your family in a position where they can say:

- "We're well governed."
- "We're connected as a family."
- "We're not defined by our wealth but we manage our wealth efficiently."
- "We're confident the business, our wealth and the family will endure for generations to come."
- "Each of us understands and respects our relationship with both the business and the wealth."'

'I must say,' says John, 'I am relieved this process exists. Even more so that it has been tried and well tested. Up to this point I thought two things: firstly, that I would have to solve this problem (I guess that's my MO) and secondly, that I would have to invent the solution somehow. I really thought it would be a combination of good lawyers and good luck. It appears I don't need to count on either! What you are demonstrating is that, like building a block of apartments, there is one best way to do this, and it works, and it is sustainable.'

'Yes!' confirmed the advisor. 'Collectively, this is the solution. It is always the solution. And it can eradicate the vast majority of complexity, uncertainty and hostility or dysfunction that is so often viewed as inevitable or normal in family business. And it can ensure the continuation of love, loyalty and wealth. All you need to decide is whether you are ready to do the work.'

CHAPTER 16

Governance Variations

All the commentary in chapter 15 assumed that John Jackson was willing and motivated to find a solution to ensure the business transitioned from one generation to the next. This is not always the case, and it's worth exploring the various governance options for other situations.

Founder Not Willing

In the case of John Jackson, he was at least partially interested in stepping back and finding a way to hand the business on to G2 that didn't cause chaos for the business or the family. But there are founders who are simply not willing to consider succession. This is fine. You can still put a governance framework in place with the intention that it will be activated when G1 dies.

I have met several founders over the years who would fall into this category. They are often larger-than-life charismatic figures who are in charge and everyone knows it. They may have a notion of succession or may even like the idea that their children will inherit and run the business, but that often tenuous future often pales into insignificance against what they want to do with the business today. Such an approach rarely comes from a place of malice; it is simply an expression of undiminished ambition. It's their business, their baby and no one can run it as well as they can. The unspoken theme of this is: 'once I'm dead my children can fight over the future of the business and ownership.'

But, even if that is the case, there is nothing to stop those children from getting together to institute a governance framework before the founder's death so that there is no fighting. That framework could include how the business will operate once G1 is gone. Clearly, a thorough governance framework may need to understand the nature of the estate but that can still be negotiated. I'm aware of situations for example where the founder has said, 'I'm not going to spell out my estate – you'll find that out when I'm dead – but I will let you know if you're doing something that's not going to succeed in the framework I have in place.'

Again – that's totally fine. No drama. Most founders, even unwilling or uncooperative G1s, don't want everything they've built to fall in a heap the minute they die. Governance that is therefore activated after death can be hugely appealing because it allows them to continue running the business the way they want but protects its survival as well as family relationships once they are gone.

I'm also aware of founders providing total transparency to say, 'This is the estate and this is how I'm going to manage the estate.' In one case, there was even a post-founder death three-year plan where the transition had already been agreed. It was the best example of governance from the grave I've ever seen. Not only was the founder unwilling to entertain succession in any meaningful way, she insisted on a three-year transition *after* her death before G2 could take over from the employed staff that she'd put in place. This G1 was afraid that G2 would come into the business, boot out all the loyal and capable staff she'd worked with for years and derail her strategy. She wanted the strategy to survive, whether she was alive or dead, and she ensured that her children signed off on all the documentation to defend her approach. As for G2, initially they hated the idea but that passed very quickly and they have instead been liberated by it. They know exactly where they stand, they know what's going to happen and are managing their own affairs, governing their own wealth and taking responsibility for their own lifepaths. They are relieved because when their mother dies, they can grieve in peace as the weight of business responsibility will stay in the business as their mother intended before eventually migrating to them via a properly constituted board, where G2 have a fair and influential voice based on their capabilities and not their surnames. By the end of the three years G2 will have built the relationships with, and endorsed the continued engagement of, G1's chosen loyal people, in which case G2 may leave them in place as employees even though they are now in total control. Alternatively, G2 may decide they are not happy with their performance over that three-year period and decide to take the business in a different direction. The founder's view is that if she can ensure that nothing rash happens for three years, then everyone in the business, including her children, will have learned what they need to learn. Everybody will have grown into the roles that they should have. And the employed staff that contributed to G1's success will have been given the best opportunity to demonstrate their capability to G2 and thus stay in place.

There is also a hybrid possibility if G1 is unwilling. In this case the business leadership role might transition, but the management and ownership of the wealth might not. For example, there could be a situation where a family has done a lot of work to agree to a governance framework, but it hasn't been activated yet. Each year the family assesses the situation to determine if it is ready to activate any of the framework. The assessment depends on the family state of health, balance sheets and the economy. But having the framework ready to go has mitigated the uncertainty and complexity the family would be living under otherwise. And, even better, the hostility between the siblings which was causing everyone pain and unhappiness has disappeared.

In this situation, some of the wealth was divested from G1 to G2, which empowered G2 to run their own race. G1 still has 10 to 12 times what G2 inherited and remain in control of this wealth. Eventually G1 will probably apply a portion of their wealth to a PAF and another portion into a futures fund for the next generation. At that point, they might invite G2 to join them in managing that wealth so they can see that it's in safe hands before they die.

Let me be crystal clear: the only way a founder can ever be certain of protecting the wealth and keeping the family connected beyond their lifetime is to have governance in place and working, independently of them, before they die.

As a parent we teach our children to ride a push bike by adding stabilisers and holding on to the seat until they gain enough balance and confidence to ride without support. Expecting G2 to manage money well when G1 has never let go of the financial bicycle seat is madness. Any G1 who expects G2 to learn how to manage wealth must allow them to witness G1 managing wealth and be involved in the decision-making process. If G1 hasn't seen G2 managing wealth successfully or even relatively successfully on their watch then the family is on the road back to shirt sleeves. It's virtually inevitable. G1 is basically creating a 'lottery win' situation for their own children. Lottery wins rarely end well because the people who win the money have no real-world experience with that type of wealth and end up making poor choices, driven by short-term euphoria, quirky passions (like buying football clubs) or hubris and ego. This is not the position any responsible G1 wants to put their children or grandchildren in. And it's certainly not the position they should put them in if they genuinely want to create a legacy.

THE ONLY WAY A FOUNDER CAN EVER BE CERTAIN OF PROTECTING THE WEALTH AND KEEPING THE FAMILY CONNECTED BEYOND THEIR LIFETIME IS TO HAVE GOVERNANCE IN PLACE AND WORKING, INDEPENDENTLY OF THEM, BEFORE THEY DIE.

Next Generation Variations

If a G1 is unwilling to institute governance or take succession seriously it is very unlikely that G2 will be ready. G2 only become ready when a founder is willing. G2 may become ready outside the family business but they will almost certainly be hindered by G1 in the family business. Even if they do demonstrate capability an unwilling G1 will rarely recognise that capability. Again, this points back to the incredible influence that parents have on their children. Remember, the single biggest lie that any parent can tell themselves is, 'I never influenced the career choices of my children.' Every parent influences their children: they are either influencing them towards a particular business or industry or away from it, but there is no such thing as neutral.

In the eyes of G1, especially an unwilling or uncooperative founder, their children are always their children. It doesn't matter how old they are, they are viewed as 'children'. That is why objectivity is necessary in the assessment of the capabilities of those children. It's why a trusted advisor is so useful in this process, because they can provide an independent view of real capabilities versus imagined capabilities (by G1 and G2). I've lost count of the number of times where, as a result of the work we've done in the family business, G1 has come to terms with the fact that G2 is far more capable than they imagined. Often, this is a revelation.

Performance contracts, the implementation of proper commercial relationships between the employed family members and the business together with a clear strategic plan allows G1 to appreciate the inherent value in their children. And they can finally see the capabilities that they can so readily see in their children's friends or friends' children but not their *own* children.

Whether the next generation are ready or not largely comes down to G1 and their attitude.

Next Generation Ready?

Of course, 'ready' is not like a light switch where we flick a switch and G2 goes from not ready to ready. The real question isn't 'are they ready?', it's 'do they demonstrate enough qualities and enough skills to prove that, with the right encouragement, they will eventually be ready?' If the answer is yes, they're ready – because whatever G1 puts in place, the owner of the assets is going to have the final say over what happens to them.

And to the extent that G1 still owns the assets, handing over and engaging with G2, watching them make decisions and being the auditor and the safety net, means that it doesn't matter whether they are 20 percent ready or 30 percent, 40 percent, 70 percent. If I ask a G1 to give me a percentage of G2's readiness, whatever they say I double it. Besides, tools such as performance contracts will illuminate whether they are ready or not. Either way governance is the solution.

The governance framework is the same. The objective is always the same – separate the three circles. And the process towards that outcome is always the same. First the business gets a voice of its own as articulated by the strategy. The current employees, including employed family members, are then assessed against what's needed to deliver that strategy. Performance contracts will objectively determine whether G2 are ready and/or capable for the roles that are required to deliver the strategy. The personal plans give every family member a voice; they highlight where each family member wants to be. The Family Charter (the family voice) sets out how shared decisions are made, including whether a family member is ready and how they can get ready if they are currently deemed 'not ready'.

If the G2s are highlighted as not ready to take on the leadership role then either G1 stays in place as the leader or a new leader is appointed based on the Family Charter. Once G1 dies or steps away from the business or if that new leader fails, G2 meet in the boardroom and engage in an orderly search for an appropriate replacement. They activate their prescribed asset fund; activate the rhythm of meetings; and they schedule time to celebrate the founder's achievements through the Family Retreat (this also gives spouses and the generations that follow a voice). They initiate a search for a new business leader based on the strategy, the business and the evidenced capabilities of G2.

In one family I work with there are five siblings, all of whom have worked in the business at some time. The oldest is the CEO and was given that role based on his capabilities and past performance. There are very clear expectations of what the CEO must deliver over a set period of time. If he does not deliver, he must step down and a new CEO will be appointed based on the same clearly defined capabilities. Everyone knows the process they must go through to appoint senior positions. There's no debate or argument. There's nobody saying, 'Hang on, isn't it my turn to be CEO now?' Any G2 is a potential CEO of the business if they want that role BUT there is an agreed process to go through for selection, as outlined in the Family Charter. The family has agreed that if a family member is equal in capability and experience to other applicants, then the family member gets the job. Or, if the family member commits to the professional development required to take on that role, they are given a provisional period in the role to demonstrate their capability – provided they also undertake the professional development necessary to close any capabilities or skills gaps.

If performance contracts and skills assessments demonstrate that G2 is ready and a role needed to deliver the strategy is open and the role matches their capabilities, then they are given the role and their performance is monitored in the same way as any other employed staff member. If performance contracts and skills assessments suggest that G2 is ready but there is no role open that is needed to deliver the strategy then they can choose to take a lesser-paid role that matches their capability and wait until something opens up, or they can leave the business for a time. At least they know exactly where they stand

and can make decisions based on their personal plan and the current opportunities in the business. In truth, impatience dissolves when governance is in place because G2 can see that they are influencing every important decision anyway. As such they are much more willing to bide their time until the right position opens up.

If G2 are not ready governance provides them with an unpressured pathway. They can volunteer for roles in the business that meet their capability and take their time moving up through the ranks as they gain greater experience and capability. And they can potentially accelerate their promotion prospects through professional development.

G2 can also volunteer that they're not ready and will *never* be ready. And the founder can then make intelligent decisions that support the business and all their children.

Family Dynamics

Every family exhibits some level of dysfunction. It's impossible not to. Add a business to the mix and the usual trivial spats can easily escalate into something more challenging. The limitations of the mind mean we are almost constantly triggered by our family and are transported back to early childhood emotional responses. None of this is helpful in business or in fostering connected loving bonds. That said, not all family members will like each other. It is very possible to have a deep affection for a sibling but not necessarily like them or want to spend time with them as a friend. That is fine. What we are seeking to avoid or eliminate is deep-seated hostility.

If the hostility is such that members of the family can't or won't be in the same room as each other, the family needs to understand the root cause of it.

First, is the root cause commercial or personal? If it is commercial then governance will solve it. If it is personal then it may require governance and some clinical intervention. But even in that case, governance can be created around that individual and activated as soon as they are no longer in the picture in the same way as an unwilling founder.

Having now worked with family businesses for over 35 years, I can count the number of clinical cases I've come across on one hand. The irony is that exceptionally successful founders can sometimes exhibit traits that nudge them towards a clinical diagnosis such as psychopath, sociopath or narcissist. Their behaviour may upset those around them but they also have the choice to disengage from the relationship. G1 must respect G2's right to take their own financial path or cease involvement in that relationship or the business if G2 finds G1 intolerable or vice versa.

But again, governance allows people to opt in and out. It allows people to volunteer their level of involvement and engagement. If G1 or G2 is suffering from a personality disorder that robs them of their rationality, then no real progress will be made to institute governance. Governance moves the power away from an individual to a shared decision-making framework that is properly influenced by all.

In most cases, the hostility that sets in motion a slow (or in some cases swift) poisoning of the family relationship can be traced back to some commercial issue. For example, two siblings are at war because their mum and dad paid for one sibling's remedial coaching when they failed the first year of university but wouldn't provide a car loan for the other sibling. Governance always solves the issue and the hostility dissolves like a snowball on a hot plate.

While it is certainly useful to track down the root cause of festering hostilities, there is very little to be gained from endlessly casting up past real or imagined inequities. One technique I use a lot is the concept of an imaginary roller door, like the ones many of us have on garages. Part of the transition process as governance is being enacted is that there must come a point where all family members choose to put grievances and slights behind the roller door. They need to recognise that the resolution of those inequities is almost always impossible to do mathematically, with all variables becoming equal. However, if they're committed to finding an outcome that everybody can live with, then family harmony and business success are possible. I make the statement, 'Everyone can live with'. Yes, it's easier to say than do. Exactly how we explain this appears in the Family Charter that we will discuss in part V, and you can find the Jackson Family Charter in appendix C. One of the greatest joys in my life is when I hear a G2 say to another G2, 'that's behind the roller door'. Any angst that might have been attached to that issue is voluntarily relinquished for the greater collective good.

Trusted Advisor

Whether or not a family has any meaningful relationship with trusted advisors often determines how likely they are to find the solutions they are searching for. If a family has a history of engaging successfully with trusted advisors, this demonstrates an openness to learn and a willingness to plug any capability gaps that the group may have.

When we think about most founders we see individuals with very narrow but deep expertise. Managing a balance sheet and diversified wealth requires broad-based capability. Recognising what's missing and recruiting what's missing into the portfolio is therefore a litmus test to future governance success. So much so that when I meet a family in distress I always enquire about their experience with consultants. If there is limited experience of external advisors and the family is suspicious and cynical – that's a red flag. If they are not prepared to trust outside experts, they might not be prepared to trust each other inside and putting governance frameworks in place becomes difficult. The advisor's value is not just about any advice that may be forthcoming; their greatest gift to any family is their automatic injection of objectivity. It is impossible for a family in business to be subjective and objective at the same time.

Bottom line: a trusted advisor can be an accelerant to a family's pursuit of good governance by dint of the fact that they bring objectivity, so their questions are not immediately polluted by internal reflex responses.

G1, G2 and beyond can't possibly know everything about everything. No one in the business would say, 'Okay, we need a trust drawn up – I'll just knock that up after lunch' (unless the business is a law firm). We know that when it comes to law, we need trusted advisors. If we need to do our taxes, we tend to gather the information and let a trusted advisor do the rest. In a family business an independent external person is able to bring much-needed objectivity to otherwise largely subjective conversations. I am frequently invited to family business meetings, for example, because, 'If you come, everyone will behave.' Governance is not instant – it requires effort and pushing through intense and challenging conversations – but once it's done, it's done. And the business and the family are forever liberated by that effort. This means the advisor is often no longer needed.

If you want your family business to be governed properly, an external independent trusted governance advisor works in the same way as a lawyer or an accountant.

It's not compulsory to give the advisor control of implementing the governance, just assistance in creating it. Once created it is possible to identify how much you can do internally and close the gap with somebody capable. The objectivity the advisor brings is always useful regardless of how much they do or don't do regarding the implementation. Remember, governance is answering the question, 'How do we make decisions?'

REMEMBER, GOVERNANCE IS ANSWERING THE QUESTION, 'HOW DO WE MAKE DECISIONS?'

If the family agrees on how decisions are made, how do they decide where to take the business? They prepare a strategic plan and it's endorsed by the family. How do they decide whether they appoint staff members? They prepare a performance contract and assess applicants' capabilities, family and otherwise, against that performance contract and the skills matrix. How do they determine what everybody in the family wants? Each family member presents a personal plan and that personal plan identifies their ambitions for the foreseeable future – including the relationship they want with the business, if any. The Family Charter – created and agreed collectively by the family with the help of a trusted advisor – then spells out how every legacy decision is made. Once this is in place most of the everyday dysfunctions and family tensions and hostilities will disappear.

Whatever the problem, governance is the answer.

PART V

If you are still reading to this point, you almost certainly recognise the chaos in these pages; or you have glimpsed the *potential* for that chaos in your future and are invested in finding a solution *before* it materialises – ideally, before the family, business or wealth are negatively impacted. Part V unpacks how that is done through the four voices – again, using the Jacksons to illustrate how this is actually achieved.

To successfully separate the three circles of family, business and wealth, the following four voices must be heard and understood in the business and family:

1. The business must have a voice (strategic plan).
2. The individuals (founder and family members) must have individual voices (personal plans).
3. The family must have a collective voice (Family Charter).
4. The family community (spouses and generations that follow) must have a voice (Family Retreat).

The aim is democracy in all matters save for the defence of the rights of the asset owner, and the protection of those rights.

We touched on this in chapter 13 but democracy in this context is important. It represents our highest hope.

The evolution of decision-making started with anarchy, followed by tribalism, mod-rule and kleptocracy.[71] But in business, especially family business, it usually starts with the next level up – autocracy. Many family businesses are effectively autocratic dictatorships, where the founder's decision is final. If there is a founding couple the decision-making protocol may have evolved slightly to embrace a coalition or co-leadership. If the business refuses to hear the four voices, as soon as the founder or cofounders die the decision-making protocols and the business itself will descend into anarchy, tribalism and mob-rule – the sibling that is most aggressive with the loudest voice will nullify the rest, often with disastrous consequences for love, loyalty and family wealth. This is almost inevitable.

The big leap forward is only possible through the appreciation and articulation of the four voices. That evolutionary leap is democracy. Each progression is characterised by the number of voices that are listened to and valued.

Part V explores the four voices, in the context of the Jackson family. After learning what was possible in chapter 15, John decided to do the work. Part V demonstrates exactly what that work looks like. But first we will unpack engineered objectivity so you can better assess any advisor that you may engage and be reassured that they bring that much-needed objectivity to the table.

CHAPTER 17

Engineered Objectivity

Throughout this book I have sought to make it clear that while family business is notoriously complex and challenging, hoping that succession or ongoing success just somehow works itself out through typical business best practice is a mistake. The family and wealth components make the business component exponentially thorny.

I also hope I have made it clear that this doesn't have to end badly. There is a best way, a proven way, to systematically unravel the Gordian Knot I mentioned right at the start of the book. And there is a best way to facilitate the effective management of love, loyalty, family wealth and succession across multiple generations.

This chapter explains the science behind that best way. It is the explanation of engineered objectivity – a key component in solving just about anything. If you want to know why this approach works then read it. If you don't care why it works and just want to get to the 'how', feel free to skip forward to chapter 18.

The best way to hear the four voices is through engineered objectivity.

Let's just remind ourselves of the limitations we face. We are not in charge of our thoughts and are easily distracted. We have myriad default settings that automate our responses even when we believe we are making rational, logical choices. Our emotional responses often bear no resemblance to reality because of these default settings.

Our communication is constantly polluted because we don't have a universal unambiguous dictionary. And we find it impossible to be objective and subjective at the same time. When we truly understand our human challenges, it is possible to access our authentic voice.

The business must also be able to emerge through the complexity and uncertainty to express its voice. And the way we untangle this mess of neurological and biological human weaknesses as well as business complexity is to apply thinking systems or engineered objectivity.

As I said earlier, in business the temptation is to believe that each business, especially family business, is unique. They are not. The challenges are universal; it is the content or details of the challenge and *only* the content that is unique.

Take a moment to see if you recognise any of these songs or artists:

- *If I Could Turn Back Time* (Cher)
- *Don't You Love Me Anymore?* (Joe Cocker)
- *I'll Be Your Shelter* (Taylor Dayne)
- *Let's Make it Last All Night* (Jimmy Barnes)
- *Because You Loved Me* (Celine Dion)
- *A Smile Like Yours* (Natalie Cole)
- *Faith of the Heart* (Rod Stewart)
- *Have You Ever* (Brandy)
- *How Can We Be Lovers* (Michael Bolton)
- *I Don't Wanna Live Without Your Love* (Chicago)
- *I Don't Want to Miss a Thing* (Aerosmith)
- *I Get Weak* (Belinda Carlisle)
- *I Turn to You* (Christina Aguilera)
- *Blame It on the Rain* (Milli Vanilli)
- *Could I Have This Kiss Forever* (Whitney Houston and Enrique Iglesias)
- *Give Me You* (Mary J Blige)

- *How Do I Live* (Trisha Yearwood)
- *I'd Lie for You* (and That's the Truth)' (Meat Loaf)
- *Music of my Heart* (Gloria Estefan and NSYNC)
- *Painted on my Heart* (The Cult)
- *Through the Storm* (Aretha Franklin and Elton John).

Regardless of your musical taste you will recognise many of them – either the song or the artist or both! You can almost imagine the moment of inspiration as the writer walked along the beach at sunset – infused by passion, tragedy or a broken heart. The initial whisper of a melody, fragments of a song and the occasional poetic lyric coming together in the night air. Back at the cosy beach house the artist reaches for their trusty guitar and tinkers with the muse. A masterpiece is created and the droplets from heaven are recorded for the world to enjoy.

Sounds magical, but it's a complete myth. All these songs were written or co-written by a songwriter named Diane Warren: a one-woman music business! Warren is one of the most successful songwriters of all time, with scores of international top-10 hits across pop, country and R&B charts. There is also Desmond Child, a man I became aware of as the cowriter on a Kiss album. These two song-writers have written an incredible array of amazing songs for artists across all genres of music.

Quite obviously, songwriting is a system that is based on a formula! I am not disputing the natural talent both Diane Warren and Desmond Child have, but there is obviously a right way to write a hit. To the audience these songs are born of pain or passion that strikes a chord in the hearts of millions (usually triggering a default setting or associative memory). To the writer they are the result of following the system or formula for writing a hit.

The same can be said of successful sitcoms. We laughed at *Seinfeld* and thought that it was such an original and unique idea. But was it really? Compare it to *The Mary Tyler Moore Show*. There's a relatively normal one (Seinfeld, Mary); a headstrong woman (Elaine, Rhoda); a zany one (Kramer, Ted Baxter); and a quirky one (George, Murray).

Or, in more recent times, consider *Friends* or *The Big Bang Theory*. The normal one was Chandler or Ross in *Friends* or Leonard in *The Big Bang Theory*. The headstrong woman was Monica or Rachel, or Bernadette or Penny. The zany role was Phoebe or Sheldon. The quirky roles fell to Joey and Phoebe or Raj, Howard or Amy. But the combinations (or the ingredients) were the same.

Thinking systems are the context or formulae for business success, whereas the answers to the questions posed in the thinking systems are the content. To reach the optimal solution to any problem we need to account for our human failings and remove them from the equation and that is best achieved by thinking systems and someone, ideally a trusted advisor, who can separate the context from the content.

Best thinking requires another mind *and* ideally requires that mind to be equipped with a formula, a *thinking system*, that quickly uncovers the solution to that particular problem. If Dianne Warren and Desmond Child could create a winning formula for writing hit songs, is it possible that there is a winning formula for diagnosing common family business challenges that would work every time regardless of business, industry or size? Is there a winning formula for eliciting the four voices in any business?

The answer is a resounding yes.

If we look at anything long enough and study it hard enough, simplicity emerges from the chaos. It's like those magic 3D diagrams that used to appear in the weekend supplement of the newspaper. You hold them up to your nose and then draw the picture away slowly until the true picture embedded in the chaos pops out as clear as day.

We need two things when wrestling with any challenge and striving to produce our best thinking: clarity of *context*, which is how you think about something; and clarity of *content*, which is the thoughts themselves. The clarity is attained by being conscious of their sep-arateness *and* by realising that *context* requires *objectivity* and *content* requires *subjectivity*.

Due to our human limitations, it is impossible to be subjective and objective at the same time. This is often because we are not in charge of our thoughts, we are constantly triggered by default settings because of the family component of family business and our emotional reactions can so easily cloud our judgement.

What is needed is a second mind in the form of an objective facili-tator or trusted advisor who is focused solely on the context or asking the right questions about the problem the business is facing. This frees those who are knee deep in the situation to worry about the content by answering those systematic questions rather than worrying about why their brother is asking them the questions! As a result, the path toward the solution is faster, smoother and comes with much less angst.

A thinking system is *a series of questions which, when answered with integrity, will lead to the best next step*. It doesn't matter who you are or where you live – if you have a particular problem the *context* or framework required in order to solve it in the best possible way is, like a creative formula, always the same. Only the *content* varies.

If, for example, a different person in a different situation has the same problem, the solution might be different but the route to the solution is always the same. The answers always sound unique but the questions that uncover those answers are not. It's the same with the songs from earlier – they all sound different and unique, but the formula for creating them was not.

As a simple example, imagine two of your friends suggest to you, in a way that clearly invites your assistance, that they are unhappy with their home environment. You suggest a thinking system approach and conduct the following discussions with each of your friends ...

Context	Content	
The Thinking System	**Friend 1**	**Friend 2**
Are you happy with your environment?	No	No
What bothers you about your environment?	Too tidy	Out of date
What would it take to fix it?	Negotiate with flatmates	Renovate the loungeroom
Is this something you can do?	Negotiation is difficult for me	I don't have the money
Could you get help?	My friend is a good negotiator	I could get a loan
What stops you from doing that?	I'm a little shy	My credit rating
What could you do to fix that?	Ask my flatmates what you just asked me	Talk to my parents about helping me out

The questions asked to unveil the issues are exactly the same for both friends. More importantly, you don't even need to know what the challenge is before you start. The real solution will come from their answers, and those are always unique. The questions are the *thinking system* and the answers lead to the solution. But getting those questions wrong can be costly both in time and resources. The right answer to the wrong question is still the wrong answer!

**THE RIGHT ANSWER TO THE WRONG QUESTION IS
STILL THE WRONG ANSWER!**

A useful analogy to illustrate this concept more clearly is a sporting contest. You have the rules, which are the context; and you have the players and the game, which are the content. In order for the game to work everyone must know the rules, but rules can be broken in the heat of the moment so we have a referee, who is the guardian of the context.

The referee is the trusted advisor for the game – the objective filter who observes the game without bias – and is the guardian of the rules. As soon as they have a personal stake in the outcome their involvement is flawed and so is the game and its result. Objectivity is dissolved by emotion. If we have no particular attachment to any one side, we can observe the game from the purity of the rules and the game. When we are not emotionally involved in the outcome, we can observe the game for the level of skill shown by the players.

The same is true with an external advisor using thinking systems or a proven formula. The external advisor or coach is the guardian of the context. They provide the template for thinking (the context) and then each family inserts their own individual content to allow the business to draw the necessary and right conclusions for each family member, the business and the wealth.

This is very different from the consultant approach. If you have ever employed a consultant to assist you in your business you would most likely be given recommendations based on the consultant's experiences, which may or may not be very similar to the situation your business is currently facing. When it comes to governance, I think it is far more valuable to guide a family to their own conclusions and solutions based on their specific situation. The trusted advisor is therefore the master of the context, leaving the family to be the masters of the content. Surely this makes more sense. No one knows your business, your family and your balance sheet better than you and your family. You just need some objectivity so that you can all get out of your own way and find the best possible solutions for each individual, the business and the wealth.

On a good day, a consultant may be able to illicit the business voice, but not the other three.

On a good day, a clinical psychologist, a popular 'solution' for family challenges, may be able to illicit the voices of the founder and individual family members, but not the other three.

All four voices are needed for a complete solution.

Thankfully, the route to the solution, just like the route to creating a hit song, is always the same. The resulting solution will always be different, just like the songs. When a trusted advisor applies thinking systems, the route to the solution is formulaic but the solution is not.

If the only tool you come to a problem with is a hammer, then the solution always looks like a nail. A trusted advisor armed with the right governance thinking systems comes with the right questions that will illuminate the right solution for your business.

As we dive into the context, holding nothing back, the pages ahead explain the solution, the context and the approach we use to illicit the four voices.

The key to assessing any proposed solution before execution is simple:

- Does the solution follow a proven path or winning formula?
- Does the solution engineer objectivity into the process? (At least until those in the family and business appreciate and put the governance systems in place to bake that objectivity into the business and into the future.)
- Does the solution ensure that the engineered objectivity covers all the crucial bases that will allow the four voices to be heard?

CHAPTER 18

The Business Must Have a Voice

The first voice that must be heard is the voice of the business.

Initially, this will be the voice of the operating business through the creation of a strategic plan. The strategic plan gives the business a voice independent of the family, including the founder. If the business is successful, a plan for the balance sheet of the family will also be required. This is also true if the business ceases to exist but the balance sheet remains. Whether it's an operating business or a balance sheet, that entity must have a voice.

Through the creation of a robust strategic plan, the business is given its own voice, making clear to the stakeholders and owners where it wants to be and what it needs in order to get there. This first voice then creates a context for family, employees and potential hires to decide the professional relationship they want to have with the business.

In family business there is typically significant confusion about where the business ends and the family begins and vice versa. If you own a business and none of your family is involved in the business and you decide to replace or employ someone, the process is simple: clarify what's needed and find the right person with the right skills. If the business is a family business, there may be pressure to employ a family member to that role, and if that family member does not have the requisite skills, then a problem is created in the family because the appointment is likely to create dissatisfaction or unhappiness as well as escalate complexity. And, the appointment is likely to compromise the business because the family member doesn't have the capability to do the job properly.

It is therefore critically important for the business to define in the deepest, richest possible terms where it wants to be, where it wants to go and how it plans to get there. This is the strategic plan. Any strategic plan worth the paper it's written on will incorporate the vision for the business as well as the operational plan, which will define all of the things that the business will focus on in the next 12 months to achieve that vision or get closer to it.

In order for the strategic plan to give the business a voice it must cover four essential elements:

- pressures
- reckoning
- RadarLock™
- strategic milestones.

If you plan to involve an advisor in the creation of this crucial document, make sure they cover each of these four elements. Without them it is not a strategic plan that genuinely gives the business a voice.

The key to a potent strategic plan is to create a strategic planning group. The group must include people who provide a cross-functional representation of the business and who have a broad range of industry-specific as well as business-specific skills. This way, the industry as well as your business is represented and objectivity can be applied to the strategic process. Together the strategic group must then work through the four elements of the strategic plan.

Pressures

The first step is to ask the leadership in the business to articulate a clear understanding of the pressures the business currently faces and may face in the future. There are two types of pressures: external pressures that we cannot control (like financial markets) and internal pressures that we can control (like our own financial management). We cannot control the labour market; it is an external pressure. But we can influence the people we hire. People, performance and culture is therefore an internal pressure.

These pressures, external and internal, will shape the landscape in which we operate.

To illustrate what this looks like in practice, I've pulled out some examples of each element taken from the Jackson Developments & Construction Strategic Plan. The full strategic plan can be found in appendix A.

Here is the complete list of pressures the strategic group identified on the business and in the business for Jackson Developments & Construction.

Presssures

We considered the forces, internal and external, that shape the world in which we do business.

In the Business (Internal)

- Strategic planning and organisational structure
- Governance and compliance
- Brand and marketing
- People and culture
- Financial management
- Acquisition pipeline
- Development management
- Property management
- Built environment
- Operations and IT

On the Business (External)

- Legislation and regulation
- Economy
- Suppliers and contractors
- Joint venture partners
- Financiers
- Councils and state government
- Demographic and social trends
- Buyers and consumers
- Infrastructure
- Real estate agents
- Competitors
- Technology

Reckoning

The second step is reckoning, where the strategic group digs into each of the pressures identified inside and outside the business. This is an opportunity for the group to share their depth and richness of thinking so as to demonstrate that they truly understand the current position of each of the identified pressures.

For example, in the Jackson Developments & Construction Strategic Plan each pressure is taken in turn and unpacked in greater detail. This depth is captured for each identified pressure.

Reckoning

Through reckoning, we brainstormed everything we saw, thought and felt that was relevant to each pressure.

Strategic Planning and Organisational Structure

- We need to publish this plan.
- We need each division to understand the role they play in the overall strategy.
- We need a 'version' for each audience.
- We need a system for monitoring, funding and delivering on the strategy.
- A strategic plan taskforce needs to be established.
- Need to clarify the priorities from the shareholders with measurable KPIs.
- Need to be flexible and ready to adapt when opportunities present themselves.
- Shareholders need to be involved in the right forums.
- Need to scale up resourcing to deliver on the strategy and for when projects go live.
- Executive Leadership Team needs more development and mentoring.
- Succession planning and key person contingency planning needs to happen.

Governance and Compliance

- Need a WHS approach, procedure and review cycle.
- Formalise JD&C governance; board, leadership, reporting and meeting timetable.
- Need to clarify who attends what meetings.
- Need to better define the Executive Leadership Team with clear KPIs.
- Formalise our guarantees and framework.
- Improve our compliance reporting at all levels.

RadarLock™

The third step is to write down a rich, highly detailed story or narrative about where the business will be in five to 10 years' time. This narrative must be real and tangible and give the reader the feeling that the business has already achieved it. It must also be ambitious and creative – offering up a target for the future – hence the name 'RadarLock™'. The full RadarLock™ for Jackson Developments & Construction can be viewed in appendix A, but the start looks like this ...

RadarLock™

Using the data from our reckoning, we described a 'Future of Choice' – one that describes an organisation that clearly understands where the world around us is heading. We describe a future state that demonstrates we understand the market and set ourselves up perfectly to capture and make the most of it – creating a successful enterprise that respects our customers, our people, our community obligations and our shareholders' needs.

We call this Future of Choice our RadarLock™.

It is five years from now, and we are celebrating the best year in the history of Jackson Developments & Construction (JD&C). Success by any measure.

Great success is underpinned by a solid commitment to **STRATEGIC PLANNING** and having the right **ORGANISATIONAL STRUCTURE** to support our vision. We published our plan and meet as an Executive Leadership Team monthly to work on the implementation. We review our plan continually and it is a living and evolving document.

The synergy between all divisions is strong, enabling us to deliver a solid financial performance across all fronts.

All new sites are bringing solid revenue from property services.

Our structure has evolved with depth in project management, development, construction and planning. We have some great talent employed who are well connected. We have steered support towards acquisitions and administration.

We have appropriately qualified leaders to manage each division and service.

Our property management business now has over 300 properties on the books.

We make sure our strategy considers emerging **TECHNOLOGY**. We stay in touch with trends, having tasked key team members with the responsibility of watching for new technologies and embracing those that make commercial sense.

We make sure we are exposed to overseas trends through travel and networking with colleagues in our industry in the right markets.

Our own technology platform is fit for purpose. We have also embraced construction technologies that give us an edge over our competition.

Strategic Milestones

The final element of the strategic plan is a well-tested set of shorter-term deliverables (typically to be achieved in 12 months), which shape the business, taking us a step towards our RadarLock™ image of the future. The milestones for strategy planning are shown below and the full plan can be seen in appendix A.

Strategic Milestones

To achieve our 'Future of Choice' we agreed that the following statements should be true in 12 months' time.

We call these objectives our strategic milestones.

Strategic Planning and Structure (SS)

Milestone: within 12 months we will be able to say:

Ref	Milestone	Priority	Owner
SS1	JD&C Strategic Plan 1.0 was signed off by board and shareholders	Critical	JJ
SS2	SLAs are in place between each business division	Critical	RK
SS3	We have a meeting rhythm and agenda for the JD&C board	Critical	PJ
SS4	We have a meeting rhythm and agenda for implementing the strategic plan	Critical	PJ
SS5	We have identified and communicated who the Executive Leadership Team is	Critical	PJ
SS6	We have developed and implemented a complete rhythm of the business	Important	PJ
SS7	Our strategic plan has been communicated in a relevant format for each audience	Critical	PJ
SS8	We confirmed our HR resource needs for this year and recruited to the gaps	Critical	RK
SS9	We have investigated a managed service arrangement for our IT	Important	SS
SS10	We developed an offshore study tour program and have a business case for it	Preferred	NJ

Brand and Marketing

Milestone: within 12 months we will be able to say:

Ref	Milestone	Priority	Owner
BM1	Our website is complete, leading edge and properly maintained	Critical	IB
BM2	Our company profile is in digital and hardcopy and represents our brand	Critical	IB
BM3	All of our collateral conforms to our brand guidelines and style guide	Critical	IB
BM4	Our celebration of successes program has been planned and budgeted	Important	IB
BM5	We have quality internal and external marketing resources to support our activities	Critical	IB
BM6	We published and implemented a group marketing plan and budget	Critical	IB
BM7	Our approach ensures that each development site is properly branded	Important	SS
BM8	We have allocated the leadership team to several agents as ambassadors	Important	PJ
BM9	Ambassadors know what is expected of them to build and maintain relationships	Important	PJ

The above is an extract. The full suite of milestones spells out *everything* that must be done in the first 12 months of the journey towards the future envisioned and brought to life by the RadarLock™.

This helps everybody understand what the business is, where it wants to go and what it takes to get there. This type of robust four-point strategic plan gives the business a voice. It's no longer 'John's Company', it is now Jackson Developments & Construction, existing independently of John, with its needs and Future of Choice clearly articulated. No doubt the story told in the full plan (appendix A) would put a smile on John's face.

Magical things happen when you give your business a voice via this type of strategic planning. Family members can be heard saying, 'Oh wow. I didn't really appreciate how much you did and what your job involved.' Nathan, for example, finally sees and fully appreciates and acknowledges Christopher's vital contribution to the business and recognises that his architectural education and experience does give him greater understanding and insight on certain aspects of the business. The professional input of each sibling and other key employees is laid bare, which fosters greater respect and helps to turn down the volume of the sibling input.

THE PROFESSIONAL INPUT OF EACH SIBLING AND OTHER KEY EMPLOYEES IS LAID BARE, WHICH FOSTERS GREATER RESPECT AND HELPS TO TURN DOWN THE VOLUME OF THE SIBLING INPUT.

The other bonus is that once the business has a voice, each key employee including employed family members are able to form a very clear view as to whether or not they are truly personally aligned to the business's ambitions. If it's facilitated properly the story of the strategic plan tells itself as you break it down into those four steps. The only way that a person can manipulate the last step which focuses on milestones and actions – what people are going to do – is to be able to predict the outcome of the first three steps, which is impossible.

What *sometimes* happens is that people leave the business as a result of a strategic plan. What *always* happens is that vacancies, when they appear, are more accurately filled by applying the plan in the selection process! People might leave because they realise there's nowhere to hide anymore. Or they might leave because they recognise that there is nothing left for them beyond what they are doing now. Or they may realise that in order to go further they will need to engage in additional study to gain any missing qualifications. And that may not be something they want to do. Commercially and professionally, these are all good outcomes.

In over 35 years of facilitating plans like this, I've never had anyone who has exited a business through this process come up to me to say I have ruined their life. But I'd love a dollar for everyone who said it was the best thing that ever happened for their career. They got clarity, not only about themselves but about what the business wanted and needed. This liberated them to move on to something that was more suited to their capabilities and aspirations. Often, they were acutely aware they no longer 'fit' and felt awkward about it. Or they simply recognised that the business was not heading in a direction that was aligned with their values or personal goals.

It is no longer about the family business and family members trying to or being expected to shoehorn themselves into a role. Once the family business has a voice and has clearly defined what it is and where it wants to go, everyone in the business, family or non-family, has the opportunity to get behind that vision and make it a reality. If that is not where the family member wants to go or they recognise that they don't have the skill and don't want to engage in the additional education to gain that skill, then the path out also becomes clearer. And that is a gift.

Founder's Folly

Founder's Folly, as the name suggests, is the mistaken assumption by the founder that this type of in-depth strategic planning is unnecessary. The reason, which they are rarely aware of, is that all the four elements – pressures, reckoning, RadarLock™ and strategic milestones – are intuitively engineered into a founder's mindset. Most of it is in their head; they take it for granted and therefore don't see the need for 'pages of documentation' or 'another talkfest'. And when the founder is fit and well, they may have a point. It is their business after all. But when the business needs to migrate from the founder to G2, or the founder becomes unwell and is unable to run the business, the system breaks down because there was never a process to get the strategic plan from the founder's head onto paper.

The strategic plan is not about replacing the founder or the founder's intuition and experience; it's about making sure that what's in the founder's head is known and shared with the rest of the business.

Typically, what happens is that because the founder never writes anything down, they develop a faulty perception that somehow, the business planning process is an unnecessary bureaucratic burden rather than a way to liberate the business and ensure what's in their head lives on long after they have gone.

When checking in with one billionaire founder about the strategic process, he said, 'Yeah, it was good but there was a lot of waffle.'

I had heard this argument before so I played along. 'Waffle – really? That disturbs me. What part was waffle?' He replied, 'Oh, that future part' (the RadarLock™).

I suggested that we go through that line by line so we could get rid of any waffle. I proceeded to read every sentence of the RadarLock™ and waited for him to respond. 'No, that's fine' … 'Okay yes, that can stay' … 'That's important, keep that' … After about five minutes, he said, 'Okay, okay, I get your point.'

What he was actually reflecting on was his irritation at having to go through the process of writing it down because he never had to in the past. But the difference now is that what was in his head – owned by him, understood by him and defended and protected by him – was now owned, understood and defended by all. Of course, this can be a double-edged sword for the founder. Some founders enjoy that control and ego-based power of having it all in their heads. Some recognise this, but realise it is holding the business back and want to be coached out of it. Others recognise it and defend it aggressively – as is their right. And there are some founders who don't even realise they are guilty of it.

CHAPTER 19

The Founder and Individual Family Members Must Have a Voice

The second voice is the voice of the individuals, specifically the voice of the founder and each of the individual family members.

Making sure that every individual in the family has a voice ensures that everyone is able to sit at the table, represent themselves coherently and be heard. The effort applied towards this outcome also evidences that each family member is engaged in a life that is self-determined.

Typically, what happens is that the founder starts the business. Their ambitions for the business are indistinguishable from their own personal ambitions. This passion and dedication leaks into all areas of their life including family life. As a result, the founder completely misunderstands or underestimates the influence they have on their children, especially around career choice and whether or not they will enter the family business. Often there is an inevitability of involvement baked into family and business life. And, as I've said previously, this inevitability is rarely the free pass it's often seen as by non-family employees. Instead, it can lead to a lack of engagement and self-determination which is never good for the individual or the business.

OFTEN THERE IS AN INEVITABILITY OF INVOLVEMENT BAKED INTO FAMILY AND BUSINESS LIFE. THIS INEVITABILITY IS RARELY THE FREE PASS IT'S OFTEN SEEN AS BY NON-FAMILY EMPLOYEES. INSTEAD, IT CAN LEAD TO A LACK OF ENGAGEMENT AND SELF-DETERMINATION WHICH IS NEVER GOOD FOR THE INDIVIDUAL OR THE BUSINESS.

The second voice is the antidote to this potentially negative outcome via the completion of a personal plan that seeks to get each individual in the family, including the founder, to articulate their own *personal* hopes, dreams and ambitions.

Each individual family member must be invited to complete a personal plan regardless of whether they work in the business or not. If they are in a committed relationship that personal plan is done jointly with their partner. As a personal plan, it makes sense to include a life partner as many personal goals and aspirations will involve their spouse and the world they've created together.

Again, the plan works through four key elements. You may notice that there's very little difference in the thinking system applied to the business and the one applied to the individual. This is the power of thinking systems. The 'steps' or questions along with the form of enquiry must stay the same; we simply change the 'labels' so that if both a strategic plan and a personal plan are in play, everyone knows which one is being discussed.

For personal plans, the four elements are referred to as:

- what matters
- download
- Future of Choice
- stakes in the sand.

What Matters

Each individual must consider what matters to them personally in their life. What's interesting about what matters is that most of the time, it includes much the same things. And this is true for everyone regardless of personal situation or wealth.

I've included examples of two personal plans in appendix B – John and Ayesha's, which I'll snapshot below, and Anika and Tom's. If you would like to see more examples, they can be found at fourvoicesadvisory.com.

For John and Ayesha …

What Matters

- Health and fitness
- Our relationship
- Lifestyle and leisure
- Our children
- Our grandchildren
- Jackson Developments & Construction (JD&C)
- Our homes
- Future Fund
- Family Council
- Foundation

Download

The second element is the download, which seeks to identify how the individual thinks and feels about all the things that they identified under 'What matters'. This is the personal version of reckoning.

For John and Ayesha …

Download

Health and Fitness

- We are in good shape, just need to maintain.
- More time for golf.
- More tennis with the girls.
- Share a passion for walking.
- Love getting to the beach house and ski lodge.
- Would like to add yoga to our routine.
- Would like to do more motorbike riding.
- Reduce alcohol intake.
- Maintain rhythm with medical checks.
- Monitor cholesterol.

Our Relationship

- Like to work towards more structured timetable allowing us to block out Mondays and Fridays just for us.
- Our relationship is solid.
- We share genuine interests with each other – theatre, ballet, sports.
- JD&C and the children can take over our lives.
- Ayesha wants more time with friends and the children.
- John prefers less time.
- More driving holidays just the two of us.
- More time on the boat.
- We have slightly different opinions on how much we enjoy looking after Ben two days a week.

Future of Choice

The third element of the personal plan is where the true power of the process lies. It ensures that every individual has a powerful believable voice that puts their hopes and aspirations into context and explains what drives them. Each individual is taking responsibility for clearly expressing where they see their future. Like the business RadarLock™, the personal Future of Choice should be highly detailed and tangible. It should also read as though the individual or couple has already achieved it.

The start of John and Ayesha's Future of Choice is outlined below and you can read it – as well as Anika and Tom's – in full in appendix B.

Future of Choice

It is five years from today, and we are reflecting on the most rewarding year of our lives – rewarding by any measure.

Having turned 69 and 65 respectively, we are both as fit and healthy as we choose to be. We keep fit by doing a lot of walking, yoga and swimming. John is also enjoying golf three times a week while Ayesha enjoys her ocean swims and meditation. We still enjoy cooking healthy meals at home with the children. We also love to dine at 'our table' at Anika's restaurant.

We get on famously just as we did the first day we met. We enjoy four-day breaks visiting places in Australia and of course our own properties. Our principal home remains Bellevue Hill. We spend as much time as possible at Sinhala which is truly a sanctuary.

We spend Australian winters in Europe and New York and love hosting friends and family at both properties. Our lifestyle is relaxed and rewarding. Between the properties and boat, we have the right balance.

We are well connected with the family. John calls Uncle Marvin at least every month or so to check in and update him. We have been able to financially assist all of our important extended family members including nieces and nephews.

Stakes in the Sand

Stakes in the sand, like business milestones, spell out everything that must be done in the first 12 months of the journey towards the future envisioned and brought to life by the Future of Choice.

This type of robust four-point personal planning gives all the individuals a voice.

For John and Ayesha ...

Stakes in the Sand

- We enjoy yoga together twice a week.
- John plays golf three times a week.
- Ayesha meditates twice a day.
- We spend time together and as a family at our holiday home, Sinhala, once a month.
- We invested time and funds in Sinhala's garden.
- We remodelled the guest house at Bellevue Hill.
- We enjoy four-day escapes to new places and favourites around Australia.
- We supported the agreed family members with education funds for their children.
- We enjoy visiting the ski lodge on a regular basis during winter.
- We settled on Mayfair London.
- New York is all set up and we enjoyed a three-week holiday in the fall.
- The business has a solid five-year plan and funding model in place.
- The Executive Leadership Team and my children understand my future plans.
- Castlereagh development delivered set objectives.
- Christopher and John golf together once a month.
- Priya has a meaningful role in the business.

- Nathan understands his options at leadership in the business.
- Nathan and John enjoy an annual rugby trip.
- Anika is financially stable.
- We supported Anika with an au pair.
- Anika and Ayesha play tennis together once a week.
- We supported Anika with what she needed.
- Ayesha spends quality time with the children one on one.
- We supported the children in balance sheet management.
- John is still working in the business three days a week.
- Quarterly Family Council meetings are a success.
- The Jackson Family Foundation was formalised, business plan developed and funds secured.
- The Future Fund is managed effectively and has delivered set results this year.
- Our wills have been updated.

And again, magical things happen when everyone has a voice.

Most of us are fully aware that in families, often one person carries the conversation more than they should and perhaps for all the wrong reasons be it eloquence, birth order or extroversion. In the worst of all cases, the one that gets listened to the most is the one no one wants to upset.

Sometimes an individual will carry the conversation because they are the founder. Sometimes they carry the conversation because, as the founder's partner, they are determined to control the dinner table in the absence of their influence at the board table. There are always complex dynamics at play. For the Jacksons the conversation carriers are John followed closely by Nathan. Nathan is the loudest, the crudest and the most aggressive and prior to the personal plans both Christopher and Priya had learnt to just ignore it. After the personal plans everyone had a voice, not just Nathan.

When every individual, including the founder and all the individual members of the family, is given a voice through the completion of their personal plan all the voices are heard and equalised. And the only way to do that is for each individual to prove that they have thought through their position.

This does three things. First, it engenders confidence that everybody's being honest about their aspirations. Remember, this reduces complexity and uncertainty. Think of it in pure mathematical terms. If I don't know what you aspire to, it could be one of an infinite number of alternatives, and I will be left to guess. Once you declare your ambition and evidence your commitment, infinity becomes one. That is complexity reduced!

Second, it allows each individual to pause, step back and consciously consider whether their newly articulated aspirations align with the strategic plan of the family enterprise. Is what they want to do and achieve in life also needed by the business, or not?

Third, it arms each individual with a narrative. This goes a long way to equalising the personality advantages that the loudest or most articulate enjoy, and personality disadvantages of the most vulnerable.

I've lost count of the number of times I've witnessed an extroverted, dominant or articulate sibling constantly steal the limelight and decision-making reins from their less 'verbal' siblings. On one occasion that springs to mind I was facilitating a session where both sons of a successful founder were to share their personal plans with G1. The two sons could not have been more different physically or in their nature. The oldest was into sport, athletic and fitness conscious, affectionately referred to by the family as the 'big unit'. He was quite introverted, took his time to speak and hated to be rushed or put on the spot. Words and self-expression didn't come naturally to him. His younger brother was the opposite: much smaller physically, but he could talk the back legs off a donkey and spoke at a million miles an hour. Words just flowed for him. In our discussions, it was pretty obvious that the founder had drawn various conclusions about his sons from their respective physicality and personality types.

When it was the older son's turn to present his Future of Choice to the family, he stood up and delivered a passionate and flawless PowerPoint presentation to the group. I watched as this unfolded and particularly enjoyed the founder's barely hidden surprise. Once his son had finished, the founder said, 'So, the "big unit" does have a plan.' It was a revelation for both of them. The son found his voice and because he'd done all the thinking ahead of time and created his presentation, he was able to speak as articulately and with just as much enthusiasm and confidence as his younger brother. It allowed him to move away from the complex family history and the role he'd been pigeonholed into to take his rightful place as a self-actualised adult outlining his personal and professional ambitions. And his dad recognised this and immediately recalibrated some of his misjudgements about his son. That one exchange completely changed the dynamic between father and son. This becomes possible once every individual has a voice.

CHAPTER 20

The Family Must Have a Voice

The third voice is the voice of the family. This is achieved by the creation of a Family Charter, where the family unites and creates a set of principles and guidelines that speaks for the family as a collective. You will see some of the text in this chapter again in the sample charter in appendix C but it is important to put it in context here.

The Family Charter

The Family Charter is essentially a document of guiding principles agreed to by the family members. It spells out the family's relationship with the family business and the rules for governing any and all shared assets.

A Family Charter can be thought of as the 'fundamental understanding' of the business that reflects both the family values and the business values. It addresses issues that tend to be the most controversial and most crucial to the future of the family in business. Charters address issues such as who will lead the business, who will work in it, how family members in the business will be compensated, and how these decisions are made and reviewed.

An important outcome of the planning process and communication objectives must be to document in the Family Charter all the potentially contentious issues that may arise. When family consensus is obtained, it represents a clear and agreed statement of values, and therefore minimises the potential for conflict.

Consensus in this context is defined in these terms: 'While not agreeing entirely with the decision, I can live with it to ensure we make decisions together – decisions that keep us moving forward.'

A Family Charter can help to minimise, and even avoid, many of the problems confronting a family in business.

It is not always possible for all family members to agree on every single issue. Accordingly, formulation of the Family Charter document may evolve over a period of time and may require a number of family meetings.

The concept of consensus is a key element in assisting family members to retain a cooperative and educated approach to resolving challenges within the family and within the business.

Ultimately, not all family members will agree with every provision of the charter, but all working and retired family members should be provided an opportunity to influence this document at dedicated Family Charter meetings. In this way, the binding principles and practices contained in the final charter will have been carefully thought out, discussed, written down and contained in an easy-to-understand document.

The Family Charter sets the principles and practices to be observed by the family with regard to the management and ownership of the family businesses. The charter also helps family members understand the rights and responsibilities that come with ownership and management and to clarify the boundary between family and business. In this way it is the physical expression of both the recognition and commitment to the three circles of family, business and ownership (wealth). The charter is a confidential family document. Signing the document reinforces that each family member has contributed to the charter and is in agreement with the details it contains.

Typically, there are two situations requiring slightly different types of Family Charter:

- When there is an operating business and significant assets.
- When there is no longer a business but significant assets, which I have referred to as the balance sheet.

The Purpose of the Family Charter

- Assist the family as shareholders of the family enterprises and other family companies to develop and maintain alignment to the company/business vision and mission.
- Clarify family members' roles and expectations of them.
- Clarify the relationship between the Family Council, shareholders, board of directors and Executive Leadership Team.
- Create a forum to discuss the issues people typically avoid.
- Explain what happens when the unexpected happens.

Family Council Defined

The Family Council is the group of family members charged with the responsibility of managing the interaction between the family and the enterprise or balance sheet. Essentially, they are there to keep the Family Charter alive and ensure its principles are applied.

The Family Council exists to:

- develop and maintain alignment to the company/business vision and mission
- create a commitment to the family being a family in business, or governing shared wealth
- ensure the Family Charter provides a basis for interaction with the family business enterprise or external advice framework presiding over the balance sheet

- ensure the business will be enduring and managed for generations that follow
- ensure the business provides reasonable returns to shareholders, current and future.

Differentiating Between the Roles

The table opposite should provide some assistance to family members in differentiating between the roles of the Family Council, trading company board, owners and Executive Leadership Team to ensure everyone focuses on the issues at hand wearing the proper hat.

The Family Charter is vital as it facilitates the third voice. The family comes together ahead of any live issues to formulate an agreed set of guidelines around the family business and the assets. This ensures that:

- the family communicates about the business and the family
- relationships are enhanced instead of potentially eroded or destroyed
- the business identifies and manages new opportunities
- the family has collectively agreed guidelines designed to reduce the possibility of conflict
- wealth creation is assisted and supported around shared values and rules
- there is clear, agreed direction in the business and family
- any differences of opinion are pushed back to the Family Charter for confirmation of agreed rules
- the business and the resulting assets are managed for the wellbeing of future generations
- family wealth strategies are addressed
- the family maintains influence on the business board.

A full copy of the Jacksons Family Charter can be found in appendix C.

Circle	Role	Obligations	Benefits	Qualifications
Family	Family Council member	· Set the ultimate family destiny · Advise the board on dividend policy and directors' fees · Advise the board on strategic investment and governance issues · Advise the board on ownership, succession and estate plans · Attend Family Council meetings · Develop and review the Family Charter	· Annual Family Retreat activities	· Elected by current Family Council members
Ownership	Company shareholder (via the ownership board)	· Owner's plan · Provide capital · Manage board performance, selections and terminations · Support decisions of the board · Attend shareholders' meetings	· Dividends as set by board of directors	· Owner of shares · Family member

Circle	Role	Obligations	Benefits	Qualifications
Ownership cont.	Company director (via the ownership board)	• Set long-term corporate vision (the 'what') • Govern the company • Set company risk appetite and policy • Approve medium-term strategy • Employ, evaluate and advise CEO • Monitor the company's performance • Balance the company's interest versus shareholders' interests • Attend directors' meetings	• Director's fees benchmarked to Australian Institute of Company Directors (AICD) survey	• Specified skill levels and experience • Elected by shareholders
Business	Executive Leadership Team (ELT)	• Set medium-term corporate strategy (the 'how') • Run the company and develop business plan • Manage company risk appetite and policy • Employ, evaluate and advise staff • Reach company's targets and KPIs • Attend management meetings • Develop management succession plans	• Salary package benchmarked to Australian Institute of Management (AIM) survey • Inclusion in Key Employee Share Plan (KESP)	• Specified skill levels and experience • Employed by the CEO

I've included two excerpts below to reinforce the game-changing nature of a Family Charter in business and family prosperity. Without a document that outlines how decisions are made and by whom (and in what forum), dysfunction is inevitable. But if all the guidelines around key decisions, especially potentially thorny ones, are outlined and agreed ahead of any need to apply those guidelines, then the likelihood of family harmony increases exponentially.

From field experience, the two excerpts I've selected to include here are most often the source and solution to resolving common dilemmas around investment in non-employed siblings, and employment of family members. Note: the approach you read below was one such example (the Jacksons) where the question was answered by the family.

For our purposes, the important issue is that the question was asked (context) and that the family, through facilitation, answered it together (content). The nature of their answer may not appeal to you. That's not important. The way your family answers the question would have a unique tone that reflects your history and ethos. As such it will reflect your past, present and chosen future.

Every charter is constructed the same way. Yet every charter is different as the language of the family authoring it is evident throughout.

Business Case Requirements

All members of the Family Council may bring investment opportunities to the council for consideration.

These will be identified as 'general business' matters for consideration, discussion and determination.

A family member may benefit directly and individually from such opportunities; however, all interests must be disclosed in advance.

The following must be included as a minimum for an opportunity to be discussed at a Family Council meeting; it is not intended to be exhaustive and further information may be requested:

- What is the idea or purpose?
- Where did it come from?
- What resources does it require?
- Who is involved and in what capacity?
- What specialist input has been applied to test the idea?
- What benefit will you derive?
- What benefit will the family derive?
- What exactly is being requested (money, time, contacts)?
- What precedents are there for the idea?
- What risk is involved and how will it be mitigated?

Family Employment

From time to time, skills, knowledge, experience and time itself will need to be applied to the management of the family's wealth.

Family members may be considered for employment in the stewardship of the balance sheet.

The family member must have, or be in the process of acquiring, the requisite skill to fulfil any duties for which they are appointed.

Should this be the case, they will be eligible to compensation at a market rate.

A market rate is represented by the compensation required to retain a non-family member with similar skills and qualifications, to complete the tasks or fill the role.

The position must be supported by a position description which clearly articulates the responsibilities and time commitment of the role.

CHAPTER 21

The Family Community Must Have a Voice

The final voice that must be heard is the voice of spouses and the generations that follow. We've covered the idea that each G2 and beyond has one vote via their personal plan. If they are in a relationship, they still have one vote, only now that single vote is shared with their partner 50/50. Assuming they have a rational and reasonable partner, 50 percent of their vote then belongs to their partner. That partner's voice is therefore heard in the preparation of joint personal plans. Their voice is also sought and welcomed, along with the generations that follow, via the Family Retreat.

It is essential for family harmony and long-term legacy-building that a conduit is created to ensure that partners or spouses and the emerging generations can be heard, integrated, initiated, inducted and orientated to the family business. The Family Retreat is aimed specifically at those individuals who may inherit a solution to a problem that most of us spend a lifetime trying to solve – ensuring our financial security.

More importantly, they will also learn to apply that privilege to the best interest of themselves, their family and their wider social community.

The Family Retreat

The primary tool for ensuring that spouses and the generations that follow have a voice is the Family Retreat. It's a fun day or weekend where all the family, including extended family, partners and children, get together and enjoy some quality time together – to talk and share stories about the business and beyond.

As well as keeping the family connected and bonded it also serves to demystify the business for partners and G3 and beyond. If you are the one who created the wealth, you have the benefit of zero mystery. You were there. You know how it happened. You know what it took and the sacrifices you made. If you watched the wealth being created by a founding parent or partnership, you also benefit from limited mystery. Chances are you were dragged in to help at weekends and after school so you witnessed the business in action. If you are born into an already wealthy family or marry into an already wealthy family, you won't have witnessed or endured any pain in regard to the accumulation of that wealth. That creates mystery for both spouses and the generations that follow. Demystifying the journey can help avoid problems down the track for both the partners and the generations that follow. For partners, there is a greater understanding of the business and what went into creating the wealth, which can foster greater financial intelligence. And if the generations that follow are unlucky enough to be allowed to travel through life thinking that the wealth is just some miracle that they're entitled to, then demystification can help to prevent that entitlement. Otherwise, they are probably on their way to becoming a statistic – shirt sleeves to shirt sleeves in three generations.

It's essential that the business that created the wealth and the various assets that have been accumulated are demystified. You must also engage G3 and beyond in the business to secure the legacy.

The Family Retreat reminds everyone what happened, how it happened and why it happened. The result is that it starts to teach partners and G3 and beyond about the responsibility that accompanies the opportunity. Where appropriate or agreed in the Family Charter, it also provides pathways for them for leadership and engagement in the management of the wealth, and it brings the business itself to life for them. By the time G3 are in the picture a successful business will almost certainly have grown and diversified, offering all sorts of expanded career choices and potential pathways for the family community.

For the Jacksons, their Family Retreat includes Christopher and Rya's children, Milly and David; Nathan and Georgia's children, Lia and Lucy; and Anika and Tom's child, Ben. The business is no longer restricted to building works. The business has its own accounts department, approvals (legal compliance) division as well as an architect suite that is leased to Christopher's firm and hosts two employees who work exclusively on Jackson projects. There is also a design centre, and there are countless opportunities in the supply chain or with contractors. Who knows – one of the children may decide to create an ancillary business and hire out construction equipment!

I'm working with a G2 who has revolutionised his father's business. His dad left school at 13 and built two successful businesses. He was not well educated but he saw a gap in road building and went for it. His son is university educated and he has invented equipment that makes what his dad developed safer and easier. He's turned a sweat and muscle business into a brain business. And that would never have happened if he hadn't been introduced and orientated into the business from an early age.

But as a business grows, it's no longer, 'Okay, you have to join the business, we need you', it's 'Come and join the business in an area that you find interesting.'

You can find an invitation to the Jacksons Family Retreat in appendix D(a).

CHAPTER 22

The Key Characteristic of Governance

For governance to work as a solution to complexity and uncertainty and as a way to combat the problems that arise from the five human limitations it must pass five tests. It must:

1. be agreed in advance
2. be designed independently of a live issue
3. be documented and referenced
4. be tested
5. be designed to grow and evolve with the family.

The governance framework that decides how decisions will be made needs to be agreed before it will be needed. This means that the framework must be designed independently of a live or current issue. If there is a current matter that is under dispute, we are now debating and negotiating, not governing. If the answer to the question 'Have we discussed this topic and how to address it before?' is yes, then we can reflect on the previous resolution and apply the approach. That is governance.

When the answer to 'How do we address the issue?' is determined *before* the issue arises, that means there is a documented governance framework in place that describes how to tackle the issue. We can then consult the documentation and proceed on the agreed basis.

If we have not discussed the issue already then we are not governing, we are arguing. We have missed the opportunity for governance.

Let's go back to the Jacksons for a moment to illustrate these specific characteristics in practice.

In the development of the Family Charter the question was raised about whether it would be possible for G3 (the grandchildren) to work in the business. Rya asked, 'When one of our children turns 16, how would we involve them in the business? What rights would they have to be involved in the business should they want to be involved?' As the family recognised the merit of strong governance early enough the question was asked and answered with an agreed protocol documented before G3 were anywhere near 16 years old. The Family Charter therefore already lays out whether children of G2 and beyond will be encouraged to work in the family business when they turn 16 – perhaps after school or on weekends. This way the business can orientate G3 into Jackson Developments & Construction should they want to be involved in the hopes that the business continues down the generations.

If, however, this discussion has been initiated when Christopher's daughter Milly turned 16, it would have been too late for governance around this issue. At that point it would become a debate or a negotiation that would have been unavoidably influenced by personalities and family dynamics. The discussion would have changed considerably if the question went from, 'When one of our children turns 16, how would we involve them in the business?' to 'When Milly turns 16, how would we involve her in the business?' Suddenly it's all about Milly – her personality, her skill set, her relationship with the founder, her father and his relationship with the founder plus a whole host of subjective issues that start to pollute the discussion and colour the outcome. That is not governance.

It's only governance if the conclusion about what opportunities to afford 16-year-old children of G2 and onwards is debated and agreed upon by G1 and G2 before anyone in G3 is eligible to take up those opportunities. As such it is agreed long before the issue becomes a live issue which further removes any potential subjectivity from the debate.

The resulting governance framework must also be *documented* and *referenced*. If it's not documented, it's not governance. It's hearsay and influence but it's not governance. It's John's influence, or it's 'Mum getting her way again'.

It becomes governance the day it's applied in the first instance and survives. In this case, it becomes governance when Milly, the first child of G2, turns 16 and is presented with a number of pre-agreed options for her involvement in the business should she wish to take them up. Once another child reaches 16 and the same rules are applied then it becomes enduring and tested governance. No upset. No emotion. No drama.

Governance is a journey. It begins with agreeing to have governance. It progresses with the help of a trusted governance advisor who will help the family identify all the issues and matters that will require governance, followed by debate, discussion and documentation. Finally, it's governance when it's been applied and tested.

Once proven it becomes an enduring legacy of the developing family asset pool. It becomes one less issue that the family or those in the business might otherwise have to discuss or debate. The rules create clarity that, in turn, dials down the uncertainty and the complexity, all while allowing the frontal lobes of each family member to stay switched on rather than allowing the fear-based amygdala to take over and trigger some irrelevant and distracting default setting.

No one needs to worry that Milly's start in the business might be based on anything other than the fact that she has turned 16 and is interested in a few hours' work in the business for some pocket money. There will be no paranoia about her being a spy for Christopher or getting preferential treatment because Christopher is John's favourite or Milly is grandpa's 'favourite grandchild' (according to Nathan's wife

Georgia). When Priya, Nathan and Anika's children turn 16, they will be afforded the exact same opportunities – and while they may choose to work in a different department or capacity, the terms of that employment are consistent.

You know governance is enduring when a G3 child says to his parent, 'Now that I'm 16, can I also get a job in the business?' Governance has an amazing ability to influence the way people think. Without governance a situation as relatively innocuous as whether a child of a family member can work in the business turns into a lose/lose situation. If the decision is that Milly is too young or there is no proper role for her, without governance Christopher is almost certainly going to interpret that as, 'That is just typical. Dad's never trusted me and now he's taking it out on Milly. I bet if it were one of Nathan's daughters, it wouldn't be an issue.' And all of those worst-case default responses would rear up to hijack rational thought and fuel underlying tensions.

Each of these types of interactions have the potential to become aggravators. Each family member has the potential to become an aggravator. And, whenever we ignore or sideline an aggravator in a family engagement, we are burying a seed of destruction. Whenever we ignore an issue or an inference from a family member, we are burying another seed. We can ignore those seeds and wait for them to grow into something substantial or we can better understand the dynamics and institute governance to prevent the bulk of them from even germinating.

When all five of the tests I listed at the beginning of the chapter have been passed, we have governance. Governance calls on us to bring our neocortex to the table. Better-quality thinking means fewer default settings and reflex responses are triggered. The more governance the less complexity and uncertainty, which provides the opportunity for ongoing family connectedness, harmony and happiness. Remember, we are not in charge of our thoughts and are easily distracted. We have myriad default settings that automate our responses, even when we believe we are making rational, logical choices. Our emotional response often bears no resemblance to reality because of these default settings and reflex responses. Our communication is constantly polluted because we don't have a universal unambiguous dictionary. And we find it impossible to be objective and subjective at the same time. Is it really any wonder that navigating life is so challenging, never mind the multiple additional layers of complexity that reside in a family business?

The way we untangle this mess of neurological and biological human weaknesses is to understand and apply governance and stewardship. This allows us to separate thoughts from thinking so as to elevate the thinking and nullify the five human limitations – thus, removing the primary catalyst for angst. In addition, governance ensures that the business has a clear vision and all employed family members are in roles they are suited to and paid properly for their contribution. All family members are then able to sit equally at the ownership or wealth table regardless of whether they work in the business or not. No one is sidelined and everyone is making and pursuing their own life goals, which may or may not be connected to the business. And perhaps more importantly, governance liberates the family and the business so that everyone and the wealth can thrive in a loving connected family.

To paraphrase author Michael Singer, it's truly a great cosmic paradox that one of the best teachers in all of life, turns out to be death … Someone who has died could immediately remind you of the insignificance of the things that you cling to or teach you that men and women of all races are equal and that there is no difference between the rich and the poor because death instantly makes us all the same.[72]

Let's not wait for death to teach us that. ALL the voices are valuable and must be heard for the effective management of love, loyalty, family wealth and succession through the generations. Those voices bring democracy. Democracy may or may not have a place, in your mind, in your operating business – but inclusiveness and effective leadership must have a place in business. Democracy in the family governance framework is fundamental; it is about giving people, all people, a voice. In the management of family wealth, democracy is achieved when we listen to and acknowledge four specific voices, hence the title of the book.

When the four voices are heard, enduring success – bound by blood, underpinned by wealth and lived in harmony – is possible.

Jackson Developments & Construction Strategic Plan

JACKSON DEVELOPMENTS & CONSTRUCTION
Strategic Plan: July 2021

Attendees

John Jackson	Founder and CEO
Christopher Jackson	Property Management
Priya Jackson	General Manager
Nathan Jackson	Development Manager
Jeff Cox	Chief Financial Officer
Simon Snape	Operations Manager
Rob King	Legal and HR
Isaac Button	Marketing Manager

Coach

John Vamos

Table of Contents

Your Objectives

- Know where Christopher, Priya and Nathan want to take the show.
- From a family point of view, manage the family interaction.
- Clear direction for JD&C and priorities.
- Know how best to serve and support each business division.
- A clear brief and path to work towards.
- Clarify style of projects we want to be involved in.
- Get the transition clear – a more 'deliberate' process.
- Our people need to understand our direction.
- A 'script' to inform all our team.
- See a higher level of clarity and collaboration amongst the Executive Leadership Team.
- Engage the leadership to empower them to help lead the business.
- Be clear about the procedures and the disciplines for a business of our size and scale.
- A strategy for the public message – a 'good news' broadcast.

Memorable Moments

We reflected on the events, accomplishments and challenges for which the last 12 months would be remembered.

- Phil leaving.
- Bondi getting council approval.
- Julie's 20th anniversary lunch.
- Bilton starting.
- Delphil acquisition.
- Presales on the Residences.
- Joint venture partner for Macquarie.
- Finishing Double Bay.
- Commencing property management business.
- Fit for purpose staff.
- Improvement in culture.
- Positive discussion so far on transition/succession amongst Executive Leadership Team.

Pressures

We considered the forces, internal and external, that shape the world in which we do business.

In the Business (Internal)

- Strategic planning and organisational structure
- Governance and compliance
- Brand and marketing
- People and culture
- Financial management
- Acquisition pipeline
- Development management

- Property management
- Built environment
- Operations and IT

On the Business (External)

- Legislation and regulation
- Economy
- Suppliers and contractors
- Joint venture partners
- Financiers
- Councils and state government
- Demographic and social trends
- Buyers and consumers
- Infrastructure
- Real estate agents
- Competitors
- Technology

Reckoning

Through reckoning, we brainstormed everything we saw, thought and felt that was relevant to each pressure.

Strategic Planning and Organisational Structure

- We need to publish this plan.
- We need each division to understand the role they play in the overall strategy.
- We need a 'version' for each audience.
- We need a system for monitoring, funding and delivering on the strategy.
- A strategic plan taskforce needs to be established.

- Need to clarify the priorities from the shareholders with measurable KPIs.
- Need to be flexible and ready to adapt when opportunities present themselves.
- Shareholders need to be involved in the right forums.
- Need to scale up resourcing to deliver on the strategy and for when projects go live.
- Executive Leadership Team needs more development and mentoring.
- Succession planning and key person contingency planning needs to happen.
- Organisational structure too flat.
- Need to have fewer direct reports to CEO.
- There is no People and Culture Lead – we are growing fast.
- IT needs a lead and we may need additional skills – BIM and CAD.

Governance and Compliance

- Need a WHS approach, procedure and review cycle.
- Formalise JD&C governance; board, leadership, reporting and meeting timetable.
- Need to clarify who attends what meetings.
- Need to better define the Executive Leadership Team with clear KPIs.
- Formalise our guarantees and framework.
- Improve our compliance reporting at all levels.

Brand and Marketing

- Need to review our company profile on all print and digital platforms.
- Need to define our brand equity and essence while promoting our legacy.

- Need policies around promotion of partnerships.
- Need to refresh brand guidelines and style guides.
- Engineer our quality of design and finish into our branding.
- Extend it to website and all collateral.
- Promote our talent.
- Build relationships with our community.
- Consider event and industry sponsorship to build profile.
- Pipeline management to drive acquisition opportunities.

People and Culture

- Need to define the JD&C approach for selection, appointment, induction, review, remuneration and incentives.
- Our JD&C culture needs to be defined.
- Career path planning for key roles.
- Review our employment contracts and ensure they're updated.
- A solid social agenda that includes everyone to be established.
- Better management of leave.
- Better utilisation of technology to support collaboration and working from home.
- Program for training, development and pathways.
- Short and long-term incentives for Executive Leadership Team reviewed and updated if needed.

Financial Management

- Think about diversification.
- Look at held income-producing assets.
- Need to have a set of parameters for key financial ratios and decisions.
- Improve financial literacy for Executive Leadership Team.
- Better management of key suppliers.
- Need more automation/more paperless.

- Financial pack for shareholders to be defined for the Family Council.

Acquisitions

- Identify a target number of key contacts in this space.
- Develop relationship management KPIs to enhance this activity.
- Assign and set KPIs for each acquisition.
- Define the selection criteria and financial resources required.
- Clarify our geographic areas to focus on.
- Explore land banking opportunities with income.

Development Management

- Need to better coordinate and manage consultants.
- Review the teams' workloads, current and future, and address gaps.
- Establish regular meetings with agenda and minutes.
- Find a way to monitor, manage and address performance issues.
- Ensure a good mix of consultants.
- Understand when it makes sense to take legal action.
- Expand the options for project management.
- Build a database of customers.
- Revise our marketing collateral.
- Define our customer care approach.
- Need a policy and audit process for bonds.
- Update feasibilities regularly.
- Get banks on site to see projects.

Property Management

- Should we be in it?
- Should we outsource or sell it?
- Need to understand the ROI.
- Full business case required.

Built Environment

- Need to decide if we should renovate or acquire neighbours.
- Office recently given a facelift.
- Business case geographical locations.
- Need a parking solution.

Operations and IT

- Need a technology road map for the next five years.
- Launch new phone system.
- More training on Microsoft Teams.
- Consider removing the server and going cloud based.

Legislation and Regulation

- Becoming more complex and changing all the time.
- Even the consultants lose track of the 'process'.
- Council mergers are increasing the complexity.
- Looking at how strata schemes can be 'consolidated'.
- Everything getting more expensive.
- Building warranty changes and increased hold back.
- Impact on fund flowing out of China.
- Authorities passing costs to developers.

Economy

- Low/steady growth.
- Australian dollar will remain low.
- A lot depends on China.
- Property market linked to China.
- Property market is flattening due to supply.
- Capital availability will tighten a little.
- Covid-19 impact.

Suppliers and Contractors

- Managed well through tender and engagement process.
- Materials cost pressures upwards creating shortages.
- Valuers are incredibly conservative.
- Not a lot of mid-tier players (big players that acquire the next tier down).
- High turnover of people.
- Opportunity for technology innovation.

Joint Venture Partners

- Need clear terms of engagement.
- Need a clear policy of when to joint venture and when not to.
- Need a review process pre, during and post.
- Consider vendors?

Financiers

- Likely to continue with stringent approval terms.
- Under competitive pressure themselves.
- APRA changes the cash and liquidity requirements.
- Relationships are key.
- Constant policy reviews and changes.
- New sources emerging.
- Need to understand 'the mix' and where they fit for us.
- Need to maintain relationships.
- Consider alternate supply line if market weakens and banks tighten.

Councils and Government

- Councils can be inefficient.
- Need active industry policy.
- State Government serious about improvement.
- State committed to infrastructure.

Demographics and Social Trends

- Diverse multicultural markets in Sydney are growing.
- Sydney has been primary focus.
- A lot more families prepared to live in apartments.
- Ageing demographic still needing to be catered for.
- Less reliant on car transport.
- Growing affordability issues.
- Technology facilities decentralisation.
- Federal Government looking at first homebuyer stimulus.

Buyers and Consumers

- Affordability is an issue.
- Want quality and reputation.
- Educated market.
- Want transport options, amenities and services.
- Want prospects for capital growth and rental returns.
- Need to consider needs of both owners and investors.
- Rely on real estate agents for guidance.

Infrastructure

- Big focus for New South Wales.
- New airport in Badgerys Creek.
- Second rail crossing Sydney Harbour.
- New hospitals.
- New rail links.

Real Estate Agents

- Tending to do more 'global' marketing versus domestic.
- Good ones are getting better, mediocre falling away.
- More online marketing.
- Wanting to partner.
- Big Four agencies doing a lot more.

Competitors

- Supply is a critical issue.
- Quality is getting better.
- Want to be the benchmark.
- Need to conduct deep analysis of their activity.
- All competing in getting sites.
- Market perception matters.
- Pressure on us to stay ahead of the market.
- Talent in demand.

Technology

- Driverless cars.
- Prefabrication technology.
- Virtual reality.
- Tailored digital marketing.
- Remote access/the cloud.
- Virtual conferencing that works.

RadarLock™

Using the data from our reckoning, we described a 'Future of Choice' – one that describes an organisation that clearly understands where the world around us is heading. We describe a future state that demonstrates we understand the market and set ourselves up perfectly to capture and make the most of it – creating a successful enterprise that respects our customers, our people, our community obligations and our shareholders' needs.

We call this Future of Choice our RadarLock™.

It is five years from now, and we are celebrating the best year in the history of Jackson Developments & Construction (JD&C). Success by any measure.

Great success is underpinned by a solid commitment to **STRATEGIC PLANNING** and having the right **ORGANISATIONAL STRUCTURE** to support our vision. We published our plan and meet as an Executive Leadership Team monthly to work on the implementation. We review our plan continually and it is a living and evolving document.

The synergy between all divisions is strong, enabling us to deliver a solid financial performance across all fronts.

All new sites are bringing solid revenue from property services.

Our structure has evolved with depth in project management, development, construction and planning. We have some great talent employed who are well connected. We have steered support towards acquisitions and administration.

We have appropriately qualified leaders to manage each division and service.

Our property management business now has over 300 properties on the books.

We make sure our strategy considers emerging **TECHNOLOGY**. We stay in touch with trends, having tasked key team members with the responsibility of watching for new technologies and embracing those that make commercial sense.

We make sure we are exposed to overseas trends through travel and networking with colleagues in our industry in the right markets.

Our own technology platform is fit for purpose. We have also embraced construction technologies that give us an edge over our competition.

Our **BRAND** essence is clear in the market and top of mind for our target marketplace. Our **MARKETING** activities across all digital platforms are leading edge and on point, attracting large groups of audiences that we can easily convert. We host our associates, consultants and advisors on a regular basis and share our journey and successes with them.

Our interactive website showcases a range of social and commercial activities that promote the great culture and achievements of JD&C.

Our brand and marketing guidelines are clearly articulated and well supported by our people. We have a great team of resources that support us by building our brand essence, developing our guidelines, and positioning our brand both in the industry and within each of our target markets.

We have a strategy for engaging with agents that allows JD&C to be their first choice. All Executive Leadership Team members take responsibility for building and maintaining these pipeline-generating activities. Our pipeline is always full, and our activities are properly resourced.

Great **PEOPLE** are attracted by our **CULTURE** which is the envy of the industry. All are clear on what is expected of them, and they get quality feedback on performance. We have a meaningful performance review program with career path management.

Remuneration and incentives are designed to align to our strategy. We have a fantastic social agenda that is supported by all team members and reinforces our positive culture.

Today, our culture is described as fun, supportive, hardworking and rewarding. Everyone is proud of what JD&C delivers and each understands their contribution is valued. We have a high percentage of 'employee customers' who own JD&C product.

All the team and industry acknowledge the legacy and great work of the founder and are now equally impressed with how the company successors have taken the reins for the next evolution of the business.

Our **ACQUISITION** activities are disciplined. We have clear guidelines within the group that support the effective acquisition and integration of new opportunities.

We have bought high-yielding land banks in Sydney's southwest and south regions.

Monthly acquisitions meetings are supported by dedicated staff. This has improved the quality of our research, the speed of decision-making and allowed us to be proactive. We have targeted some excellent geographic areas that will benefit from government infrastructure, taking options on a range of potential development sites.

Our pipeline is converted in part through the great support we enjoy from our **FINANCIERS**. We set an internal loan to value ratio (LVR) limit that we work towards continuously. We have great relationships with the key financiers and private financiers who will look at funding on a case-by-case basis.

All of our partners match a clearly defined profile and allow us the freedom to do our job.

We have shared our strategic plan with the banks and our shareholders and remain committed to our future course.

We have mitigated our exposure by negotiating out of personal guarantees where practical.

We have a great relationship with **REAL ESTATE** agents that can bring us opportunities. We know how they operate in these contemporary times, and they respect our understanding of their challenges and ambitions.

We keep abreast of **DEMOGRAPHIC** and social trends, doing research prior to each strategic review. We rely on a quality panel of service providers, farming all their data to ensure we build a strategy that is relevant for the times.

Because of the procedures put in place five years ago, our regular monthly reviews of projects, pipeline and project management ensures that we are working from the best **ECONOMIC** market intelligence.

Some projects that were successfully acquired underperformed only because of unforeseeable circumstances. However, due to the processes in place and our cash reserves we were able to see them through.

Our **DEVELOPMENT MANAGEMENT** is now of world-class standard. We meet monthly, report weekly, minute all promises, audit and track delivery. We have a well-documented process for governing the development cycle and we improve it after every project delivery.

We have a great panel of **SUPPLIERS AND CONSULTANTS** that give us depth and access to the best quality service. We have knitted them into a 'community' and engage socially with them to evidence our appreciation.

We have a better understanding of how to use the law to secure a better outcome in the approval process.

We have significantly upgraded our **MARKETING, SALES AND RELATIONSHIP** development performance. Our database is massive, and it is accurate. We have developed a system for staying in touch with buyers and keeping our brand top of mind. This initiative has helped with presales and promoting a positive reputation amongst our community of buyers.

We watched the **REGULATION AND LEGISLATION** landscape and were the first to adjust once council rationalisation happened. We built and maintained relationships, showed empathy for our council friends affected and ended up with some supporters from the process.

We constantly review all we bring to market, considering the buyer and consumer's needs and again 'framing' the intelligence of our suppliers and contractors to design to the market's emerging needs.

We delivered on our 2020 **DEVELOPMENT PORTFOLIO**.

Our **FINANCIAL MANAGEMENT** systems are robust and have stood the test of time. We have confidence that our approach ensures our $15 million portfolio is properly and profitably managed with the right portfolio allocation.

We have a **COMPLIANCE** officer in place and the appropriate WH&S systems to support the business.

Our **COMPETITORS** demonstrate their respect through constant invitations to consider being acquired. We refuse the offers because we wish to preserve the brand and maintain the lifestyles we aspired to.

We are proud of our **BUILT ENVIRONMENT**. It is fit for purpose and large enough to cater for our growth in the next five to 10 years.

Today we retain an active portfolio. It includes those still underway from 2020 with a growing land bank that includes several sites across New South Wales.

Mapping

Mapping is the visual expression of the answer to 'What are the pressures?' ON refers to the activities related to the running of any business. OF refers to the delivery of what the business does for its marketplace.

It is useful to reflect on the map as the DNA of the business. It shows another example of removing complexity – everything comes back to one of these headings.

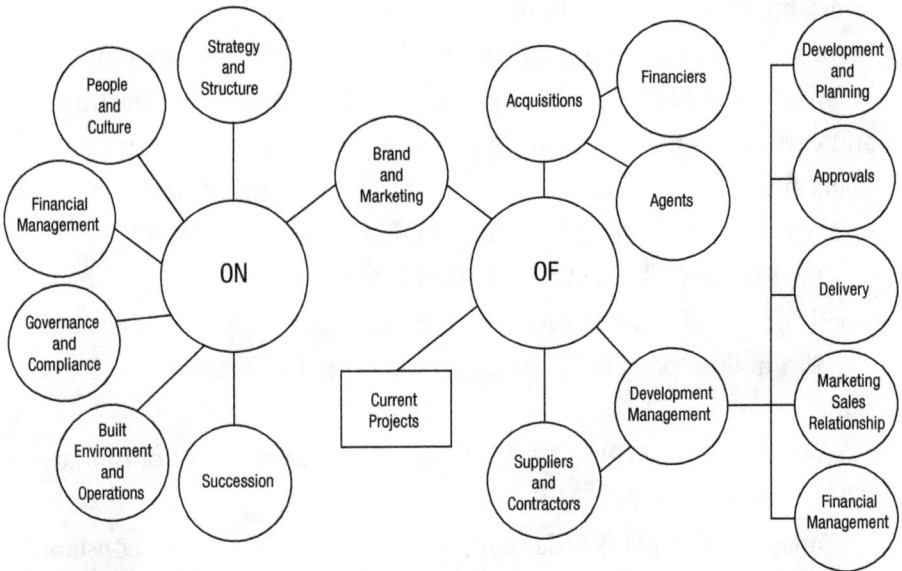

Strategic Milestones

To achieve our 'Future of Choice' we agreed that the following statements should be true in 12 months' time.

We call these objectives our strategic milestones.

Strategic Planning and Structure (SS)

Milestone: within 12 months we will be able to say:

Ref	Milestone	Priority	Owner
SS1	JD&C Strategic Plan 1.0 was signed off by board and shareholders	Critical	JJ
SS2	SLAs are in place between each business division	Critical	RK
SS3	We have a meeting rhythm and agenda for the JD&C board	Critical	PJ
SS4	We have a meeting rhythm and agenda for implementing the strategic plan	Critical	PJ
SS5	We have identified and communicated who the Executive Leadership Team is	Critical	PJ
SS6	We have developed and implemented a complete rhythm of the business	Important	PJ
SS7	Our strategic plan has been communicated in a relevant format for each audience	Critical	PJ
SS8	We confirmed our HR resource needs for this year and recruited to the gaps	Critical	RK
SS9	We have investigated a managed service arrangement for our IT	Important	SS

Ref	Milestone	Priority	Owner
SS10	We developed an offshore study tour program and have a business case for it	Preferred	NJ

Governance and Compliance

Milestone: within 12 months we will be able to say:

Ref	Milestone	Priority	Owner
COM1	We have a WHS Compliance Officer and the WHS Manual is up to date	Critical	SS
COM2	All attend the meetings as scheduled and for which they are required	Critical	SS
COM3	We have implemented a governance framework and three-circle model to ensure our businesses success	Critical	JJ

Brand and Marketing

Milestone: within 12 months we will be able to say:

Ref	Milestone	Priority	Owner
BM1	Our website is complete, leading edge and properly maintained	Critical	IB
BM2	Our company profile is in digital and hardcopy and represents our brand	Critical	IB
BM3	All of our collateral conforms to our brand guidelines and style guide	Critical	IB

Ref	Milestone	Priority	Owner
BM4	Our celebration of successes program has been planned and budgeted	Important	IB
BM5	We have quality internal and external marketing resources to support our activities	Critical	IB
BM6	We published and implemented a group marketing plan and budget	Critical	IB
BM7	Our approach ensures that each development site is properly branded	Important	SS
BM8	We have allocated the leadership team to several agents as ambassadors	Important	PJ
BM9	Ambassadors know what is expected on them to build and maintain relationships	Important	PJ

People and Culture

Milestone: within 12 months we will be able to say:

Ref	Milestone	Priority	Owner
PP1	Every role has an up-to-date position description with KPIs	Critical	RK
PP2	The responsibility for People and Culture has been properly assigned	Critical	RK
PP3	The remuneration and incentive program for the Executive Leadership Team is established	Critical	RK

Ref	Milestone	Priority	Owner
PP4	The remuneration and incentive policies are defined and understood by all	Critical	RK
PP5	We have a social program that helps build our culture and the professional relationships we want	Important	RK
PP6	We have a leave planner to ensure resources are always there to lead the business and each project	Important	RK
PP7	We have defined the culture we want and the behaviours to encourage	Critical	RK
PP8	Succession plans have been established for critical roles in the business	Critical	RK

Financial Management

Milestone: within 12 months we will be able to say:

Ref	Milestone	Priority	Owner
FM1	The JD&C Financial Reporting Framework has been agreed and delivered	Critical	JC
FM2	Treasury targets have been established	Critical	JC
FM3	The research available to us on the economy and markets is applied to active projects in acquisition strategy	Critical	JC

Acquisition Pipeline

Milestone: within 12 months we will be able to say:

Ref	Milestone	Priority	Owner
ACQ1	We have a good discipline in place for assessing all acquisition opportunities	Critical	NJ
ACQ2	Monthly acquisition meetings are underway with agendas and minutes	Critical	NJ
ACQ3	Our search criteria are clearly defined allowing us to focus on the right agents and locations	Critical	NJ
ACQ4	We have engaged properly with all joint venture partners to resolve potential acquisition opportunities	Critical	NJ
ACQ5	We regularly review other developers' products (quarterly visits)	Important	NJ
ACQ6	We have a formal pipeline reporting process and targets in place	Critical	NJ

Development Management

Milestone: within 12 months we will be able to say:

Ref	Milestone	Priority	Owner
DM1	We have templates for project meetings with all reporting adhered to	Critical	NJ
DM2	Project meeting schedules were set and observed; activity is tracked	Critical	NJ

Ref	Milestone	Priority	Owner
DM3	We have appointed a new Development Manager with a planning background	Critical	RK
DM4	We identified relationships within the authorities and engaged appropriate activities to build trust and support	Critical	NJ
DM5	We have access to a panel of quality consultants and suppliers	Critical	NJ
DM6	We have advice on how we may leverage the legal process to facilitate the approval process	Important	RK
DM7	After assessing our project marketing needs, we identified our requirements and have resourced it effectively	Important	RK
DM8	We have a 'JD&C Buyers' community database and actively market to it	Important	IB
DM9	Every project has a defined frequency for a feasibility update	Important	NJ
DM10	We had a proactive response planned and implemented it once council amalgamations were announced	Important	RK
DM11	We have invested time in our valuer panel to build relationships and secure support	Critical	PJ
DM12	With the support of relevant consultants, agents and architects we take time to build our understanding of consumer and buyer trends	Critical	IB

Built Environment

Milestone: within 12 months we will be able to say:

Ref	Milestone	Priority	Owner
BE1	Our brief for our premises refurb is complete and costed	Important	PJ
BE2	Our office amenities are on board and welcomed by all	Important	PJ

Financiers

Milestone: within 12 months we will be able to say:

Ref	Milestone	Priority	Owner
FIN1	We have formal relationship development activities with each bank to strengthen partnerships	Critical	JC
FIN2	We proactively search for any feedback, intel or clues in relation to bank policies or key HR changes	Critical	JC
FIN3	We take our bankers on site regularly	Important	JC
FIN4	We have a panel of potential private partners and have an indication of their appetite for risk and the models in which they would engage	Critical	JC
FIN5	We secured our private partner for Badgerys Creek	Critical	JJ
FIN6	Commercial terms are in place with all private lenders	Critical	JC

Ref	Milestone	Priority	Owner
FIN7	Our LVR targets for 2020–2025 are defined and short-term objectives set	Critical	JC
FIN8	A strategy for funding is in place for Bondi	Critical	JC
FIN9	A financial board pack was prepared and delivered for the Family Council Quarterly Meeting	Important	JC

Current Projects

Milestone: within 12 months we will be able to say:

Ref	Milestone	Priority	Owner
CP1	We secured access rights to The Manor through adjoining properties	Critical	CJ
CP2	Stage 6 is developed, completed and 100 lots have been sold at Macquarie	Critical	CJ
CP3	Mascot is complete	Critical	CJ
CP4	Highfield is at Stage 2 construction; Stage 1 has sold out	Critical	CJ
CP5	Coffs is DA approved, rezoned, and pre-sale marketing commenced	Critical	CJ
CP6	Alexandria is rezoned for mixed use and DA is underway	Critical	CJ
CP7	Oran Park has completed, we have 80 units under management	Critical	CJ

Ref	Milestone	Priority	Owner
CP8	Chatswood is under construction and100% pre-sold	Important	CJ
CP9	Allambie Heights is rezoned, and DA approved	Critical	CJ
CP10	Our property management portfolio has reached 150	Important	CJ
CP11	Our property management systems are ready for scale in management, enquiry handling and landlord relations	Important	CJ

APPENDIX B

Personal Plans

We have included the personal plans for John and Ayesha (G1), and Anika and Tom as an example of G2.

PERSONAL PLAN FOR JOHN AND AYESHA JACKSON

What Matters

- Health and fitness
- Our relationship
- Lifestyle and leisure
- Our children
- Our grandchildren
- Jackson Developments & Construction (JD&C)
- Our homes
- Future Fund
- Family Council
- Foundation

Download

Health and Fitness

- We are in good shape, just need to maintain.
- More time for golf.
- More tennis with the girls.
- Share a passion for walking.
- Love getting to the beach house and ski lodge.
- Would like to add yoga to our routine.
- Would like to do more motorbike riding.
- Reduce alcohol intake.
- Maintain rhythm with medical checks.
- Monitor cholesterol.

Our Relationship

- Like to work towards more structured timetable allowing us to block out Mondays and Fridays just for us.
- Our relationship is solid.
- We share genuine interests with each other – theatre, ballet, sports.
- JD&C and the children can take over our lives.
- Ayesha wants more time with friends and the children.
- John prefers less time.
- More driving holidays just the two of us.
- More time on the boat.
- We have slightly different opinions on how much we enjoy looking after Ben two days a week.

Lifestyle and Leisure

- The balance is not right.
- John is still working too hard.
- John even works on holidays.

- Need to get the balance right between us time versus children time versus grandchildren time.
- Want to buy a New York apartment/house.
- Ayesha wants to holiday again in Sri Lanka.
- Would like to buy a house in London.
- Plan is to travel two to three months away each winter, with London as our base.

Our Children

- Christopher
  - He still does not get it.
  - Not adding value in the business.
  - Is this truly his passion?
  - We need to help him and not ruin the relationship.
  - Not spending a lot of time with him outside of work.
  - Have been some dramas but getting there.
  - Ayesha wants to do more social things with him.

- Priya
  - Same as with Christopher, but smarter.
  - She is so headstrong but could not imagine the business without her.
  - She argues back but this is getting better.
  - Not sure how she will manage one day with marriage, children and work.
  - Spends a lot of time on her sport and preparing for marathons which distracts her from work.
  - Has done some great things at work. Reliable and delivers.
  - Team respect her.
  - Would like to surprise her with a honeymoon.

- Nathan
  - Very demanding.

- Can sometimes act entitled which we need to keep in check.
- So similar to John.
- Need to monitor his behaviour at work.
- Has made his future very clear to us.
- Makes us laugh.
- Can be very caring.
- Want to continue our rugby cup annual trip tradition just us.

- Anika
  - Enormously undemanding.
  - There are no eggshells, no tension, she is very sweet and career independent.
  - Love that she has found her passion.
  - Proud of her path.
  - Is a little reliant on us with the baby.
  - Is starting to ask lots of questions about our assets.
  - Has indicated she wants to start another restaurant.
  - Need to make sure all the children stay connected.

Our Grandchildren

- Love our time with them.
- Children need to invest in au pairs. Happy to support them financially with this.
- Need to start thinking about education funds.
- Would like to take them to Europe as they get older. Just us and one grandkid at a time.
- Need to arrange family night once a quarter with everyone.
- More time on the boat with everyone.

The Business

- Business plan is fantastic.
- All major developments are tenanted.
- Missed out on Alexandria site.

- Working on Castlereagh opportunity.
- Going from strength to strength.
- Finance is in place for all majors.
- Business still cannot run without me.
- Not sure who will run it when I am gone.
- Executive team rely on me too much.
- Need to ensure my long-standing employees are looked after.

Our Homes

- Never want to sell Bellevue Hill.
- The holiday home, Sinhala, is used often by all the family.
- The ski lodge costs a lot to maintain but it's worth it.
- Wish to finalise New York and London purchases.
- Have great support at all properties.
- Every home has a beautiful garden.

Future Fund

- Need to get advice on how the 'value' in current assets can be applied to the Future Fund.
- Five major investments are at least two years away.
- Our children want to understand this part more.
- Advisors sometimes are not helpful.
- Priya is the smartest to help with this.

Family Council

- Process has only just started.
- A little forced but know it will be beneficial in the long run.
- Want to convene another in September.
- Next meeting all should be on deck.
- No dial ins.
- Would like to learn how other families do this well.

Foundation

- Donations are continual.
- Want to keep supporting the youth.
- Currently being capitalised.
- Not large amounts of money floating around.
- Need to get it active.
- Need to further progress our wills.

Future of Choice

It is five years from today, and we are reflecting on the most rewarding year of our lives – rewarding by any measure.

Having turned 69 and 65 respectively, we are both as fit and healthy as we choose to be. We keep fit by doing a lot of walking, yoga and swimming. John is also enjoying golf three times a week while Ayesha enjoys her ocean swims and meditation. We still enjoy cooking healthy meals at home with the children. We also love to dine at 'our table' at Anika's restaurant.

We get on famously just as we did the first day we met. We enjoy four-day breaks visiting places in Australia and of course our own properties. Our principal home remains Bellevue Hill. We spend as much time as possible at Sinhala which is truly a sanctuary.

We spend Australian winters in Europe and New York and love hosting friends and family at both properties. Our lifestyle is relaxed and rewarding. Between the properties and boat, we have the right balance.

We are well connected with the family. John calls Uncle Marvin at least every month or so to check in and update him. We have been able to financially assist all of our important extended family members including nieces and nephews.

All of the grandchildren are growing up and are enjoying the properties and boat. We spend five to seven days at the ski lodge at least once each winter. We now enjoy ourselves more while our lifestyle is costing less. The savings have in part been re-invested in Ayesha's art collection. Despite our busy lifestyle we stay in touch with all of our friends.

JD&C's reorganisation was a huge success. Christopher, Priya and Nathan are all doing a fantastic job running the business. When I decided to step back two years ago the right successor was evident and is doing a great job.

Nathan is heading up his own Property Portfolio Division and has built businesses of a scale and style that suit his personality, priorities and professional aspirations. Christopher has decided to engage in further studies in architecture and we are supporting him through this process. The boys are doing great under Priya's leadership.

All the children have strong balance sheets and are supported when business plans and cases are presented that make commercial sense.

We have continued to grow and secure wealth in both our Foundation and the Future Fund. A strategic divestment allowed us the best of all worlds: a cashed-up bank, a Foundation that was capitalised (it had money to give) and a significant development holding.

In John's role as Chair of the Family Business the opportunity is there for him to mentor each of the children. New opportunities have been considered with all styles of engagement in place to allow the family to invest in and manage development opportunities.

The children are now in full charge of their professional lives.

Anika is working three days a week in the restaurants. She has won numerous awards and has received many write-ups and we are incredibly proud of her.

It is noticeable that time we spend with each of the children is now more Jackson rather than business centric.

This separation has meant that the children's spouses can now enjoy updates on the business through our quarterly family luncheons. At this event we also talk about the Foundation and its ambitions.

We have found Christopher is more communicative. It took some time, but he now trusts his view is being heard. Christopher and Nathan provide a valuable contribution. They have grown to understand their differences and respect each other. All children are independently wealthy, and this lack of financial pressure has adjusted their priorities.

Priya is doing a great job as CEO. She is well known in the industry and recognised for a range of award-winning projects.

We love our grandchildren. One weekend each season we host all of them at Sinhala. They are in our lives a lot and we have them over regularly though we enjoy some help to allow us to concentrate on them. We involve them in our pursuits, and we turn up to important moments in their lives.

We also activated the Foundation, which has been capitalised and is active. There have been a number of liquidity events in the last five years that allowed us to build each family's balance sheet and that of the Jackson bank.

Our balance sheet has improved. We have reached a personal net worth of $150 million net asset with no debt. Our community contribution continues through the Jackson Family Foundation.

We have an active Family Council that keeps our family together in managing wealth. The Family Council liaises with the business board and between the two, strategies for the *business* and our *balance sheets* are debated and resolved.

Stakes in the Sand

- We enjoy yoga together twice a week.
- John plays golf three times a week.
- Ayesha meditates twice a day.
- We spend time together and as a family at our holiday home, Sinhala, once a month.

- We invested time and funds in Sinhala's garden.
- We remodelled the guest house at Bellevue Hill.
- We enjoy four-day escapes to new places and favourites around Australia.
- We supported the agreed family members with education funds for their children.
- We enjoy visiting the ski lodge on a regular basis during winter.
- We settled on Mayfair London.
- New York is all set up and we enjoyed a three-week holiday in the fall.
- The business has a solid five-year plan and funding model in place.
- The Executive Leadership Team and my children understand my future plans.
- Castlereagh development delivered set objectives.
- Christopher and John golf together once a month.
- Priya has a meaningful role in the business.
- Nathan understands his options at leadership in the business.
- Nathan and John enjoy an annual rugby trip.
- Anika is financially stable.
- We supported Anika with an au pair.
- Anika and Ayesha play tennis together once a week.
- We supported Anika with what she needed.
- Ayesha spends quality time with the children one on one.
- We supported the children in balance sheet management.
- John is still working in the business three days a week.
- Quarterly Family Council meetings are a success.
- The Jackson Family Foundation was formalised, business plan developed and funds secured.
- The Future Fund is managed effectively and has delivered set results this year.
- Our wills have been updated.

PERSONAL PLAN FOR ANIKA JACKSON

What Matters

- Health and fitness
- Tom and Ben
- Parents and siblings
- Family and friends
- Restaurant
- Travel, hobbies and interests
- Asset accumulation
- Balance sheet management

Download

Health and Fitness

- Want to do more yoga.
- Need to get a regular masseuse.
- More time to cook healthier meals at home.
- More cooking with Mum.
- More family walks.
- Want to increase my meditation.
- Would like to do a regular health retreat with Tom.
- Drink less alcohol and reduce amount of coffee.
- More time for tennis with the girls.
- Maintain three PT sessions each week.

Tom and Ben

- More one on one time with each other.
- Would love more time to experience fine dining and latest dining trends together.

- Love our adventure holidays together – skiing, hiking, sailing etc.
- Want to support Tom more with his career and work.
- More midweek romantic getaways.
- More family walks.
- Ben is great.
- Need to confirm his place at Scots.
- Need to check Mum and Dad are still happy looking after him while I'm at work.
- More time with his cousins.
- We are thinking about baby number 2.

Parents and Siblings

- Love spending time with Mum and Dad. Together and separately.
- Worry that Dad is working too hard.
- Need to support Mum better.
- Need to stay across of all the family governance matters to protect my interests.
- Need to check in regularly with Chris, Priya and Nathan.
- Need to check in more with all my nieces and nephews.
- Host more family get togethers at the restaurant.
- Want to support Priya so she knows that I back her 100%.
- Need to check in with Chris regularly. Keep him talking.
- Nathan and I to catch up for dinner on a regular basis to ensure our relationship stays intact.

Family and Friends

- Love our annual family holidays with Mum, Dad and everyone.
- Being treated like the baby is getting boring. Need to address this.
- Need my siblings to understand that I am not getting a free ride.
- Need my siblings to understand that I work hard.
- Have a great network of friends. Mostly from school, cooking and through Tom.

- More regular catchups with our friends.
- Would love to take the boat for my 35th birthday with friends to Hamilton Island.
- Would love to host alumni event for my culinary school grads.
- Expand our social network through Ben's friends' parents.
- Lots of friends are super supportive of restaurant. Need to keep this balanced.

Restaurant

- My pride and joy.
- Site is completely established now in Rose Bay.
- Atmosphere and casualness are really appealing, although menu is innovative and high end.
- Current team are fantastic.
- Hard to find talent, but once we do, they are great.
- Need to engage with more social influencers to drive market attention.
- Would love more media pieces and publications.
- Would like to extend licence. Need help with this – maybe Chris or Priya could help.
- Want to maintain 30 to 40 hours a week with managers to plug the gap.
- Would love to host more intimate events, products launches etc that attract celebrities.
- Food costs need close monitoring.
- Would love to do more to support women in hospitality.

Travel, Hobbies and Interests

- Continue visiting France once a year.
- More wine trips with friends around Australia, New Zealand and Europe.
- More time to read and chill.

- More time at the beach as a family.
- Would love to go to Tassie.
- Want to tie in sourcing providore supplies with getaways, e.g. visiting truffle farms.
- Would love to be more active with Priya. Maybe bike riding and more tennis.

Asset Accumulation

- Have never worried about money.
- Tom and I prefer life experiences than material possessions.
- Need to make sure we have a funding plan in place for Ben's education.
- Restaurant is making a good profit and repayments to Dad and Mum are on track.
- Would like to understand more about the family's balance sheet and how this is managed.
- Have never worried but need to start paying attention as I am not in the family business.
- We own our home in Paddington.
- Would love a hobby farm.
- We are good at managing the finances for the restaurant.
- Would love to look at a second restaurant. Maybe in the Highlands.
- Want to update my family on how the business is performing so they know I am okay.

Future of Choice

It is five years from now, and we are celebrating the most fulfilling year of our lives.

Our relationship is solid. We keep it that way with weekly date nights and open conversations where we share our experiences, challenges and successes. We have two weekends away, just us, each year.

We have a great structure built around our personal lives providing the support we need.

Tom is as healthy as he wants to be. He exercises three times per week which is programmed well in advance. He maintains a healthy weight and his lifestyle is active enough to ensure diet is not an issue. Anika is fit and healthy. Her routine includes a range of exercises including gym, tennis, yoga, bike riding and swimming. Her healthy meal preparations ensure she and the family can comfortably stay healthy and fit.

Ben and his little sibling are both happy and healthy. Ben is seven years old and is attending Scots. He is an active little man who loves sport and playing with his friends. He is very academic and loves reading, learning but mostly cooking with Mum.

We live in our renovated home in Paddington which is now five bedrooms. The renovation was completed in 2023 and more than meets our needs. It is the home our children will grow up in. We have built our assets. We have acquired some investment properties along with our share portfolio which has a 'long-term' investment mix. The house today would be valued at $10 million.

We have a full and rewarding lifestyle. We go skiing overseas once a year. We go on an island escape every year and try to make sure that one of our parent sets are with us on that vacation. Every year we have a girls/boys weekend away and alternate a full week. Tom and I love our annual health retreats.

We are close to all our family. We stay engaged with my parents and enjoy weekly dinners together. Tom's parents are doing great, and we see them in the Southern Highlands regularly. Our children have strong relationships with their cousins, and we all regularly meet as brothers and sisters socially. Our network of friends is part of our lives, and we love hosting them at the restaurants. We expanded our network including the parents of our children's friends.

The restaurant in Rose Bay is thriving and receiving many awards and accolades. Our second restaurant was launched in 2021 and is a thriving success. Both businesses are profitable, and I enjoy spending my time at both locations being creative in the kitchen.

The Jackson Family Foundation is well established. There is a fund that is fully 'subscribed' and available for investment. The family manages the funds carefully to ensure that what we hold still grows. All the right systems are in place. Meeting disciplines are formal, and the board is balanced and well governed.

Tom is loving his work and has finally achieved the right work–life balance. We have a great support network that ensures our family and businesses can run smoothly.

Stakes in the Sand

- Tom and I enjoy a weekly date night at a new and exciting restaurant.
- Tom and I enjoy two annual weekend getaways just the two of us that always involve good food and wine.
- PT three times a week and weekly yoga at the beach keeps me in check.
- I play tennis with the girls once a month.
- We have talked about baby number two.
- Ben is enrolled at Scots.
- I enjoy spending two full days a week just with Ben.
- Mum and Dad love looking after Ben two days a week.
- We have engaged an architect for the renovation on Paddington.
- We are managing our share portfolio effectively and have grown it by 20 percent.
- We enjoy an annual ski trip as a family.
- We visit Tom's parents once a quarter in the Highlands.
- I have started looking into acquiring a truffle farm.

- We regularly catch up with our closest friends.
- The Rose Bay restaurant has grown in sales and value and has received multiple awards.
- I take the team offsite once a year to set our plan and goals for the year ahead.
- We have identified a second restaurant site.
- We achieved our extended liquor trade licence.
- We understand the Jackson Family Foundation better and now know the role we play in this.
- I actively provide updates to my siblings on how the businesses are performing.

APPENDIX C

Jackson Family Charter

THE JACKSON FAMILY CHARTER

Preamble

This charter is intended to define and formalise the governance of wealth shared by the family.

The charter is not a legal document. The legal protection of and entitlements to family wealth are covered by the various trusts, wills and related documents. Some of these documents are directly referenced herein.

Every problem or matter for resolution presents two independent challenges. These two challenges are firstly the solution and secondly how the solution will be determined. When both are addressed at once, you have complexity and debate. This charter is intended to resolve the second question (how) before the first question (what) arises.

Our Guiding Philosophy

Wealth can be a catalyst for happiness, or an enemy of it.
Which one it becomes is a matter of your attitude to it.
Wealth does not define you nor does it make you special.
If your attitude is right, then it can become an asset and can
accelerate your ambitions and success.
– Ayesha Jackson, March 2021

PART ONE –
THE FAMILY CHARTER PURPOSE
AND CORE ELEMENTS

Purpose

Family Charter Defined

The Family Charter is a document that describes the guiding principles agreed to by family members, essentially defining the family's relationship with the balance sheet and related trading enterprises.

A family-in-business charter can be thought of as the 'fundamental understanding' of the wealth that reflects both the family values and their business values. It seeks to address issues that tend to be the most controversial and most crucial to the future of the family in the governance of wealth. A charter can address issues of who will lead in the business, who will work in it, and how family members employed by the family business will be compensated. In particular, it defines how these decisions will be made.

An important outcome of the planning process and communication objectives must be to seek consensus. When family consensus* is obtained, it represents a clear and agreed statement of values, and therefore minimises the potential for conflict.

A Living Document

A charter can help to minimise, and even avoid, many of the most typical problems confronting the family and its relationship with wealth.

It is not always possible for all family members to agree on every single issue. Accordingly, formulation of the Family Charter document may evolve over a period of time and requires a number of family meetings.

---

* We define consensus in the following terms: 'While not agreeing with the decision, I can happily live with it to ensure we make decisions that keep us moving forward, together.'

The concept of consensus is a key element in assisting family members retain a cooperative and educated approach to resolving challenges and issues within the family and within the businesses they own and influence, and their balance sheet.

Ultimately, not all family members will agree with every provision of the charter, but all working and retired family members should have an opportunity to influence this document at dedicated Family Charter meetings. In this way, the binding principles and practices contained in the final charter will be carefully thought out, discussed and documented. At subsequent family meetings key principles and parameters are set out to guide in establishing the charter.

This Family Charter sets the principles and practices to be observed by the family with regard to the management and ownership of the family balance sheet. The charter also helps family members understand the rights and responsibilities that come with ownership and management and to clarify the boundary between family, ownership and business operations. The charter is a confidential family document. Signing the document reinforces that each family member has contributed to the charter and agrees with the details it contains.

Communication and Confidentiality

A private email group will be set up for the Jackson family to:

- protect confidentiality
- record and archive correspondence
- simplify communication.

All family members will have a designated email address for family governance and charter-related matters.

All correspondence in relation to matters encompassed by this charter will be conducted on the jackson.com site.

Context

The family members who have contributed to the development of this document have agreed that the Jackson Family Charter should:

- assist the family, as shareholders or beneficiaries of the wealth, to develop and maintain alignment in the management of assets and the engagement with the trading businesses
- clarify family members' roles and expectations of them
- clarify the relationship between the Family Council, shareholders, board of directors and Executive Leadership Team
- create a forum to discuss complex issues that might otherwise be avoided or delayed
- explain what happens when the unexpected happens.

Family

To avoid any misunderstanding now and into the future, reference in this charter to 'family members' means any direct bloodline descendants of John and Ayesha Jackson.

In the first instance 'family' is defined as John, Ayesha, their children Christopher, Priya, Nathan and Anika, their children's spouses and the grandchildren of John and Ayesha.

This definition will evolve as the family grows with the addition and arrival of the next generation.

It is John and Ayesha's intention that important partners of their children will be welcomed, and a spirit of inclusiveness and transparency applied.

The Companies

Any reference to the balance sheet, assets or enterprises shall mean any enterprise John and Ayesha hold an interest in and which has been identified and named by the Family Council as falling within the shared asset pool or balance sheet. This definition acknowledges that from time to time family members may wish to engage in an enterprise independent of our family-in-business concept.

The Family Council

The Family Council is the group of family members charged with the responsibility of managing the interaction between the family and the balance sheet.

The Family Council will meet formally on a quarterly basis to tend to the requirements of managing the shared wealth. This is to ensure that any decisions are not in conflict with the family's shared vision, mission and core values, or the ambition of each family member.

There will be four meetings each year, as follows:

- **January:** Three-day Family Retreat program (standard agenda plus AGM plus professional development plus family activities).
- **April:** Half-day followed by a family activity.
- **July:** Full day to review performance of the trading enterprise followed by a family activity.
- **October:** Half-day followed by a family activity.

Agendas:

- The standard agenda will apply at all meetings. In addition:
  - A trading business detailed agenda will apply for the July meeting.
  - The retreat agenda will include a professional development component.

PART TWO –
THE ROLE OF THE FAMILY COUNCIL

Overview

Our balance sheet and experience in business gives us an advantage in the marketplace. Essentially this is because decision-making can be more easily facilitated and is more likely to take a long-term view; rather than being driven by the possibility of short-term profits at the expense of longer-term advantages.

The family members working in the business acknowledge that the Family Council and Family Retreat are not formal decision-making bodies in respect to the business.

While the Family Council may develop proposals and recommendations with a view to influencing the board and management, good board governance principles will determine board decisions.

Why Does This Council Matter in Relation to the Jackson Trading Enterprises?

- To develop and maintain alignment to the company/business vision and mission.
- To create a commitment to the Jackson family remaining a family in business.
- To ensure the Family Charter provides a basis for how we influence the business as shareholders.
- To ensure our business will be a positive legacy.
- To ensure the business operates profitably and ethically and delivers a meaningful return for shareholders.

The Value the Council Brings to the Trading Asset (JD&C)

- Promotes the family as a respected, honourable and successful family in business within all our communities (profitable, equitable, viable, long term – sustainable).
- Provides the family-in-business style of direction to our designated family representatives.
- Creates celebrations to link family and our history in business.
- Demonstrates our track record of engagement in enterprises that provide an acceptable return on capital expenditure.
- Fosters the basis of a sustainable, ethical and profitable business culture.

The Family

The Family Charter will:

- assist each family member to be true to our family values
- enable the family enterprises to provide the funds to permit each of us to make decisions for our future in alignment with our values
- provide all current and future family members with opportunity to reach their potential
- demonstrate the value of good governance in personal, family and business life.

Motivations for this Charter

We embrace this charter and its intent for the following reasons:

- It is great for communication.
- It provides a basis for shared understanding of complex matters of governance.
- It provides the next generation(s) with an opportunity to learn, understand and take responsibility.
- It ensures that everyone feels well informed.
- It develops a roadmap for new generations to follow as others pass.

- It ensures that the affairs of the estates of each generation are well managed and intentions served.
- It clarifies the activities and engagements both during and between family events.
- It mitigates the potential for family conflict.
- It provides a basis for resolving family conflict.
- It creates a common dialogue that brings each generation of peers together.
- It builds a strong precedent for generations that have yet to arrive.

Differentiating Between the Roles

The table opposite should provide some assistance to family members in differentiating between the roles of the Family Council, trading company board, owners and Executive Leadership Team to ensure everyone focuses on the issues at hand wearing the proper hat.

Our Three Circles

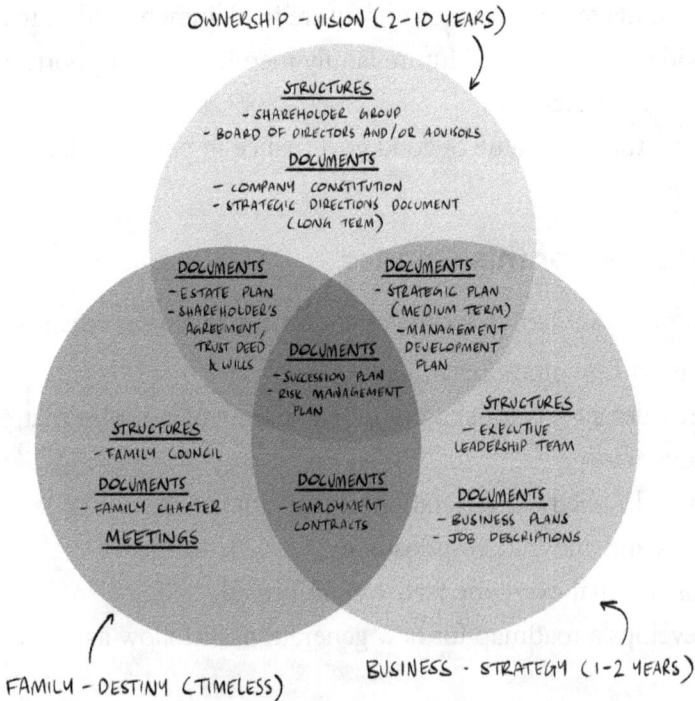

OWNERSHIP – VISION (2–10 YEARS)

STRUCTURES
- SHAREHOLDER GROUP
- BOARD OF DIRECTORS AND/OR ADVISORS

DOCUMENTS
- COMPANY CONSTITUTION
- STRATEGIC DIRECTIONS DOCUMENT (LONG TERM)

DOCUMENTS
- ESTATE PLAN
- SHAREHOLDER'S AGREEMENT, TRUST DEED & WILLS

DOCUMENTS
- SUCCESSION PLAN
- RISK MANAGEMENT PLAN

DOCUMENTS
- STRATEGIC PLAN (MEDIUM TERM)
- MANAGEMENT DEVELOPMENT PLAN

STRUCTURES
- FAMILY COUNCIL

DOCUMENTS
- FAMILY CHARTER

MEETINGS

DOCUMENTS
- EMPLOYMENT CONTRACTS

STRUCTURES
- EXECUTIVE LEADERSHIP TEAM

DOCUMENTS
- BUSINESS PLANS
- JOB DESCRIPTIONS

FAMILY – DESTINY (TIMELESS)

BUSINESS – STRATEGY (1–2 YEARS)

Circle	Role	Obligations	Benefits	Qualifications
Family	Family Council member	• Set the ultimate family destiny • Advise the board on dividend policy and directors' fees • Advise the board on strategic investment and governance issues • Advise the board on ownership, succession and estate plans • Attend Family Council meetings • Develop and review the Family Charter	Annual Family Retreat activities	Elected by current Family Council members
Ownership	Company shareholder (via the ownership board)	• Owner's plan • Provide capital • Manage board performance, selections and terminations • Support decisions of the board • Attend shareholders' meetings	Dividends as set by board of directors	Owner of shares Family member

Circle	Role	Obligations	Benefits	Qualifications
Ownership (cont.)	Company director (via the ownership board)	• Set long-term corporate vision (the 'what') • Govern the company • Set company risk appetite and policy • Approve medium-term strategy • Employ, evaluate and advise CEO • Monitor the company's performance • Balance the company's interest versus shareholders' interests • Attend directors' meetings	Director's fees benchmarked to Australian Institute of Company Directors (AICD) survey	Specified skill levels and experience Elected by shareholders
Business	Executive Leadership Team (ELT)	• Set medium-term corporate strategy (the 'how') • Run the company and develop business plan • Manage company risk appetite and policy • Employ, evaluate and advise staff • Reach company's targets and KPIs • Attend management meetings • Develop management succession plans	Salary package benchmarked to Australian Institute of Management (AIM) survey Inclusion in Key Employee Share Plan (KESP)	Specified skill levels and experience Employed by the CEO

PART THREE –
FAMILY COUNCIL FORMALITIES

Meetings and Schedule

The Family Council will meet quarterly on a formal basis. One of these quarterly meetings will take the form of an annual Family Retreat which will typically be run over a weekend.

The Family Retreat will be a gathering of families and family members at the instigation of the family for the purpose of celebration. The council shall use the gatherings as a vehicle to inform, educate and report on any family business, shareholder representative and balance sheet, and promote personal development and family connectedness.

The Family Council AGM is to be held in January of each year in line with the Family Retreat.

The AGM agenda will include recommendations concerning:

- company board appointments and reporting
- company dividend policy outcomes
- compensation arrangements of family members
- changes to the balance sheet.

The Family Retreat program will be confirmed each year at the July quarterly meeting.

Meeting Guidelines

A quorum for the Family Council shall be 100% of designated members: John, Ayesha, Christopher, Priya, Nathan and Anika.

It is acknowledged that as the family grows in numbers there is no automatic right to be represented on the Family Council.

It is anticipated that existing council members will identify potential members in retreat and nurture and mentor the candidate.

A diverse range of skills, experience, difference and diversity is sought as time passes.

Potential council members will only be considered on reaching 21 years of age.

The Family Council will consider and recommend to family members various insurances to ensure the sustainability of any family enterprise and the independence of surviving family members.

Commitment to confidentiality within the council shall be paramount.

Budgeting for Family Retreat and council activities:

- An annual agenda of activities shall be developed and maintained 12 months in advance.
- All identified activities shall be supported by an appropriate budget to be presented and approved at the council AGM.
- It is envisaged the Family Retreat will coincide with the AGM for the purposes of communication.
- It is intended that the family balance sheet will appropriately fund such activities of the Family Council to the extent that these activities may impact or influence the businesses.

The Family Council members who are not employed in the family business are charged with organising and managing the Family Retreat.

Governance of Trading Interests

For the family to be well informed it is important that regular meetings are held with the shareholder representative.

From time to time, the shareholder representative may invite Family Council members to meet with:

- company directors
- business board members
- Executive Leadership Team.

Governance Framework of the Family Interest in Trading Enterprises

The family currently holds 100% of the shares in Jackson Developments & Construction (JD&C).

JD&C board:

- John Jackson
- Priya Jackson
- Tom Klein
- Jack Blunt.

Consideration of Balance Sheet Management

The family holds a diversified balance sheet.

It is understood that specialist skills are needed to guide decision-making in relation to the balance sheet.

The Family Council will seek to secure specialist advice at commercially reasonable rates to inform, assess and help implement their decisions.

Decision-Making and Control

All assets held in the balance sheet are under the direct control of John and Ayesha Jackson.

Christopher, Priya, Nathan and Anika's role is to consider, engage, learn and influence the thinking that is applied to the family balance sheet now and into the future.

To that end the current voting rights are held by John (1) and Ayesha (1).

In time, John and Ayesha may elect to activate and extend voting rights to their children.

Additionally, they may elect to consider the views of their children to affect any 'tie break' if needed.

PART FOUR –
GUIDELINES FOR KEY FAMILY
COUNCIL MATTERS

Dividend Policy and Directors' Fees

The Family Council will review family members' financial expectations and make a formal recommendation in relation to any distributions or support.

The family business structure with quarterly accounts and notes are provided as an addendum and reviewed at the quarterly Family Council meetings to an appropriate level of detail.

Ownership

Each asset will have its own legal documentation in respect of a company constitution, trust documents, shareholders' agreements and so on; however, the principles that we wish to guide this formal documentation are:

- sale – first right of refusal between John and Ayesha, then direct to Christopher, Priya, Nathan and Anika
- death – as per wills.

Business Case Requirements

All members of the Family Council may bring investment opportunities to the council for consideration.

These will be identified as 'general business' matters for consideration, discussion and determination.

A family member may benefit directly and individually from such opportunities; however, all interests must be disclosed in advance.

The following must be included as a minimum for an opportunity to be discussed at a Family Council meeting; it is not intended to be exhaustive and further information may be requested:

- What is the idea or purpose?
- Where did it come from?
- What resources does it require?
- Who is involved and in what capacity?
- What specialist input has been applied to test the idea?
- What benefit will you derive?
- What benefit will the family derive?
- What exactly is being requested (money, time, contacts)?
- What precedents are there for the idea?
- What risk is involved and how will it be mitigated?

Family Employment

From time to time, skills, knowledge, experience and time itself will need to be applied to the management of the family's wealth.

Family members may be considered for employment in the stewardship of the balance sheet.

The family member must have, or be in the process of acquiring, the requisite skill to fulfil any duties for which they are appointed.

Should this be the case, they will be eligible to compensation at a market rate.

A market rate is represented by the compensation required to retain a non-family member with similar skills and qualifications, to complete the tasks or fill the role.

The position must be supported by a position description which clearly articulates the responsibilities and time commitment of the role.

Loans

Loans may be made to family members; they will be considered only with prior notice (21 days) when supported by a business case. An interest rate will be set that reflects the level of risk and amount of capital required. These interest rates once set will apply to all loans that are of the same class of risk. Interest must be paid and or offset against any family distribution. The business case must conform to the framework set out by the Family Council or ownership board depending on the source of loan funds.

Decision-Making

The Family Council is the forum where decisions are made that may influence the family, family members and the family wealth.

Decision-making and dispute resolution is to be based on a consensus process with unanimous agreement required to affect any agreed action or recommendation.

Any unresolved disputes shall be determined by John and Ayesha at inception.

The inaugural Family Council will include the following:

John Jackson Ayesha Jackson	Ownership and control
Christopher Jackson Priya Jackson Nathan Jackson Anika Jackson	Influence
John Vamos	Independent chair

The chair will moderate all meetings and record all minutes.
The chair is not required to be an independent.
The chair will be appointed, annually, at the Family Retreat.

PART FIVE –
CORE VALUES AND VISION

Core Values

These are the non-negotiable expectations of any family member; they are our practices and beliefs.

Personal Attributes

- Reliable
- Honest
- Ethical
- Accountable
- Sense of humour
- Courageous
- Relaxed
- Fair
- Disciplined
- Committed
- Has good values
- Open-minded
- Spiritual
- Nurturing
- Balanced
- Kind
- Strong integrity

Work and Professional Life

- Grateful
- Goal-driven
- Balance of time
- Have a go (entrepreneurial)

- Strong leadership
- Proactive
- Promotes family gatherings
- Employees with similar values
- Regular holidays
- Respect for the business
- Understands Family Charter and its intentions
- Understands the business's aims
- Understands our heritage

Life Balance

- Have fun
- Health is very important
- Be active
- Live in the now with the future in mind
- Work to live – not live to work
- The journey is more important than the destination

Self-Development

- Well read
- Continuous learning
- Achieves full potential
- Broad horizons
- Open to new ideas and experiences
- Creative and innovative

Relationships and Communication

- Accept others as they are
- Listen
- Employees as equals
- Respect people, ideas and property
- Mentoring
- Consensus decisions

- Speak out
- Non-discriminatory

Community and Environment

- Charitable
- Be an example in the community
- Care about the planet
- Community service
- Promote our family philanthropy

Some Jacksonisms

- 'Never give up'
- 'Tomorrow is a new day'
- 'Don't be perfect, be better'

Vision

What we believe we can become:

- As a family with wealth, we see an opportunity to grow a wealth opportunity for the benefit of current and future family members.
- A source of opportunity to develop through education, capabilities and values as individuals, which, in turn, enables our family members to provide for themselves and make a meaningful contribution to society.
- Assist family members to identify and create opportunities for a meaningful and successful life as an individual, for younger family members to base their inspiration and behaviours on.
- Be recognised by the 'outside world' as making a worthwhile contribution to community, environment, economy, family and individuals.
- Continue to respect the legacy of John and Ayesha Jackson as the founders of JD&C.

PART SIX –
COMMUNICATION AND EDUCATION

Communication

In all our dealings with each other, family members will endeavour to adhere to the following principles:

- Respect the confidentiality of communication within the family.
- Communicate actively with each other clearly, factually and honestly.
- Individuals must not dominate any meeting.
- We celebrate and promote diversity and difference.
- We avoid typecasting individuals.
- Lively communication is expected; however, discussions should never be personal.
- Discuss issues with a focus on outcomes and 'on the merits' (there is no bad idea, just good ideas and better ideas).
- Discuss issues that are otherwise avoided, but do not discuss complex issues without preparation.
- Respect the opinions of other family members, even if we do not agree with them.
- Quarterly 'minutes' from the Family Council meetings will be circulated.

Education

The family will promote education through the following avenues:

- Sponsorship of tertiary and further studies (business case required)
- Funding of the Family Council program
- Inclusion of professional development at the Family Retreat
- Establishment of the family library.

Employment of Family in Asset Management

Further Requirements

As explained earlier, the family is receptive to family members assisting in the management of the balance sheet providing they are able to demonstrate they have the potential to make a strong contribution, via their enthusiasm, maturity, skills and experiences.

Family members will only be offered employment on the following conditions:

- There is a position available.
- Family members view working with family as a privilege and not a right.
- They will be subject to an inclusive selection process.
- The owners will have the final say.
- It is desirable they have travelled overseas and broadened their horizons.
- Their performance is managed objectively.
- Payment for balance sheet management is not their primary source of income.

PART SEVEN –
FAMILY ENGAGEMENT AND
SHARED INTERESTS

Personal Updates

We acknowledge that everyone's life and times, ambitions and challenges are interesting and important. We allocate time at each meeting to listen, engage and support each other's journeys.

We are all more interesting than we realise.

Family Activities

Breaking bread together is important. However, it should not be the only way in which the family shares time.

Each quarter, in turn, a family member will take responsibility for convening and hosting an activity day. They will select the activity with genuine regard for the needs and expectations of all.

Outside comfort zone is encouraged, while activities known to cause angst are to be avoided.

Philanthropy and Charity

We support philanthropy and the family's philanthropic endeavours. In general, donations will be directed through the Family Council.

As a family, at the annual Family Retreat[73] we discuss and encourage family members to be actively supportive and involved in charitable activities requiring personal endeavour (such as building orphanages, third-world health improvement, tours of duty).

We seek to support individuals who are equally worthy of opportunity but denied due to lack of access to wealth and influence.

Environment

As long-standing and highly ethical corporate citizens, our family is committed to protecting and promoting the environment by:

- providing resources to implement and meet the requirements of the environmental policy
- promoting internal awareness by supporting projects that seek solutions to environmental problems in order to improve the sustainability of the global environment
- taking a leadership role in the wider community by actively encouraging our employees to promote environmental awareness outside of the workplace to family and friends
- integrating environmental stewardship into all facets of our operations
- conducting all business in a responsible manner; respecting the environment
- fostering the sustainable use of the earth's resources by careful selection of environmentally conscious suppliers
- complying with all applicable statutory environmental laws and regulations.

PART EIGHT –
ALTERATIONS TO THIS CHARTER

Ad Hoc Amendments

If a family member believes that the charter should be added to or amended, he or she should prepare a written amendment proposal, detailing the nature of the proposed addition or amendment, and the reason he or she believes the addition or amendment is appropriate.

All such amendment proposals will be considered at the next scheduled Family Council meeting and will be determined by unanimous support agreed through consensus, and formally adopted provided a quorum was present to determine the suggested changes.

Annual Review

In addition to the process above which allows for ongoing ad hoc amendments or additions, this charter will be reviewed annually at the Family Retreat.

Proposed additions or amendments will be treated in the same way as they are under the ad hoc amendment process outlined above.

PART NINE – RATIFICATION

By signing this document, all of the family members involved with the development of this charter agree and acknowledge that:

- they have had an opportunity to openly contribute to, question and discuss the spirit and wording of this charter
- the spirit and wording of this charter reflects the consensus reached by the family during its development
- they will commit to each other to support and adhere to the spirit and wording of this charter, in both actions and words
- the expectations and obligations imposed by this charter will form part of their terms and conditions of employment with the company.

Signed by the following family members on _____ [date].

John Jackson _____

Ayesha Jackson _____

Christopher Jackson _____

Priya Jackson _____

Nathan Jackson _____

Anika Jackson _____

PART TEN – CHARTER APPENDICES

Charter Appendix One: A Family History

The history of the evolution of the family balance sheet is in three parts.

The first is in the balance sheet exposé prepared by John Jackson – an extract is in the body of this charter and will from time to time be updated.

The second is the family history of both John's family in England and Ayesha's family in Sri Lanka.

The third is contained in the strategic plans prepared for the trading enterprises. These plans will be tabled at family meetings to secure their endorsement. This will be done annually, and each plan carefully archived to evidence the history of the business.

Charter Appendix Two: Asset Pool and Jackson Balance Sheet

JD&C (100%) Estimated value based on normalised EBITDA of $50m	*$400,000,000
Bellevue Hill	$20,000,000
Castlereagh Street (75%)	$35,000,000
Ski lodge	$8,000,000
Sinhala	$6,000,000
London home (under consideration – funds available)	$30,000,000
New York home (under consideration – funds now allocated)	$28,000,000
Superannuation	$5,000,000
Shares	$4,000,000
Future Fund	$2,000,000
Foundation	$1,500,000
Debt	$5,500,000
Net Worth (outside Trading Enterprise)	**$134,000,000**

* Estimate only and AUD

Charter Appendix Three: Summary of the Jackson Estate

Summary of Will of John Albert Jackson, Dated 3 October 2018

- Ayesha Jackson to be **executor and trustee of John's estate**.
- Executor and trustee are entitled to be **reimbursed/compensated for testamentary expenses/time spent** as executor and trustee of estate.
- **Executor and trustee entitled to, in relation to distribution of the rest and residue of estate:** convert residuary assets of estate to cash and distribute or distribute actual assets of estate so that they are jointly owned by intended estate beneficiaries or distribute the actual assets of estate such that intended estate beneficiaries receive all ownership interests in certain assets.
- **John's body** is to be available for organ transplant/medical and scientific research purposes.
- **Funeral arrangements** as per what the executor and trustee consider appropriate.
- **Life insurance** is not to be used to pay any estate debts.
- **Superannuation death benefits** are not to be used to pay estate debts.
- Executor and trustee to pay all estate debts and testamentary expenses.
- Christopher, Priya, Nathan and Anika Jackson are bequeathed all **shares in Jackson Developments & Construction Pty Ltd.**
- **Balance of estate** not otherwise disposed of is bequeathed to each child's trust in equal shares.
- If there are no beneficiaries of the above four trusts, the whole balance is bequeathed to the other trust.
- Executor and trustee must ensure **all tax-related records** are distributed to the same beneficiary of John's estate that is the recipient of that asset.

- **Purpose of establishing each trust** is to provide support and an effective investment vehicle for Ayesha, Christopher, Priya, Nathan and Anika and future bloodline lineal descendants of John's family.
- The trustee is to be fully aware that an important objective of John's in establishing this trust is to protect the assets of the trust from a breakdown in any personal relationship of any of the beneficiaries.
- Any **Principal's children** (if Principal is dead) shall receive the distribution of the trust fund that the Principal would have received.
- Trustee and excluded person shall not benefit from any part of the trust fund or income of the trust.

Charter Appendix Four: Family Council Meeting Agendas

Quarterly Meeting Agenda (Standard)

In **April** and **October**, a quarterly Family Council meeting will occur with the following agenda:

- Welcome and logistics
- Confirmation of minutes
- Actions carried forward
- Personal updates:
  - Christopher and Rya
  - Priya and Delvyn
  - Nathan and Georgia
  - Anika and Tom
  - John and Ayesha
- Balance sheet review
- Trading business update
- Family activity (timetable and convenor)
- General business (includes new business or investment opportunities)
- Next meeting

Quarterly Meeting Agenda (July)

In **July**, the agenda includes everything on the standard agenda, plus:

- Review of JD&C Pty Ltd trading performance
- Strategic plan review and endorsement
- Detailed update of employed family members (role, compensation and career path)

Quarterly Meeting Agenda (January)

In **January**, the Family Retreat agenda includes everything on the standard agenda, plus:

- The economy at large
- The performance of the business
- The Future Fund update
- The Family Foundation update
- Family activity, medium and long term
- Personal plan presentations
- Professional development

Invitation to the Jackson Family Retreat

Good morning family,

A short note of information for the Family Retreat coming up on 29 to 31 January 2021.

About the Timing

Just a reminder that we have chosen January to be the right timing to acknowledge and participate in the Jackson Family Retreat. January is symbolic to the Jackson family as it is the month that John Jackson's family arrived in Australia. We have also locked in a time that should be more accessible for all where construction is generally quieter, and children are on school holidays. The idea was to pick a date that would not be impacted by school. By selecting this date, we also ensure that in years to come, university student G3s will also be available for the event!

About the Program

We are asking you all to ensure that you are on site by midday on Friday 29 January. This will allow you to settle in and be ready for the afternoon program. It will also give the young children some time on site to enjoy the amenities.

The Event Start and Finish

The Retreat program includes an afternoon welcome gathering – so formal proceedings commence mid-afternoon (3:30 pm) on Friday 29 January. The last formal session will be the dinner Saturday 30 January. The retreat concludes on Sunday, though no program is in place to allow all families to enjoy the resort.

The Location

The event will be held at Lizard Island Resort located in Queensland. All transport and flights have been arranged by our private travel agent.

Key Program Features

Program highlights include:

- Guest speaker to welcome and open the retreat
- Twilight harbour cruise
- Welcome dinner
- Informal shareholder update
- Family presentations including updates on:
  - the economy at large
  - the performance of the business
  - the Future Fund

- the Family Foundation
- A family 'all-in' challenge

A detailed agenda will be available on arrival.

Logistics and Children

Some key things to remember:

- The Friday program includes everyone.
- On Friday early afternoon the shareholders only will be required for an informal update.
- The Saturday sessions for all will start at 10:00 am with the founders' traditional greeting.
- We will provide childcare for all children.
- The family 'all-in' challenge will run from 2:00 to 4.00 pm on Saturday – it will be designed to be inclusive of all ages.
- The dinner on Saturday will be a formal event.

What is Included in Your Package?

The founders John and Ayesha are your hosts for this event. John and Ayesha will cover all costs from your arrival on Friday to the conclusion on Sunday at checkout including all travel and logistics. If you would like to extend your stay, or arrive earlier, please contact the venue directly and settle your account.

Questions or Concerns

If you have any, please call John Vamos, or Mum and Dad!
    We look forward to seeing you all there for an enjoyable weekend.

Regards,

Mum and Dad (John and Ayesha)

APPENDIX D(b)

Examples of Pages from the Jackson Family Retreat Yearbook

BEACH

LEGO CHALLENGE

BIRTHDAY FUN!

SUNSET

AT THE WHITEBOARD AGAIN!

THE LAST DINNER

References

1. Khaldun I, Rosenthal F, Dawood NJ (1969). *The Muqaddimah: An Introduction to History*. Princeton University Press.

2. Hargreaves S (2014). 'The richest Americans in history.' CNN Business. money.cnn.com/gallery/luxury/2014/06/01/richest-americans-in-history/2.html.

3. Smyrnios KX, Dana L (2006). *The MGI Family and Private Business Survey 2006*. MGI and RMIT University. fambiz.com.au/wp-content/uploads/05-MGI-Aust.-FB-Survey-2006.pdf.

4. Smyrnios KX, Dana L (2010). *The MGI Australian Family and Private Business Survey 2010*. MGI and RMIT University. familybusiness.org.au/documents/item/251.

5. eMyth (2010). 'The Challenges of a Family Business.' e-myth.com/cs/user/print/post/the-challenges-of-a-family-business.

6. Smyrnios KX, Dana L (2010). *The MGI Australian Family and Private Business Survey 2013*. MGI and RMIT University. fambiz.com.au/wp-content/uploads/08%EF%80%A21-MGI-FB-Survey-20131.pdf.

7. Stewart I, Joines V (2012). *TA Today: A New Introduction to Transactional Analysis, Second Edition*. Lifespace Publishing, Melton Mowbray.

8. Nicholson N (1998). 'How Hardwired Is Human Behavior?' *Harvard Business Review*. hbr.org/1998/07/how-hardwired-is-human-behavior.

9. Harari YN (2011). *Sapiens: A Brief History of Humankind*. Penguin, London.

10. Dawkins R (1976). *The Selfish Gene*. Oxford University Press, Oxford.
11. Nicholson N (1998). Op. cit.
12. Egan K (2008). *The Future of Education: Reimagining our schools from the ground up*. Yale University Press, New Haven and London.
13. Dispenza J (2007). *Evolve your Brain – the Science of Changing Your Mind*. Health Communication Inc, Deerfield Beach, Florida.
14. Ibid.
15. Dunbar R, Barrett L, Lycett J (2007). *Evolutionary Psychology*. One World, Oxford.
16. Ibid.
17. Wilson EO (1998). *Consilience: The Unity of Knowledge*. Little Brown and Company, London.
18. Vamos P (as yet unpublished). *The Foresight Saga*.
19. Dispenza J (2007). Op. cit.
20. Hebb D (1949). *The Organization of Behavior*. John Wiley & Sons, New York.
21. Nicholson N (1998). Op. cit.
22. Dispenza J (2007). Op. cit.
23. Dispenza J (2012). *Breaking the Habit of Being Yourself: How to Lose your Mind and Create a New One*. Hay House, California.
24. Garfinkel H (1967). *Studies in Ethnomethodology*. Blackwell Publishers, Malden.
25. Lipton BH and Bhaerman S (2009). *Spontaneous Evolution*. Hay House, London.
26. Coates J (2013). *The Hour Between Dog and Wolf: Risk Taking, Gut Feelings and the Biology of Boom and Bust*. Fourth Estate, London.
27. Norretranders T (1998). *The User Illusion: Cutting Consciousness Down to Size*. Penguin Books, New York.
28. Doidge M (2007). *The Brain That Changes Itself: Stories of Personal Triumph from the Frontiers of Brain Science*. Penguin, London.

29. Lipton BH (2008). *The Biology of Belief: Unleashing the Power of Consciousness, Matter and Miracles.* Hay House, New York.

30. Ibid.

31. Coates J (2013). Op. cit.

32. Goleman D (1995). *Emotional Intelligence: Why it can matter more than IQ.* Bantam Books, New York.

33. Ibid.

34. Singer M (2007). *The Untethered Soul: The journey beyond yourself.* Raincoast books, Oakland, CA.

35. Dispenza J (2007). Op. cit.

36. Lindstrom M (2009). *Buyology: How Everything We Believe About Why We Buy is Wrong.* Random House, New York.

37. Nicholson N (1998). Op. cit.

38. LeDoux J (1998). *The Emotional Brain.* Simon & Schuster, New York.

39. Bryson B (2009). *Mother Tongue: The Story of the English Language.* Penguin, New York.

40. Haidt J (2006). *The Happiness Hypothesis: Putting ancient wisdom and philosophy to the test of modern science.* Arrow Books, London.

41. It's important not to get hung up on the number. It's only a marker – a marker that indicates a complexity inflection. It doesn't matter how many euros, dollars or yen that might be. It may be $100,000 one day thanks to inflation. What matters is the point of inflection where worry about safety and survival inflect and become complexity of choice.

42. Witters D, Liu D (2017). 'Income Buys Happiness Differently Based on Where You Live.' Gallup Blog. news.gallup.com/opinion/gallup/210011/income-buys-happiness-differently-based-live.aspx.

43. Dunn EW, Norton M (2012). 'Don't Indulge. Be Happy.' *New York Times.*

44. Csikszentmihalyi M (1990). *Flow: The classic work on how to achieve happiness*. Rider, New York.

45. Hari J (2015). *Chasing the Scream: The Search for the Truth About Addiction*. Bloomsbury, London.

46. Pink D (2009). *Drive: The surprising truth about what motivates us*. Penguin, New York.

47. Witters D, Liu D (2017). Op. cit.

48. Pink D (2009). Op. cit.

49. Harari YN (2011). Op. cit.

50. Vonnegut K (1992). *Mother Night*. Vintage Classics.

51. Leman K (2009). *The Birth Order Book: Why You Are the Way You Are*. Revell, Grand Rapids, MI.

52. Jaffe DT (2010). *Stewardship in Your Family Enterprise: Developing Responsible Family Leadership Across Generations*. Pioneer Imprints.

53. Hofstadter DR (1980). *Godel, Escher, Bach: An Eternal Golden Braid*. Penguin, London.

54. Berne E (2015). *Transactional Analysis in Psychotherapy*. Martino Fine Books, Connecticut.
Stewart I, Joines V (2012). *TA Today: A New Introduction to Transactional Analysis*. Lifespace Publishing, North Carolina.

55. Vamos J, McCreadie K (2010). *Elephants and the Business Laws of Nature*. Institute of Organisational Coaching Pty Ltd, Sydney.

56. Schilling DR (2013). 'Knowledge doubling every 12 months, soon to be every 12 hours.' Industry Tap. industrytap.com/knowledge-doubling-every-12-months-soon-to-be-every-12-hours/3950.

57. *The Economist* (2009). 'Rolls Royce: Britain's Lonely High-Flier.' economist.com/node/12887368.

58. Duhigg C (2012). 'How Companies Learn Your Secrets.' *The New York Times*. nytimes.com/2012/02/19/magazine/shopping-habits.html?pagewanted=1&_r=2&hp&.

59. Kurzweil R (2001). 'The Law of Accelerating Returns.' kurzweilai. net/the-law-of-accelerating-returns.

60. Galloway S (2017). *The Four: The Hidden DNA of Amazon, Apple, Facebook and Google.* Transworld Digital.

61. Partridge J (2020). 'Netflix now worth more than ExxonMobil as value reaches $196bn.' *The Guardian.* theguardian.com/media/ 2020/apr/16/netflix-now-worth-more-than-exxonmobil-as-value-reaches-187bn.

62. Harari YN (2011). Op. cit.

63. Garfinkel H (1967). Op. cit.

64. Kahneman D (2011). *Thinking, Fast and Slow.* Penguin, London.

65. Lewis M (2011). *The Big Short: Inside the Doomsday Machine.* Penguin, New York.

66. You can buy it from Amazon.

67. Pink D (2009). Op. cit.

68. You can see a copy of the resulting strategic plan in appendix A, and find more examples at fourvoicesadvisory.com.

69. You can read examples of these at fourvoicesadvisory.com.

70. Examples of personal plans can be found in appendix B and additional examples are available at fourvoicesadvisory.com.

71. Watkins A, Stratenus I (2016). *Crowdocracy: The End of Politics.* Urbane Publications, Kent.

72. Singer MA (2007). *The Untethered Soul: The Journey Beyond Yourself.* New Harbinger Publications, Oakland, CA.

73. For examples, please visit fourvoicesadvisory.com.